# LAWSON LIES STILL IN THE THAMES

# LAWSON LIES STILL IN THE THAMES

## THE EXTRAORDINARY LIFE OF VICE-ADMIRAL SIR JOHN LAWSON

## GILL BLANCHARD

AMBERLEY

First published 2017

Amberley Publishing
The Hill, Stroud
Gloucestershire, GL5 4EP

www.amberley-books.com

Copyright © Gill Blanchard, 2017

The right of Gill Blanchard to be identified as
the Author of this work has been asserted in
accordance with the Copyrights, Designs and
Patents Act 1988.

ISBN 978 1 4456 6123 0 (hardback)
ISBN 978 1 4456 6124 7 (ebook)

British Library Cataloguing in Publication Data.
A catalogue record for this book is available
from the British Library.

Typesetting and Origination by Amberley Publishing
Printed in the UK.

# CONTENTS

# FOREWORD AND ACKNOWLEDGEMENTS

This biography charts the tumultuous life of John Lawson, a Scarborough-born 'tarpaulin' – an ordinary merchant seaman – who played a central role in the English civil wars and Dutch wars. His extraordinary life provides a lens through which to view the personal and political conflicts of the period. In navigating his way to becoming a vice-admiral he survived political intrigue and imprisonment. Despite his radical republican beliefs he became a major actor in the restoration of the monarchy, for which he was knighted. John's subsequent actions, including establishing a defensive harbour in Tangier, locates his tale within the wider context of England's transformation into a global political and economic power.

My journey into John's life began with a house history in Alresford in Essex. I opened up a bundle of deeds held at Essex Archives, which included a copy of his will and other legal documents. I was intrigued to find that he was a vice-admiral who had received a gold chain from Oliver Cromwell in 1653 during the first Dutch War – and a pension from King Charles II.

These deeds and his original will provided a little information about John's wife, daughters and a couple of other relatives, while also revealing that he owned property in Wanstead in Essex and Scarborough in Yorkshire.

I was astonished to discover that he had played a vital role in the Restoration in 1660, yet I had never heard of him. When I found a brief account of his parliamentarian career, his exploits in the Dutch wars and in Tangier and discovered that he came from Yorkshire (my own county of birth), I was hooked. I wanted to know more about this almost forgotten hero and why he did what he did.

Part of the mystery was that, apart from naval histories and the sterling work of Scarborough local historian, Dr Jack Binns, very little had been written about John Lawson. He barely appears in histories of the civil wars and interregnum period, even those that focus on the restoration, or in the biographies of people he worked closely with. It was even more puzzling to me to find little recognition of him in his birth place. I hope that one day this omission will be rectified and John Lawson will be publicly recognised in his home town of Scarborough.

Very little is known about John Lawson's personal background and some of the primary sources that might tell us more, such as parish registers, do not survive. In searching those that do I was able to fill in some of the gaps by using family reconstitution methods. This primarily involved following up on the cousin and cousin's son named in John's will and tracing what happened to his wife and daughters. The trail led me to Scarborough in Yorkshire, London and Essex, to research in the archives in those counties and then beyond to Hampshire, Sussex, Oxfordshire and Lincolnshire.

I looked at every will and other probate records for Lawsons in Yorkshire, London and Essex between the late 1500s and the mid 1700s, including any that might relate to his wife's family. I located details of his daughters' marriages, their children and some grandchildren via parish registers, probate and legal records. I was fortunate in that Scarborough has been the subject of several local histories since the late 1700s, as well as much research by those interested in particular aspects, such as the coal trade, the civil war and the castle; also, that the North Yorkshire Archives in North Allerton have produced two calendars of parish records covering the period from 1600 to 1660.

More information came via searches for monumental inscriptions, deeds, apprenticeship and freemen records and transcripts and the letters, memoirs and diaries of contemporaries. The diary of Samuel Pepys, diurnial of Thomas Rugge, the memoirs of Edmund Ludlow, William Penn and Edward Hyde, Earl of Clarendon have provided much detail about John's life as well as background context. The Calendars of State Papers, treasury accounts, parliamentary archives and other official documentation provided fantastic insights into John's career, as well as some glimpses into his character and personal life. These led me to yet more wills, more letters, more parish registers and so on.

My first thanks must go to Mark Vesey of the Scarborough Maritime Heritage Centre, who has gone above and beyond in his assistance in this quest; and to historian Dr Binns, who I was fortunate to meet on a visit to Scarborough. I can blame Jack for this book, as it is his writings on John Lawson that I found first. His work and suggestions led me to many of the sources I have since used.

I am not a naval historian. As a result I found the histories on the subject by J D Davies and Bernard Capp absolutely invaluable. They also led me to a number of sources I would not have otherwise known about.

I have called on the skills of fellow professional genealogists to locate and retrieve documents and to undertake some research. Particular thanks must go to Kristina Bedford for all her hard work at The National Archives. This book would not have been completed without it. Hilary Clare, Sharon Grant, Les Mitchinson, Carol Kerry-Green and Kirsten English all proved invaluable in locating sources, obtaining copies of documents, taking photographs or providing useful information in Essex, Oxfordshire, London, Hampshire and Yorkshire.

There are too many archives and organisations to mention each one, but North Yorkshire Archives in North Allerton deserve a special mention for scanning and emailing me a document at extremely short notice. So do Leicester University and the National Portrait Gallery, for their generosity over granting free use of the copies of portraits they own of John Lawson.

A remarkable number of people have been generous with their time, by giving advice or feedback as the book has progressed. Among them are Dr Andrew Hopper as well as the Jarndyce Antiquarian Booksellers, who allowed me to use a letter they own.

Last, but not least, my home team of critical readers and proofreaders at various stages. Top of the list is my long suffering partner Ian Buckingham and our good friend Robert Orton, who have both devoted immense amounts of time in reading, critiquing and re-reading numerous drafts. Chris Stiven has been proof reader extraordinaire. The rest of the team are Caitlin Blanchard and Ross Orton, along with backup and support from the other wayfaring wayward women, Cate Blanchard and Pipa Clements and the Norwich Writers' Circle. My thanks also to my fellow MA in Biography students: Alison Baxter, Ann Kennedy-Smith, Deborah Spring, Lisa Eveleigh,

Rob Atkinson and Susan Burton, who have provided much invaluable critiquing.

Any mistakes or omissions are of course all mine.

## *Note on dates*

Throughout this book, I have used the modern calendar for years, but tended to use the original days and months given in original documents to avoid confusion when quoting. Until 1752 the New Year began on the 25 March. Dates that fell between 1 January and 25 March in this period therefore appear to be a year behind modern dating in original documents. For example, 1 January 1659 would be 1660 in the modern calendar. For the purpose of clarity I have used the modern calendar, so that all dates are shown as they would appear today. However, some source citations use original or double dating, e.g. 1 January 1659/60.

# PROLOGUE

On 13 December 1659, with rioting on the streets of London and the army controlling government, Vice-Admiral John Lawson led twenty-two warships into the Thames and, in defence of parliament, threatened to blockade the city. 'As becomes Englishmen', he declared, 'I am resolved with my life and fortune to pursue the restoration of our liberties'[1]. In doing so, he was about to play a pivotal role in the death throes of the republican cause for which he had fought so hard for seventeen years.

Portraits show John Lawson with a receding hairline and long, curling hair. Large, round eyes look out with a steady gaze over a long, narrow and slightly crooked nose and firm, but not over-full lips. Brief flashes of his personality emerge from the letters and diaries of contemporaries. 'A man of probity'[2] said parliamentarian Edmund Ludlow, while royalist Sir Philip Warwick thought him 'most generous hearted and intelligent'[3]. Others considered him just a rough-mannered, blunt-speaking common sailor – who had risen above his station. These were mostly people who did not share his politics[4].

Born in 1615, John's home was at the lower end of Merchants' Row in Scarborough, which ran alongside the castle dykes. Despite his reputed 'low parentage'[5] he was to become a literate and articulate ship owner and sea captain. His conversations with Edmund Ludlow during the crisis of 1659 and 1660 reveal a trusting and optimistic nature that contrasts with the steely resolve he displayed to the army leaders. He was the naval equivalent of Oliver Cromwell's 'plain russet coated captain who knows what he fights for, and loves what he knows'[6].

In the winter of 1659 high winds, heavy rain and flooding swept across England and Scotland. Harvests were ruined for the third year in a row[7]. The country's mood was desperate amidst fears of a return to the bloody conflicts of the 1640s and early 1650s. From on board his ship *The James* Vice-Admiral Lawson wrote publicly to the Lord Mayor, aldermen and councillors of London. He declared that he and his captains 'could not in all conscience tolerate the breach between parliament and army that had come to the fore since October'. Now, as their unhappy differences grew ever wider the ideals which had cost them all 'so much blood and treasure' were facing 'utter ruin'[8].

Radical elements of the army had taken control of government. In response, John Lawson was desperately trying to restore a Commonwealth government in whose defence he had already been imprisoned and exiled. This was, he asserted, a contest fought in Christ's own interest as well as his people's. If parliament could not be saved by friendly means then he and his men would use the utmost force to do so[9]. Appealing fervently to the Lord Mayor and city council to withstand the designs of King Charles I's son – Charles Stuart – this deeply committed puritan led his men into the Thames that grey December day on a point of principle. Parliament should never be subordinate. Not to the army. Not to any king, nor to any Lord Protector[10].

There is no doubt where John Lawson's sympathies lay. His fierce devotion to parliamentarianism had seen him navigate his way from merchant seaman up the ranks in the navy until he was rewarded with the Vice-Admiralty in 1653. Along the way he had publicly supported the Levellers who agitated for a radical egalitarian society (at least for men). Now he was rumoured to be a religious and political subversive. He was also immensely popular with his men; in part no doubt because he was intimately concerned with their welfare. In very modern sounding terms, he proposed making comfortable provision for disabled seamen and the widows and orphans of serving sailors, creating jobs for the able-bodied poor and giving financial aid to those 'too lame and impotent to work'[11].

Here we catch a glimpse of what shaped John. He spent a large portion of his life in a town whose fortunes – even its sights and smells – were dominated by the treacherous North Sea; learning his trade transporting coal from Sunderland to London and the continent. Almost unique among seventeenth-century naval officers in not having first been a gentleman soldier, his manner certainly found favour with ordinary sailors[12].

After months of conflict following Oliver Cromwell's death, the army in London under John Lambert's command marched to Westminster in October 1659, drove the MPs and the Speaker out, locked the doors and set guards to prevent them re-entering. A military dictatorship was now running the country in the name of the republic.

By the first week of December, the country was at 'the mercy and impulse of a giddy, hot-headed, bloody multitude'[13]. Soldiers patrolled the streets of London. On the fifth of the month came a surge of violence, as city apprentices petitioned for the removal of the army. Troops and young trainees from every trade and city guild – carpenters, grocers, butchers, tailors, scriveners, apothecaries and more – clashed near Whitehall. It is likely that Samuel Lawson, son of John's cousin and apprentice grocer to his father in Lyme Street, was one of those hurling stones, tiles and turnips[14]. The soldiers shot them down.

A number of protestors were killed and over thirty wounded. In the days that followed, soldiers pulled down city gates and carried grenadoes – explosive shells – into St. Paul's Cathedral, Sion College and elsewhere. Butchers pretending to play football attacked the guard inside Whitehall. The prisons filled[15].

This was John Lawson's moment. Declaring himself for the Rump and against the army, he and his fleet arrived at Gravesend at the mouth of the Thames on 13 December 1659. The renowned diarist Samuel Pepys began his journal at the very beginning of January 1660. On the first page, he wrote how the army officers were forced to yield while 'Lawson lies still in the river'[16].

Within three months of his bold stand to defend the Commonwealth, John Lawson had forsaken it and become a reluctant kingmaker.

# CHAPTER 1

# THE MATTER FROM THE BEGINNING

One evening shortly after the restoration of the monarchy, the fugitive parliamentarian Edmund Ludlow was invited to a banquet by the senators of Bern in Switzerland. He had escaped to that city after the return of Charles II to England, and his hosts pressed him for details of what caused the fall of the English republic. This, he answered, could only be understood 'by taking up the matter from the beginning'[1].

To understand John Lawson's role in this fall we need to go back to his beginning too. Like so many people of the time, he was an ordinary man who became caught up in extraordinary events. By mapping John's religious fervour, total commitment to the Commonwealth cause and background in trade, as well as his exposure to radical ideas, military and naval exploits, his changes in fortune and the treacheries of others, he becomes a cipher for the personal and political conflicts of a period of unprecedented upheaval.

Leading parliamentarians Sir William Penn and Edmund Ludlow thought him brave, wise and kind[2]. Ludlow's opinion is notable in that he was one of the judges at the trial of King Charles I and signed the king's death warrant. After the restoration, Edmund Ludlow spent the rest of his life in hiding abroad. To him, the men who had betrayed the Commonwealth 'rendered themselves detestable by the baseness of their crimes'[3]. Yet in his memoirs, Ludlow quite deliberately made an exception for John Lawson, despite the vice-admiral being among those who changed allegiance. Rather, he thought him essentially honourable although 'in some measure seduced by [the] subtleties of others'[4].

A more faceted image of John Lawson emerges from the writings of Samuel Pepys. He generally thought well of the vice-admiral, describing him as 'very good-natured' at one point[5]. This amiable opinion did not prevent the diarist from making occasional acerbic remarks about John's officiousness, social climbing and unwillingness to do favours for him. Pepys worked both at the Exchequer and for the politician and naval commander Edward Montagu. This meant he was well placed to chronicle the tumultuous events, as John became intimately involved with shaping the nation's future alongside Montagu and General George Monck, the Commander-in-Chief of the Army in Scotland[6].

John Lawson declared that Scarborough was his birthplace in his will, but little more is known about his background[7]. Some writers have even claimed him for Hull – no doubt because of the time he spent there in the early 1640s. His beginnings and many details of his family have remained obscure or speculative, only now revealed by a close examination of his will and other documents.

While John's birth in 1615 can be deduced from the age given on his marriage licence,[8] the Scarborough parish registers, which might have revealed his parentage, were destroyed when the church came under attack during a battle between cavaliers and roundheads. A flight of fancy might conjure a vision of John launching the cannon balls that damaged those church records during the siege of 1644.

Even John Lawson's will does not aid matters much, as the only relatives named outside of his wife and daughters were a cousin (also named John) who lived in London and that cousin's son. This cousin's brothers and father, Nicholas, can be identified through wills, apprenticeship and freemen records, but it is still not clear exactly how they connect, especially as the term 'cousin' was frequently used to denote any kinsfolk.

There could of course be any number of possible reasons that John did not mention siblings, nieces or nephews in his will, from his being an only child to estrangement. The latter would be an obvious assumption to make given the events of the 1640s and 1650s, but it is too simple. His later actions and other bequests indicate that by the end of his life, John was more than willing to put at least some of those divisions behind him.

William Penn, who became a close neighbour and friend of John's, described him as coming from a lowly background of fisher folk. He was not the only one to make this claim. Yet John Lawson was no poor fisherman. His signature, on an autographed engraving in 1659 and on letters, reveals a firm, confident and well-formed hand. The language he used in letters and public declarations signifies a man with some education, although he did not attend university[9].

Other clues to John's background emerge from local records, apprenticeship papers and wills relating to the family of his cousin John, as well as in the letters, diaries and memoirs of friends and colleagues. Despite the haphazard nature of the surviving records for Scarborough, we can glimpse John Lawson in his early twenties among the town's lists of ship owners, masters and mariners, trading coals in and out of Scarborough port. These portray a man who spent a large portion of his life in the town during the first half of the 1600s[10] and raises the question as to why some were so keen to point to John as being from poor stock. Was it a means of symbolically demoting him – or a desire to make him more appealing? From his detractors it was mere denigration. To his admirers, it established the innate qualities that enabled to him to overcome his background.

When John was admitted as a freeman by the corporation on 3 October 1639, he was described as a freeman's son who had served an apprenticeship with Henry Nicholson. Sadly, this record doesn't name his father[11]. The handful of surviving bishops' transcripts for Scarborough before 1620 – copies of the parish registers compiled annually – include just two baptismal entries for Lawson children. These records have enormous gaps, with nothing at all for the period in which John Lawson was born, or when he was having his own children. Unfortunately too, the clerks who made these copies did not see any necessity to include the wives' names, making it hard to distinguish in some cases whether one couple or two different sets of parents were being listed[12].

A little more can be gleaned from the Scarborough corporation records. A few men and women called Lawson, or Lowson as it was often spelt, appear during the first half of the 1600s. Among them were an Edmund and Robert and a William Lawson who were leasing property, paying rates, acting as parish and corporation officials or being fined for misdemeanours such as letting rubbish lie in the street. In what may be a sign of religious dissent, there were regular entries in the early 1620s relating to fines paid by William Lawson for not attending church or receiving the sacrament for a whole year at a time. The name William Lawson pops up again in the corporation records in the 1630s, for being bound over, with others, to keep the peace and prosecuted for shooting pigeons[13]. The impression one gains from these activities is that this was a young man.

It is possible that John Lawson attended the small grammar school that stood next to St Mary's church, on the hill just below Scarborough castle, overlooking the sea. Such notions are limited however by the destruction of the school records for this time period and there being little evidence that he knew Greek or Latin, which was mandatory for the school's pupils[14].

Like many bright young men who went into trade, it is probable that John learned his letters while undertaking his apprenticeship, rather than at school. There were opportunities for a bright and ambitious young man with some basic education. One celebrated example is the diarist Samuel Pepys, whom John came to know very well. Samuel was the son of a tailor and far from unique in moving up the social scale and gaining jobs and promotions through a mixture of ability, family connections and a network of friends. Although Pepys eventually went to university, this was only possible when he obtained charitable funding[15].

If John Lawson had any assistance from a relative, the most likely candidate was the master mariner William Lawson. By 1635, William owned a quarter share of one of the 155 church pews costing £1 and 10 shillings, equivalent to around £130 today. The following year, William was elected to the prestigious position of warden of the Society of Shipowners, Masters and Mariners. In October of the same year, he was one of twelve master mariners who swore a pledge to the town's bailiffs that none of his ship's company had been in any place infected with plague in the previous month[16].

Perhaps it is too easy to read significance into such small traces, but when John first registered with the Shipowners Guild in 1639 at the age of twenty-four, his name was written below William's. Whether he was John's father, brother, the 'Uncle William' named in the will of the son of John's cousin, or another relative is uncertain, but William named one of the ships he captained in the early 1640s the *John*. This William Lawson is almost certainly the same man who married Isabelle Hickson in Scarborough in 1636 and had a son called John two years later, as one of his other ships was named after his wife[17].

The fragmentary nature of the surviving records makes it difficult to discern whether the mariner William was the same one baptised in 1605. If so, he is likely to be the man who sold his share of a close of meadow known as St Nicholas Close in 1630, which he had inherited from his father. The deed of sale in the Scarborough Corporation records mentioned five other siblings, but none were named and the will referred to in the sale cannot be located[18].

Whatever John's kinship ties to the other Lawsons in Scarborough, a picture of close family ties and a background firmly rooted in trade emerges from the snippets in archives. There are the uncles and cousins who migrated to London and Essex in the early 1600s to become grocers and skinners, one with lands granted to him in Ireland, and the cousin's son, Samuel Lawson, who would die in the East Indies after sailing there on business in his good ship the *African* of London[19]. As with his contemporaries the merchant seamen Rainborowe family, a pattern emerges of intermarriages, mutually beneficial apprenticeships and trade agreements between relatives and family friends, shared religious leanings and political and financial commitments and favours binding them closely together[20].

Many of his kinsmen and associates would later join John in the navy[21]. One who very much wanted to was Captain John Thomson, a merchant seaman from Yorkshire. Thomson suffered such losses at sea in the 1650s that he decided to enter naval service hoping to serve under John Lawson, whom he described as his former neighbour. He was so disappointed that this was not to be that he pleaded with admiralty officials to place him with another fellow-Yorkshireman instead[22].

When John married twenty-three-year-old Isabelle Jefferson in January 1640, in the parish church of St Oswald in Lythe in north Yorkshire, it appears to have been a love match. With her home parish just a mile from Whitby, it is likely that they met on one of his stopovers at the harbour there, or through one of the many Jeffersons who lived in Scarborough at the time. Their enduring affection is displayed in two letters. Fourteen years after their marriage, John expressed his fondness for Isabelle and concerns for her health in a letter to his friend Sir Henry Vane. Nine years after that, she in turn took steps to protect him from the impact of hearing bad news while serving abroad. Still, if she was, as is believed, the daughter of another master mariner, it was also an advantageous marriage for John[23].

By the time he was in his early twenties, John Lawson was an experienced and successful collier. He part-owned a merchant ship called *The Adventurer,* which transported coals via Scarborough across hundreds of miles to English ports and to the continent. Part-ownership allowed merchants to spread the cost of investing in the larger, more expensive vessels being built in the early 1600s.

More goods could be transported on a single voyage, increasing profitability, but by sharing the risks they stood to lose less if things went wrong[24].

Like many other merchant mariners who prospered, John invested in land and property. In 1647, after leasing pasture land in Garlands, Weaponess and Butts Close from the Scarborough Corporation for several years, John bought a house at number four West Sandgate, adjoining Tollergate and opposite the lower end of Merchants Row. Now on or very close to the site of a car park, the house stood within sight of the sea and overlooked by the church and castle. This house and some meadowland he owned in nearby Church Close and Greengate Close would remain in the family until the last piece of property was sold by his granddaughter Anne Kinaston in 1698[25].

The port town of Scarborough was centred on one long, sloping street, somewhat confusingly named Westbrough, Newbrough and Eastbrough at different geographic points. Smaller roads running parallel to the seashore branched off to the north and south. A few of the fifteenth- and sixteenth-century black and white timber framed houses, shops and inns remain on Sandgate, Quay Street and Parkins Lane. John had a daily reminder of prevailing superstitions and fears of demons and witches in the grotesque figures carved onto the posts of the *Newcastle Packet Inn,* within sight of his home.

While Thursday and Saturday were market days, fish was sold on the sands almost daily. The sea was ever-present in the lives of Scarborians. From the earliest times, lights were placed in church towers along the coast to guide sailors into safe harbour. When John navigated in and out of the curved bay, he could clearly see the medieval church of St Mary standing on the approach to the castle gate. So too did the adjacent chapel of St Thomas, until it was demolished in the siege of 1644. Modern buildings and roads now form a tiered amphitheatre, rising up to the ruins of the ancient castle that dominates the skyline and obscures the view of the church and chapel from the sandy beach hundreds of feet below. Walking up the hill to where the closes and meadows John once leased are now overbuilt and looking out across the town, it is possible to see traces of his world more clearly[26].

In the 1630s, coal was a growth industry. It had begun to replace wood as the main source of fuel for heating and cooking in the early seventeenth century, especially in towns and cities. Scarborough had no ships in the coal trade at the beginning of the 1600s, but shortly before John Lawson was born a new pier extending from the shore to the foot of the castle mound was completed, helping to stimulate trade in the town. With no signs of any bequests from relatives to set him up in life, this trade is almost certainly how John flourished at such a young age.

By 1625, there were twenty-five colliers conveying coals from Newcastle and Sunderland to London, Rotterdam and Calais, all paying tax on every chalder of coal they shipped (or chaldron). Different weights applied in London and Newcastle and for waggons and ships. The Newcastle chalder on a ship at this time was equivalent to 53 hundredweight - around 5,936 pounds.

Most of the coal brought into Scarborough originated in Sunderland by the end of the decade. The relationship between the two towns would become even more important from the 1640s, after the royalist town of Newcastle banned the export of coal to London and Sunderland became the city's main supplier. A surviving trade agreement from 1643 between Scarborough master mariner William Clarke and Sunderland merchant Browne

Thomas describes an arrangement typical of those John would have made. Browne Thomas paid William Clarke to take a reasonable load of coals into 'Holland, Zealand or Flander' as a good wind and weather allowed. There he would stay eight working days to unload and complete his business[27].

Every merchant seaman had experience of evading pirates on their travels. In 1634, an ancient 'ship money' tax was revived by Charles I, ostensibly to pay for protection against the Barbary pirates from North African countries under Turkish control, targeting merchants and the fishing-fleets returning from Newfoundland. Those captured were sold in the slave markets of Turkey, Libya, Tunisia, Algeria and Morocco; their labour and the ransom money paid to release them being a vital part of the economy of the Ottoman Empire. Captives were encouraged to communicate with their families in order to encourage them to raise the money. Lists of pennies, shillings, and even pounds, given by local men and women from all social backgrounds towards collections issued by royal mandate for the ransom of slaves, are lodged in parish records across England, especially in coastal areas[28].

Pirates and marauding foreigners were not the only danger for seasoned seamen, particularly merchants and those in the herring fisheries based on the east coast. Colliers homeward-bound and other experienced seamen from the herring fisheries based on the east coast were deliberately targeted by navy pressgangs operating on ships out of the Medway, the Downs or Spithead.

Merchant ship owners such as John took to hiding their men or landing them on shore before they came within range of the press-ships, while local bailiffs and constables refused to assist the press-masters on land when they visited[29]. One bitter sounding report from a press-master in East Anglia to his superiors claimed 'the officers of the town were so base that they could not get a man; as fast as our people searched one part of the town, they got into the other, although they searched with candles'[30]. It is not too far-fetched to presume that the personal experiences of friends, neighbours, crewmen or relatives led John to demand the abolition of this practice of forcing or tricking men into serving in the navy or army in peacetime. He would certainly have seen the effects on families and communities of having their mariners snatched away from them[31].

Thomas Hobbes, born in 1588, the year of the Armada, commented 'My mother gave birth to twins: myself and fear.' Similarly, religious wars and political conflict across Europe formed the backdrop to John Lawson's early life. He was ten years old when Charles I came to the throne in 1625. From the very start, King Charles was embroiled in conflict with parliament. Unresolved political and religious tensions eventually led to civil wars and his execution. Despite dazzling advances in science, art, literature and architecture and the beginning of the move towards becoming a major world power, England was riven by extraordinary turmoil that affected everyone's life, not least John's.

Charles I increasingly used his royal prerogative to get his own way over raising funds for wars, first against Spain, then against the Scots. The belief that the monarch ruled by divine right and was above the law enabled him to override parliament's will on the grounds that he was appointed by God and acted in his name. His father James I had reiterated this long-standing notion when he was crowned and, with it, the principle that the freedoms of his subjects only existed through his goodwill, not as a right.

By the 1630s there was a growing rift between Charles I and his subjects over an increasingly expensive war against the Scots and the additional taxation to pay for it. Although many members of parliament objected, Charles I had dissolved parliament in 1629 and it would not sit again until 1640, so there was little they could do. It was not illegal for the king to rule personally as parliament was traditionally called to provide the monarch with permission to raise taxes. If this was not needed, then parliament was not called. To raise the money he needed without summoning the MPs, he resorted to the ancient custom of demanding ship money.

The ship tax had been traditionally used by the monarch to order coastal towns to pay towards equipping the fleet if an invasion was feared. King Charles spotted this as a means of raising funds to pay for a stronger navy to enforce British sovereignty at sea, without needing to contribute financially or gain parliament's approval. In 1635, he extended the ship tax to inland areas. As the king demanded more the following year it became evident that he planned to carry on doing so. There was enormous resentment at this extra tax across the country from an already overburdened and increasingly resistant population. Yorkshire inhabitants paid more than any other region at £12,000 - more than a million pounds today. The king's response to protests and legal challenges was to claim that he did not need parliamentary consent to raise ship money in times of national danger, on which he was the sole judge. The consequence was that more and more MPs became determined to limit the king's power to overrule them.

Rivalries with the Dutch, French and Spanish over lucrative trade routes and fear of invasion were given as reasons to restore the ship tax. The few supporters of the tax in Yorkshire may have felt vindicated in the summer of 1635, when Scarborough harbour became the scene of fights between a Dutch vessel and Dunkirk man-of-war, then between Dutch and Spanish vessels, within two weeks of each other. The town withstood an attempt by sixty or seventy of the Dutch crew, armed with muskets and pikes, to take the Spanish ship at night, but feared that the Dutch were still determined to have it. Naval warships were hastily dispatched to the town to restore order and tasked to fire and sink all Dutch ships north of Harwich. Despite this type of protection from the navy, the outrage that King Charles provoked by using the royal prerogative to implement the tax was a major contributor to the outbreak of civil war in 1642[32].

The king and Archbishop William Laud's reorganisation of the Church of England was another trigger point. Communion tables in the middle of churches were repositioned at the east end of the sanctuary and surrounded by rails as a separate holy space. In Scarborough work to rearrange the pulpit and build new pews inside St Mary's Church began in June 1634[33]. Such changes emphasised the king and archbishop's belief that worship should be devotional and sacramental. Unfortunately for Charles I, his reforms and his attempts to bring the Scottish Kirk in line with the English Church ultimately led to rebellion.

The changes made by the king and archbishop were anathema to many, especially puritans. Unlike the Protestant Church in Scotland and on the continent, the Church of England was governed by bishops appointed by the crown and ritual ceremonies of worship had remained. Most early seventeenth-century puritans still belonged to the Anglican Church. Although they were not a homogenous group, they were in general opposed to church hierarchies and rituals and felt that the Protestant Reformation was incomplete.

England had more or less shaken off the rituals of the Catholic Church by the early 1600s, apart from in a small number of recusant households. When James I came to the throne, his Calvinist upbringing had raised the puritans' hopes of further reform in the Protestant Church. This was not fulfilled. Although there was some toleration of nonconformist practice before the 1620s, James I refused to change the prayer book and a major problem arose when first James, then his son Charles, began to be perceived as allowing Catholicism to creep back.

Puritan elements within the Church of England proposed their own religious reforms and tried to counter the changes being made under Charles I. Their emphasis on self-reliance and hard work and emphatic anti-popery drew increasing numbers in the 1630s. It was notably attractive to those in trade, including merchant seamen such as John Lawson, who were exposed to new ideas when travelling and interacting with incomers from the Low Countries[34]. His own worship and beliefs were firmly protestant.

The 1640s and 1650s thus became defined by conflicts over the balance of power between king and parliament, then by the nature of government and the rights of the individual in relation to government. Questions over whether King Charles was divinely appointed to rule or putting England's protestant heritage at risk began to emerge. These were followed by new ideas about political liberty, religious tolerance, property ownership and the function of the Church of England. Religion and the bible, with its psalms and revelations, underpinned every argument. This was a battle for the very heart and soul of all England.

By January 1642 riots and rebellions were breaking out across England. After two weeks of being besieged in Whitehall Palace by angry mobs, Charles I fled to Hampton Court with his wife and children. A few days later Charles sent the queen to France for safety and in February the court was moved to York. The situation deteriorated even further until in August, King Charles declared war against parliament by raising his royal standard in Nottingham.

Ultimately, the war was about the rights of parliament versus the unlimited power of the monarch, as well as disputes over the structure and influence of the Church of England in government and private affairs, with the catalyst being Charles I using his royal prerogative to impose the ship tax. This reached directly into peoples' pockets, raising political consciousness in the most direct manner, even among those who might not otherwise have objected to the king exercising his power.

Two decades of bloodshed would follow, in which more than 200,000 people died, with equal numbers injured, imprisoned or driven from their homes. No part of the British Isles was unaffected and the clichés of brother against brother, father versus son and mothers estranged from daughters were played out, as families and friends found themselves on opposite sides. The king was put on trial and executed, followed by the abolition of the monarchy, the House of Lords and the bishops. England became a republic, all of which was accompanied by challenges to the dominance of the landed gentry and unheard of freedoms to preach and publish. This though, was in the future.

Within weeks of war being declared, John Lawson cheerfully signed up to do God's work in the fight against the king. Years later he still exulted that it was for 'the glory of God and the good of his people'. He explained how he was convinced right 'from the beginning of these times of the justice of the parliament's proceedings'[35]. From that moment on, he said, 'the Lord has kept my heart upright to the honest interest of the nation', despite banishment and the dangers to his own life and freedom[36].

John Lawson served most of the next three or four years at sea. As was the custom for merchant seamen, he was initially hired, with his vessel, to support the navy during the summer months. His tasks were to transport supplies and reinforcements, to guard against the Scots and deter any foreign power that might send help to the embattled royalists. During the summers of 1643 and 1644 and the summer and winter of 1645, John's ship of small burthen served parliament under the wonderfully named Captain Haddock on the north-east coast and under Captain Browne closer to home[37].

After eight months in the navy's service John and his family were in great financial want. It was common for captains to wait months to be reimbursed for their men's pay and victuals. By March of 1643, he was desperately petitioning the Navy administrators for £1,590 - around £136,000 in today's money - outstanding for his own pay, the purchase of supplies and the wages he had paid to his men out of his own purse[38]. As an interim measure, John prayed that the Commissioners of Excise at Newcastle be ordered to pay him £500 out of the taxes they had received from merchants trading in flesh and salt. Having met with other losses and 'suffering many times by the enemy at sea'[39] he understandably continued his own freight trade in between navy patrols. As a result 'I had subsistence'[40] he later told his mentor Sir Henry Vane.

John's faith meant he construed personal and military setbacks positively. One disaster was 'bad, because honest men have suffered, and the cause of God will be reflected upon, but if our mercies were not mixed with some bitter pills we should be either lifted up or undervalue them'[41]. Victories were signs of heavenly approval. One can almost feel righteousness seeping from the page as he wrote of hearing the news of 'how the Lord has broken and dispersed the malicious and desperate crew of cavaliers'. It was for John 'another signal of testimony of God's displeasure against that wicked interest'[42].

In September 1642, a few weeks after the war began, fellow Yorkshireman Sir Hugh Cholmley took a regiment to Scarborough to hold it for parliament. The town, castle and port were of vital strategic importance. It was defensible, a safe anchorage with established sea lanes to other ports on the east coast and the continent. Not only that, but the town was less than a day's ride from the county's capital city of York. Despite a number of skirmishes with royalist forces, Sir Hugh's troops successfully occupied the town for the next five months. The bailiffs and burgesses of the town were so well pleased with Sir Hugh's proceedings for protecting the town that they recorded their thanks in the corporation minute books. They were no doubt even further relieved by his promise to pay towards the costs[43].

Sir Hugh Cholmley and his son, also named Hugh, were both to play an important part in John's life. The older man was a leading political figure in Yorkshire. Sir Hugh Cholmley was always a more moderate and conciliatory parliamentarian than some of his fellow Yorkshire squires. He was undoubtedly influenced by most of his Yorkshire relatives, including the Hothams of Hull, being parliamentarians, but he was also virulently anti-Catholic and had played a small but significant role in the trial of the king's favourite, the Earl of Strafford. He became opposed to the ship tax in 1639–40 when the purpose for raising money changed to paying for the war against the rebel Scots instead of for warships for the Royal Navy.

March of 1643 saw a dramatic reversal as Sir Hugh defected to the royalists, taking eighty horsemen and 400 foot soldiers with him. He was then appointed royal governor of the castle and town. In a giddying turn and turnabout, the castle was reclaimed for the parliamentarians within a week. Forty seamen under the command of Hugh Cholmley's cousin, Captain Browne Bushell, accompanied by eight or nine townsmen, scaled the walls at night and surprised the guard. The names of most of the men who forced their way into the castle's keep are unknown, but few were better qualified to be among them than John Lawson, who not only had personal knowledge of the area, but had served as a master-at-sea under Bushell's command the previous year.

Then, in another unexpected betrayal, Browne Bushell was quickly persuaded by Cholmley to return the castle to him and join the king's cause. Within three days Scarborough was again in royalist hands. Sir Hugh Cholmley wisely allowed every officer, soldier and burgess to decide whether to remain in Scarborough or to depart. Most town leaders accepted this change of allegiance. John and Isabelle Lawson did not. With scarcely time to pack their possessions, they and a few other families abandoned their homes and fled south to the parliamentary stronghold of Hull. The other men noted as taking refuge there were John Harrison, William Nesfield, Thomas Gill and Peter Hodgson, all in the shipping trade and religious radicals[44].

The young couple had been married barely nineteen months and had at least one infant daughter to care for on the perilous journey, while Isabelle was either nursing another baby or pregnant with the second of their six daughters[45]. Royalist soldiers controlled the major roads on the thirty-six-mile journey between Scarborough and Hull and were quartered in towns en route. The sea was not much safer, with armed patrols loyal to the king keeping guard close to shore. But despite the greater distance involved, it was the more attractive option for a skilled sailor like John who knew the winds, tides and safe harbours.

John's brief recollection of the events between 1642 and 1648 in a letter to Sir Henry Vane therefore bears closer scrutiny. Here he speaks of the treachery of Sir Hugh Cholmley and others at Scarborough. His life being endangered, John was 'determined to keep my heart upright to the honest interest of the nation'[46]. So few words to record this war's personal and emotional impact.

Sir Hugh Cholmley held out for more than two years in Scarborough, while Browne Bushell embarked on a five-year career as a royalist privateer and gunrunner, capturing parliamentary ships for financial gain. Surprisingly, John Lawson never mentioned Browne Bushell by name when he spoke of those who were faithless to the parliamentary cause. Yet he certainly had more personal contact with Bushell than with Cholmley, having been directly under his command at sea. It is tempting to see this as due to Bushell's double-dealing having had such a deep personal impact on John that he could not bring himself to mention it directly[47].

The elder Sir Hugh Cholmley represents the changing fortunes and vacillations that occurred among many during the civil wars. Whether it was because he was embarrassed or ashamed, the former governor omitted nearly all references to his parliamentary career from his memoirs, written many years later. He stated that it was they who broke trust with him by changing the rationale for war, failing to supply him and dishonouring his name. It is understandable that he wished to gloss over his actions and motives. He, like other turncoats, was portrayed in the worst possible light as weak, womanly, ungentlemanly and cowardly[48].

John Lawson was of course one of those who bitterly condemned Sir Hugh's duplicity, not least because it cost him his home and put his and his family's lives in great peril[49].

In Hull and Scarborough respectively, both Isabelle Lawson and Elizabeth Cholmley, wife of Sir Hugh, stayed with their husbands rather than seeking safety with friends or relatives elsewhere[50]. 'Yet in the greatest danger would not be daunted, but shewed a courage above her sex,'[51] said Sir Hugh of his wife afterwards. Elizabeth and her maids nursed the wounded and sick inside Scarborough castle and refused to leave, even when the besieging commander threatened to put every man and woman there to the sword. Sir Hugh's tribute to his wife could have equally applied to Isabelle Lawson and the many unnamed maidservants, soldiers' and sailors' wives and townswomen who also endured these battles and sieges.

They were not alone in living in a battle zone. Yorkshire was England's biggest county with a population of around 400,000, roughly the same as London. Major towns and ports such as York, Skipton, Scarborough and Hull all suffered attack. Troops who could not be billeted into the garrisons were accommodated wherever there was room in local inns and houses, with locals having no choice in the matter. With the influx of soldiers and refugees seeking safety and shelter, accounts of atrocities – intimidation, physical and sexual assaults, robberies and murder, soon followed[52].

Inevitably, women bore the brunt of caring for the wounded and the sick. There were insufficient field hospitals on both sides so the majority of cases were nursed by local families – not necessarily willingly. Besieged doctors, apothecaries and women with their herbs and poultices had to adapt rapidly to treating multiple injuries in the midst of plague, typhus and other life-threatening diseases.

Most of the injuries came from three-quarter-inch musket balls hitting bodies at high velocity, causing fractures, large exit wounds and, worst of all, ricocheting internally. Despite cleaning wounds with sponges and compresses wrung out in wine or vinegar, infection was rife as the lead balls slamming into flesh pulled pieces of dirty or bloody clothing inside the body. The enormous mortality rate meant that unless they were local, most war dead ended up in burial pits rather than in the churchyard, with the attendant worry for comrades and families as to whether they had received a decent Christian burial[53].

While the royalists held Scarborough, John Lawson was able to put his skills to good use in Hull. He had a part share in the *Covenant*, a 140-ton armed ship with a crew of forty-two and twelve cannon. He used it to carry supplies in and out of the port of Hull and transported at least one cargo of lead to Scotland to be turned into ammunition[54].

The castle in Scarborough became the garrison for 700 royalist soldiers. The port from which he had previously traded was now used to intercept parliamentarian ships, inflicting serious coal shortages on London. The impact of war went far beyond the fighting. John Lawson lost much more than his home. Most of his friends, the people he did business with and, quite likely, family members had stayed in Scarborough. Whether they were motivated by pragmatism, disillusionment with parliamentarianism, or genuinely supported the king, they were now on the opposite side to him.

Among those who remained in Scarborough was the merchant William Lawson. William was elected to the town council and continued trading in and out of the town. On at least one occasion, Cholmley's shipping agent, who provided stores to Browne Bushell and other royalist privateers, commissioned William Lawson to bring in wine, prunes, raisins, iron, tar and whale and seal oil – known as train oil – from Sweden. On another, William was chosen to carry a message by sea to the king's troops[55]. Such assignments demonstrate that William was trusted by the royalist side. If, as seems likely, William was John's kinsman this illustrates the depth of divisions that the war caused between families and friends.

John Lawson still had no doubts that he was fighting in God's interest and for God's people. In a letter he wrote some years later to Sir Henry Vane, he described how after arriving in Hull he first devoted himself to serving at sea with his small ship. He managed to support his family and took great pleasure in recounting how he had been an instrument in 'discovering and (in some measure), preventing the intended treachery of Sir John Hotham'[56].

Sir John Hotham was the governor when John Lawson arrived in Hull and his son, also called John, was a Lieutenant-General at Nottingham Castle. Early in 1642 the two Hothams and their men had prevented the king from gaining access to the magazine at Hull – the second largest in the country. However even before the Lawsons took up residence in the town, father and son were becoming perturbed by parliament's increasingly radical aims. Jealousy over the appointment of Lord Fairfax as General of the Yorkshire forces and snobbish disdain over the number of Yorkshire cloth workers entering the forces edged both father and son towards the royalist camp.

When the Hotham estates were perceived to be threatened by the Earl of Newcastle's royalist army, they began corresponding with the earl. The son eventually promised to defect if parliament should act improperly and when the timing was right. He assured the earl that his father would join him, as would the inhabitants of Hull and others elsewhere in the East Riding of Yorkshire and Lincolnshire. Despite the Hothams' public condemnation of Sir Hugh Cholmley for defecting, his switch heightened suspicions about the Hothams' loyalty. The son's high-handed attitude when dealing with fellow commanders at Nottingham Castle made matters worse. He was arrested there on suspicion of treachery on 22 June 1643, but managed to escape and rejoin his father at Hull[57].

Father and son were arrested together a few weeks later. In the mêlée, Sir John Hotham was knocked from his horse and struck in the face by a musket. A large number of the Hothams' 3,000 officers were either imprisoned or kept under watch as suspicious. No details survive as to exactly what part John Lawson played in discovering their treachery, but the captain was one of the witnesses at their trial for treason, along with Colonel Matthew Boynton. Seventeen months after their arrest, father and son were both beheaded and Sir John Hotham forced to watch his son's execution the day before his own[58].

The royalist successes of 1643 were short-lived. Parliament regained the military advantage by the end of the year. The second siege of Hull in September through to October ended in humiliating defeat for the royalists and they withdrew. In the meantime, parliament made an alliance with the Scots that altered the military balance in the north. The Scottish army crossed the border at the beginning of 1644 and royalist strength in Yorkshire dissipated. Any hope of recovery vanished with their defeat at the battle of Marston Moor on 2 July 1644[59].

John Lawson continued to make his mark, serving the navy from his base at Hull by blockading the royalist ships using Scarborough port. On one memorable day towards the end of 1644, John captured a royalist merchant ship. Not content with this victory, he rapidly mounted four of the enemy's guns onto his own ship. He cut off his fly-boat to increase the *Covenant's* speed and then, in a David and Goliath effort, gave chase to and captured a man-of-war that out-sized and out-gunned his own vessel. Ever the pragmatic Yorkshire merchant, he followed up once he was back on shore by demanding compensation from the Navy for his lost boat and the maintenance of the captives on board[60]. This was his hometown that he was blockading – and his exile was not from choice. What personal conflicts he felt can only be imagined.

Taking the royalists by surprise one cold day in February 1645, the parliamentarian commander Sir John Meldrum and his troops seized 120 ships moored in Scarborough haven, cutting off any possible retreat by sea and recapturing the town. Losing only eleven men, they took eighty royalist soldiers prisoner as Sir Hugh Cholmley and his forces withdrew into the castle. Sir Meldrum and his brigade of infantrymen attacked and a twenty-two week siege began.

Indicative of the importance of Scarborough, the besieging forces brought some of the largest cannon in the land. One was named 'Sweet Lips', reputedly in appreciation of a Hull prostitute. It weighed two-and-a-half tons and was positioned at the east end of the chancel inside St Mary's Church, with a direct line of sight to the castle keep. Cannonballs, weighing from twelve to sixty pounds, battered the castle's defences. A terrible spectacle occurred after three days' bombardment, as the 100-foot high and 15-foot thick west wall of the great keep collapsed[61].

The rubble from the tower barricaded the only entrance to the castle, providing protective cover and ready-made missiles for the royalist defenders. Unable to breach the outer walls, Meldrum's parliamentary troops engaged in hand-to-hand combat around the barbican gateway. Two weeks into the siege, Meldrum took a musket ball 'in att the bellie and out of the backe',[62] lingering in agony for six days before he died. Matthew Boynton replaced him and by mid-summer the bombardment, an outbreak of scurvy and the shortage of food and water left few men fit enough to fight. News of the king's devastating defeat at Naseby came in June. When Sir Hugh Cholmley surrendered the castle on 25 July, around half of the original 500 defenders were dead. The Lawsons' banishment was over[63].

Whether John Lawson took part in the siege is not recorded, but there are clues. He had definitely returned to Scarborough by September 1645, at which time he was elected to the Common Hall's First Twelve – the town's ruling body. This was not an honour given lightly and has justifiably been interpreted by some historians as a reward for his efforts in overcoming Cholmley. A month later the corporation records include a note from an army official that mentions how diligent John had been about the town's business[64].

Nevertheless, the town was still vulnerable – and not just from the royalists. 'The pirates doe still continue their mischiefes upon these coasts having taken nine ships within eight days since the 21st of March',[65] warned the town council in a letter to John at the beginning of April 1646. It would undo all trade unless some speedy and special care was taken for Scarborough's relief. Seven warships had to be deployed from elsewhere to see them off[66].

By May 1646, repairs had been made to the castle and on the sixth of that month John Lawson was rewarded with a captaincy in the New Model Army. Alongside his civic duties, he commanded a hundred men to be maintained in the town under the new governor, Colonel Matthew Boynton[67]. His move from merchant seaman to army captain was not as unusual as it might appear, especially for men who had proven their worth, whether that was at sea or on land. Loyalty and audacity were prized qualities in the new force.

The New Model Army (or New Modelled Army as it was first known) was formed only a few months before John's appointment. It was designed to replace local militia companies with full-time soldiers under a single command and Sir Thomas Fairfax was appointed Captain General. Leaders were appointed on ability not social standing and prohibited from having seats in parliament, in order to keep the army separate from political and religious factions. Exceptions were however made for four men, including Oliver Cromwell and his son-in-law Henry Ireton, due to their military skills.

The soldiers were a mix of veterans and conscripts, press ganged from parliamentary-held areas and large numbers held dissenting puritan convictions. Recruits were sworn to pull down Babylon, cleanse the nation of popery, reform corrupt and superstitious clergy, advance Christ's kingdom, bring the enemies of church and state to justice and uphold parliament.

The Presbyterian army chaplain, poet and hymn-writer Richard Baxter was among those disquieted by the ardent religiosity permeating the new army. He wrote of how the newsbooks and broadsheets had spread the news across the country that there were swarms of Anabaptists in our armies, 'but we thought it just a lie'[68]. Baxter was not alone in using the term Anabaptist so pejoratively. It was a convenient label for all kinds of nonconformist religious subversives, typified by those vehemently against the government, a state-sanctioned church and being forced to financially support the Church of England. Baxter went on to say that when he joined Cromwell's army that he 'found a new face of things', of which he had never dreamt: plotting heads hotly determined to pursue ideas which indicated their intention to 'subvert both church and state'[69].

The creation of the New Model Army marked a milestone in the civil war. It was no longer just about limiting the power of the monarch and subduing Catholic leanings within the Church of England. It was now an overtly political and religious revolution. Victory after victory for the parliamentarians followed. So too did the ransacking of towns and villages and atrocities by both sides. After Naseby in 1645, Oliver Cromwell proclaimed the victory to be by the hand of God, while the king's correspondence, which was seized after the battle, purportedly revealed him to be in alliance with Irish papists and under the influence of Henrietta Maria, his French Catholic wife.

By late 1645, England was almost completely under parliamentary control. Puritan zeal would be expressed by obliterating religious images in churches across the country. Christmas should be a fast day not a feast, preached the ideologues. No more puddings and pies, garlanding homes with holly, singing or acting out mummers' plays. 'Christmas was killed at Naseby fight. Likewise then did die roast beef and shred pie', went one protest song[70].

As the royalist forces suffered overwhelming defeats, John strove to help Scarborough recover from the destruction wrought on the castle, church, school and town. Over the next couple of years he frequently travelled to London on behalf of Scarborough council, to lobby the government for war damage compensation. Staying regularly at the Three Cups Inn in Holborn and elsewhere, John's letters to the corporation convey his frustration at how long it took for matters to be heard. The ease with which John Lawson slotted back into the community is worth remarking on. There is no hint of animosity between him and the leading townsfolk, who had continued to work with the royalists while he was in Hull. Rather, John threw himself wholeheartedly into working with them for the benefit of the town. Two of his apprentices were accepted as freemen and he rented a large piece of farmland on the edge of the town[71].

Despite John's obvious willingness to fight on the parliamentary side from the very beginning, it is only in his surviving comments, in letters and declarations from the 1650s onwards, that we hear John Lawson's own, unquestionably radical words on religion and politics. We can therefore only wonder how defined these opinions already were, or whether he became more politicised in the years to come.

Although John Lawson's politics were firmly aligned on the radical edge of republicanism, it is not known exactly when the rumours began that he was an Anabaptist[72]. John's actions reinforced this perception. He publicly supported the election of radical MP Luke Robinson in 1645 and forcefully opposed any suggestion of a single ruler above parliament. At the same time he demanded liberty of conscience – no one should meddle in another's religious practice[73]. These views were highly suspect, even among many parliamentarians, having been popularised by the Quakers and the radical political movement that became known as the Levellers. The army provided a nurturing environment for the development of Leveller notions of religious freedom, equality and political responsibilities. While the Levellers were not a homogenous or uniformly cohesive group, they played an increasing role in the radicalisation of public opinion between 1646 and 1650.

By 1647, the king was under arrest and the army had become a political force in its own right. Pre-existing divisions between different strands of parliamentarianism increased rapidly. In the autumn of that year, the famous 'Leveller Debates' took place at St Mary the Virgin church in Putney. In the midst of meetings between representatives of the New Model Army's ranks and officers over what to do with the king and what form of post-war government should be established, the Levellers in the army made startling and dangerous demands for the extension of suffrage. They presented a vision of a fairer society, based on the supremacy of parliament, independence of the judiciary, freedom of speech and religious toleration. While this inspired large numbers of those present, the debates also revealed fundamental divisions among parliamentarians[74].

Available records do not reveal whether John was ever directly involved with the Leveller agitations of the late 1640s. He did however spend his time captaining a company of foot soldiers in the New Model Army, right at the moment when Leveller ideas had their strongest impact within the ranks[75]. Moreover, many of the military, naval and merchant men he knew well were Leveller sympathisers. John's own experiences of exile and the defection of friends and commanders to the royalist cause might make even the most moderate person open to new and increasingly radicalised concepts.

What John and the Levellers had in common was rhetoric and religious principles. Much of the Leveller protests were originally focussed on religious grievances, notably the lack of 'liberty of conscience' and the requirement to pay tithes – the tax that supported Church of England clergy. They began to advocate political reform as their grievances with parliament and the army increased. The would-be reformers emphasised the notion of 'natural law', although interpretations of this varied from it being 'traditional' common laws of England or the Magna Carta, to the laws of God and laws innate to human interaction.

However it was expressed, one message was clear: people had a duty to defend their kingdom against destructive leaders. The Levellers were not the only group to espouse such ideas. Quakers and more communistic egalitarian groups such as the Diggers shared many of the same ideals and rhetoric. They also used many of the same tactics to bring these to a wider audience via thousands of cheap and easily produced tracts, petitions, pamphlets and broadsheets[76].

John Lawson left very few words to explain how and why he was so often willing to risk his life, his family's safety and financial stability. For him the fight against the royalists was simply righteous and just. His belief was that the just foundations of a godly government could only be achieved through freedom of worship. This conviction was intrinsically bound up with his own later demands to abolish tithes, suggestions for economic improvements by removing excise duty and how to aid the poor and sick who were unable to support themselves through no fault of their own[77].

The experiences and writings of people from similar backgrounds offer deeper insights into John's faith. He and his fellow parliamentarians believed they had God on their side. It was a cause that attracted nonconformists who were immersed in a culture of godliness, fostered through intense group bible study and lengthy prayer meetings. Their personal relationship with the bible and God as well as their political ideology was heightened by gatherings in which lay people openly disputed scriptural interpretations[78].

One man that John Lawson had much in common with was Captain Lieutenant William Bray, a junior officer in the New Model Army. Bray came to public attention in the 1640s through his letters and petitions and was imprisoned for supporting the Levellers in 1647. Echoes of his words can be heard in the letters and declaration John published during his confrontation with the army in 1659 and 1660. In distinctly millenarian terms, Bray wrote of how a vengeful God would judge the wicked deeds of those that conspired in power and corrupted England's fundamental laws[79].

John would need all his faith and unswerving commitment to the cause once more before the decade was out. In 1648, after five years eluding all attempts to capture him, the renegade Browne Bushell was reported to be at the mouth of the River Tyne seizing the goods of Newcastle colliers on behalf of the king. John Lawson was ordered to sail the *Covenant* north to bring his former commander in. Bushell's subsequent execution was deliberately timed by the Rump Parliament to coincide with the eighth anniversary of his betrayal of Scarborough castle[80].

Any satisfaction that John might have felt at Bushell's imprisonment was undone in July. Draping a red flag over the curtain wall of Scarborough Castle and declaring for the king, his commander Colonel Matthew Boynton joined the turncoats. A second siege began. This was the other betrayal that John Lawson spoke of when reflecting on his parliamentary service. With his life in danger once more, John Lawson again quit his home and took his family back to Hull[81].

On 6 August 1648, letters arrived in Hull from General Fairfax addressed to Colonel Overton, the governor there and to Captain John Lawson. Colonel Overton was requested to give John Lawson his best assistance.[82] To John Lawson, Fairfax wrote:

> Captaine:- By the power and authority to me given by both houses of parliament I doe hearby constitute and appoint you captain of the foot company lately under the command of Colonel Boynton in Scarborough castle he being revolted[83].

Captain John Lawson set forth once more on behalf of God and parliament. Furnished with two drummers and a hundred men armed with muskets, pikes, powder and shot he marched to Scarborough to assist the forces there to reduce the castle[84].

# CHAPTER 2

# A VERY HIGH TRUST

On 19 December 1648, Captain John Lawson and his company of soldiers watched as Colonel Boynton, his officers and men marched out of Scarborough Castle with colours flying and carrying their loaded muskets. The royalist troops headed down the hill to the accompaniment of beating drums and, when they reached Scarborough common, laid down their arms. John was appointed to witness the official surrender, signing the agreement alongside Christopher Legard, Lieutenant Colonel William Spence, Colonel Barrington Bourchier and Captain Nicholas Conyeres. The town itself had been recaptured a few weeks before, so the whole of Scarborough was in parliamentarian hands once more. One can only imagine the satisfaction John felt at defeating Matthew Boynton, the second traitor he named as causing him, his wife and children to have fled Scarborough for their lives. Now they could all return home from Hull[1].

The parliamentarian cause to which John had committed himself six years earlier was at a turning point. Two weeks before the surrender of Scarborough Castle, MPs hostile to plans to put the king on trial for treason arrived at the Palace of Westminster to attend parliament – only to find the entrance guarded by a troop of musketeers commanded by Colonel Thomas Pride. As other regiments patrolled nearby streets, one of their fellow MPs, Lord Grey of Groby, stood on the steps holding a list of around 180 of those whose interests were not aligned with what the army wanted. He pointed out each man on the list as they arrived and Pride's troops forcibly turned them away. Around forty-five MPs who resisted were arrested and guards were posted to prevent them all from gaining access.

This military coup became known as Pride's Purge, a name that rather understates the event. It ended the Long Parliament that had sat since 1640. Barely seventy serving MPs remained, giving rise to the name the Rump Parliament – its back end – the source of many bad puns and ribald comments. Rump MPs were mostly independents whose support enabled the army chief, Oliver Cromwell, to usher in the Commonwealth republic the following year. This parliament, this republic, was what John Lawson would carry on fighting for. For him, it was the most true and godly form of government[2].

Contemporaries and historians have had much to say about Cromwell's actions and motivations after this event. The royalist Sir Philip Warwick, former MP and secretary to Charles I, summed up the feelings of many on both sides of the political divide when he described Cromwell as 'extraordinarily designed for those extraordinary things [which he] successfully and greatly performed'[3]. Warwick's additional portrayal of Cromwell's 'wickedness and fanatical frenzies'[4] is the subject of as much argument today as it was then. In the centuries since there have been numerous epithets applied to him, ranging from fanatical regicidal dictator, instigator of religious persecution and war crimes, to reforming idealist and a founder of Britain's modern parliamentary democracy.

Oliver Cromwell's military prowess, charisma and talented political acumen had enabled him to rise from relative obscurity as MP for Huntingdon to Lieutenant-General of the parliamentarian army and, eventually, the first republican head of state. His son Richard would be the second and last. Cromwell had come under the influence of puritans during his early years, especially at school in Huntingdon and at Sydney Sussex College in Cambridge. He joined the parliamentarian cause because he believed, like so many others, that Charles I was turning the country back towards Catholicism.

By the late 1640s, Cromwell's brilliant military tactics had helped him become one of the key players in political affairs. Although Cromwell was absent when Pride's Purge took place, it began a process that enabled his rise to the top of government. Saviour or wrecker of the republican cause? There were many, including men that John Lawson was closely associated with, who would go on to openly accuse him of wanting power for its own sake.

On 30 January 1649, a few weeks after Pride's Purge, King Charles I stepped out of a long window on the upper floor of the Banqueting House in Whitehall onto the scaffold built outside. As the masked executioner swung the axe down, a great groan came forth from the crowd of men, women and children watching. Upon hearing the details, the scholar John Aubrey wrote 'the world since then is utterly changed'[5].

The next few years would see England transformed at every level within the new order, but political and religious fault-lines soon appeared. Discontent with the government escalated, especially over religious matters[6]. The majority of MPs seemed more concerned with imposing godliness than freedom of worship and there was little reform of the church. Harsh punishments were enacted for adultery, fornication before marriage and profane language, while the Act against blasphemy was deliberately framed to curb more extreme sectarians such as the libertarian Ranters, who caused a moral panic with pamphlets promoting promiscuity, drinking and a personal relationship with God.

It was part of a wider suppression of entertainment and jollity in the name of the Lord. Worst of all for enormous numbers of people was the outright ban on celebrating Christmas, going far beyond previous attempts to destroy traces of the pagan solstice celebrations and Roman Catholic trappings. Soldiers alerted by the smell of a goose roasting on a fire seized festive food. Those discovered playing cards, dancing or singing carols in private were arrested. In Scarborough before the wars, inhabitants had been fined for not going to church. No one checked people's attendance any more, but those who did not observe the Sabbath as a holy day of rest were prosecuted for drinking ale, playing shovelboard, tables and cards and taking part in various games including coits and football on a Sunday[7].

Even the clergy holding services were not immune to violence and intimidation. Nothing however was done about the vexatious question of tithes, whereby most of the population were compelled to give the clergy ten per cent (or the equivalent in money) of whatever they grew; their cattle, sheep, milk, eggs and wool or other produce, as well as the same percentage of any earnings from labour.

John would spend the next two years in command of a foot company moving between army bases in Scarborough and Boston in Lincolnshire. Boston's location and port made it extremely importantly strategically. As well as being strongly parliamentarian, there was also a long history of nonconformism among the residents as large numbers of the earliest American pilgrim settlers were from Lincolnshire, with several influential figures from Boston itself. Anti-royalist feeling in the area had been fuelled by the draining of the fens, which had been authorised by Charles I and had damaged the livelihood of many in the area.

Despite his army command, John Lawson's seafaring skills would continue to be of service to his hometown. He carried on as a merchant seaman alongside his army duties. Moreover, the people of Scarborough were so worried about attacks from royalist privateers that they asked the authorities to give John and his fellow captain, William Nesfield, a frigate each in order to better protect the town's coast. John's growing reputation for audacity was only enhanced in May 1649, when he sailed into the Danish port of Gluckstadt to retrieve a stolen collier for its Scarborough owners. Within sight of an armed fortress, John boarded the collier and towed it away before the guards could fire a shot[8].

Piracy was, as it always had been, a constant problem, particularly from royalists. Sailors and merchants from Scarborough and nearby fishing villages were captured and kept in Dunkirk until an exchange could be agreed for royalists or Dutch prisoners held in York prison[9]. In December 1649, royalist pirates/privateers seized a ship full of barley and took it towards Jersey. Unfortunately for them, a storm drove it into Scarborough where it was recaptured[10]. A few months later, a man-of-war from Dunkirk was noticed on the coast and Robert Colman, a fisherman from Yarmouth who was in Scarborough with his vessel, offered his services to Governor Bethell, even though his boat was still laden with fish. With the help of soldiers from the garrison and seven of his own men, they refused the command to 'strike ye doggs for King Charles'[11] and captured the man-of-war after 'a very hot skirmish'[12]. In the same year, the wife of Moyler Vanarke of Dunkirk was reported as keeping Robert Vickars of Scarborough a prisoner under three locks until her husband was released[13].

John was not quite living in a brave new world. Despite having bought land and a house at Sandgate in Scarborough, money was a constant worry. Parliament's financial position was no better than it had been when he served as a merchant seaman. Throughout 1648 and 1649, John regularly begged the army administrators to reimburse him for his company's pay and the cost of quartering them. This included most of the expenses incurred after the defection of Colonel Boynton up until after the town and castle were retaken.Scarborough had suffered badly during this latest siege, as they had during the town's earlier upheavals.

The burgesses had previously petitioned Colonel Boynton when he still held the castle, to consider the heavy costs they had to bear for quartering the soldiers, providing food, bedding, timber, candles for the guards, thirty eight pecks of coal a night and other supplies for the castle. On top of that was the matter of his troops requisitioning their hay, cattle and horses without giving due compensation. Trade, said the burgesses, was in decay as a result.

Things were not much better once Boynton was ousted, with complaints and heartrending stories from the townsfolk of people on the verge of starvation merely being redirected to the new governor, Colonel Bethell. The town council asserted that they would rather pay money to the governor directly than submit to the intolerable burden of quartering soldiers[14]. One altercation in May 1649 between William Catline, a gunner based in the castle and George Moore of the town, typifies the tensions. Moore refused to sell Catline corn at the price he wanted. After Catline accused Moore of trying to tax him, Moore pushed him backwards, grabbed his sword and cut him on the head. Moore's defence was that Catline had tried to appropriate corn and rye meant for the governor and that Catline pushed him first[15].

Six months after being commissioned to lead his troops to besiege the castle, John Lawson was still waiting for all the monies he had spent on behalf of the army, as well as his own pay. So too were the people of Scarborough. Scores of complaints began to be filed in the corporation's records chest from townsfolk who had not been reimbursed for supplying food and accommodation to John's men during the same period. One set of vouchers, for billeting over fifty men in John's company for the three months from March to July 1649, lists various sums of between two and thirty shillings for quartering his men for between one and ten weeks. The cost to the widow Chapman for hosting Anthony Gye for three weeks was eight shillings, while Richard Stamp had a Thomas Rowell lodged with him for nine weeks at a cost of twenty-four shillings[16].

The following quarter, another list of moneys still owed to fifty householders ranged from three to eighteen shillings. The petitions demanding to be reimbursed sent by the bailiffs and burgess of Scarborough to the committee for the army pointed out in no uncertain terms that they had been left with insupportable burdens and losses as a result of their willingness to serve parliament by lending money and allowing quarters to the soldiers of Colonel Bethell and Captain Lawson when they were too destitute to pay. A little money trickled in over the next couple of years, but unredeemed bills for around fifty of John's men remain unpaid to this day[17].

The man to whom John sent his own appeals for money was Adam Baynes, who had served under General Fairfax and in early 1649 became the Northern Brigade's financial agent and attorney in London. When Captain Baynes presented one of John's petitions for three months' pay and other costs to the committee for the army, he was told that they could not possibly repay it as they did not have enough money in their treasury. Again and again, John pointed out the hardship these debts caused for his family, but the country was essentially bankrupt[18].

Even when he was evidently frustrated, John Lawson always addressed Baynes as his dear friend and signed off by sending him his love. Starting from 1649 onwards, this affectionate farewell was frequently followed by John declaring himself to be the Commonwealth's faithful servant or similar[19]. This expression of affection between men was by no means unusual for the time. While it was often merely a convention, it could also represent a bond that encompassed a love of God, loyalty and shared endeavours and John really did consider himself bound in blood, sacrifice and ideology to the Commonwealth.

At the beginning of December 1649, John was forced to borrow sixty pounds to pay his officers and soldiers. Ten days later he was still entreating his commander to arrange repayment – and by the latter half of the month, he was running out of patience[20]. On the nineteenth, he wrote again to Captain Baynes, this time to ask why the money from the treasury for the garrison at Scarborough castle was not forthcoming when Major Cotterell had received his at Boston. He signed off by sending his love to Captain Baynes and Captain Margetts. Then, without any further explanation, John took the time to add a postscript to his letter to say he assumed that John Lilburne 'lives still and is att liberty'[21]. It is the only time in his correspondence with Baynes that John makes any comment on matters not directly relating to the army or the money he was owed.

John Lilburne was the nominal head of the Levellers. Although from different backgrounds, the two men were roughly the same age and shared many of the same principles. Lilburne had a long history of agitating for political and religious reforms. Having joined the New Model Army in 1640, he became a Lieutenant-Colonel and was a leading figure during the Putney Debates of 1647. A zealous supporter of parliament until the army suppressed the Levellers, Lilburne would become one of parliament's fiercest critics before the decade was out[22].

Lilburne's escalating attacks on the army, parliament and former allies saw him imprisoned numerous times throughout 1648 and 1649. Each time he was released, Lilburne and his friends increased their propaganda efforts, mainly via the publication and distribution of broadsheets. Many of the Leveller ideals were shared by other radical and visionary groups, such as the Ranters who rejected all formal worship and the communistic Diggers, who called for the earth to be treated as a common treasury for all. But none of them came together in any kind of coherent movement strong enough to challenge parliament[23].

A Leveller mutiny in the army was crushed in May and, by October 1649, John Lilburne was on trial for treason. The following month he was acquitted and released from custody yet again. By the time John Lawson wrote to Adam Baynes and asked for news of Lilburne, two years had passed since the Putney debates. Now Lilburne and other Levellers were openly questioning whether anything had fundamentally altered since the king's execution and vigorously denounced the Rump for seizing power from the people[24]. This is where John Lilburne and John Lawson differed. While Lilburne condemned it, John Lawson would remain a devoted servant of the Rump and of the Commonwealth republic it created.

Despite having much popular support, the Levellers were losing their potency as a force for political change by 1650. Their highest point of agitation, support from common soldiers and appeal to the wider populace had already passed and within a couple of years they would be spent. Nevertheless the radical notions that came under the umbrella of Levellerism philosophy did not just disappear. The Levellers' central demands became a refrain repeated by many other activists for years to come[25]. Indeed, their words would be heard in John Lawson's own public declarations in later years, in which he demanded freedom of worship, the cessation of tithe payments and no monarchy or any other single ruler over parliament[26].

John Lawson obviously thought Lilburn's freedom was important enough to comment upon when he wrote to Adam Baynes in the winter of 1649, but left no clue as to why[27]. His pressing concern was, again, financial. Parliament had come up with a scheme to raise funds to pay the army. Instead of paying the northern officers, they assigned them debentures – certificates – for the money owed. In 1649, parliament ordered the sale of crown lands to pay the army. The debentures could be exchanged for these lands, with the amount of land granted dependent on the level of arrears[28].

Understandably, many soldiers were unhappy at being giving the equivalent of a credit note to exchange for land. Large numbers sold their debentures to speculators at a fraction of their value in return for cash, receiving on average of between one shilling and sixpence and twelve shillings in the pound. Captain Baynes was one of those who benefitted, as he obtained thousands of pounds worth of debentures from 109 soldiers and officers, including most of his own men, at well below what they were worth and used them to purchase a valuable manor[29].

It all took time. In December, the tone of John's letters shifted from just asking for reimbursement to entreating Adam Baynes to find out if he was to receive any debentures. If so, he wanted to know what their value was in the pound and whether Baynes could deliver them to him soon[30]. In January 1650, John wrote again asking for around two hundred pounds-worth. He explained that he had agreed to use the debentures as part purchase towards land in the manor of Wyberton, which lay just on the edge of Boston in Lincolnshire. John was acting on behalf of the existing tenant, who could not buy the land directly as it was owned by the crown. In return for using his credit, John would receive a small parcel of land. However, he needed more in order to meet the asking price and instructed Baynes to purchase new ones for him, so long as it was at a good rate[31].

Shortly afterwards John received his debentures. In February he signed a three-way transaction with Thomas Tooley, the owner of Wyberton Manor and his tenant Thomas Graves. John's land credits were £660, estimated at around £50,000 today, though you wouldn't now get what John did for the money – a cottage, twenty-eight acres of pasture land and another five acres that were leased to tenants[32]. No precise account survives of how much John made out of the arrangement, but he said that if he had been willing to buy all of it in exchange for fifty pounds a year to the owner, that he would make about eighty pounds a year on top of that from the leases, with more to come as the land was improving. John hoped that if Mr Tooley and Mr Graves broke off their arrangement, then

Adam Baynes would purchase the manor along with Mr Graves, for it would be a 'special bargain'[33].

The timing could not have been better. His years of chasing the army authorities for what he was owed were almost over. John's foot company was disbanded within weeks and he was, as he put it, 'called to employment' in the navy[34]. An intriguing, undated and unsigned draft letter in the Scarborough town council records seems to refer to John leaving the army. Among the litany of complaints from its authors about the condition of the castle and its governor Colonel Bethell's mismanagement of the garrison, they were deeply regretful that 'Capt L is now going for London to gett his discharge from his employment here and wee can no wayes prevayle with him to continue'[35].

The navy had experienced its own mutiny, purge and reformation almost in tandem with the army's, mainly over political differences. The Rump Parliament had quickly seen that a strong navy was essential for survival. It was remodelled after 1648 with three army colonels – Popham, Blake and Deane – appointed as Admirals and Generals at Sea. The Council of State, the Rump's executive body, retained ultimate control but established a new Admiralty Committee to oversee it. The king's execution had horrified other governments in Europe, many of whom were unwilling to recognise the new regime. Apart from this posing a threat to England's overseas trade, there was the possibility that some of these countries would actively aid the Stuarts in their attempts to regain the throne[36].

This insecurity was compounded by the Rump initially wielding little power outside of England and Wales. Scotland proclaimed allegiance to the king's son and most of Ireland was in royalist hands. Without a strong, trustworthy and efficient navy to protect the republic, its survival was doubtful. The sales of confiscated royalist lands and fines brought more than seven million pounds to the new republican government between 1649 and 1653. Although much of this went towards paying their debts, including army and navy arrears, it also helped to finance military incursions in Ireland and Scotland and the building up of a new Commonwealth navy.

Although the navy had a crucial part to play in protecting England's shores against the royalists, pirates and brigands of any nature or motivation, the major victories occurred on land. Soldiers and officers in dramatic battles such as Naseby and Marston Moor gained honour and fame – or infamy, depending on their actions or which side the observer was on. Whether or not such large-scale bloodshed, decimation of communities and deep fissures along political and religious lines should be seen as glorious, the land battles and the army were the stuff of legend and folk tales.

In contrast, the navy's role as a deterrent and assisting with the transport of troops and supplies during the civil war was far less glamorous. As a result the navy was (and by some still is) seen as of only secondary or limited importance, and even overlooked completely in some accounts. But the Rump soon saw the commercial potential of using a strengthened navy against the Dutch. The consequence was that the English navy would eventually become the most powerful in the world and a couple of years after John Lawson signed up, he became an active participant in England's most fruitful and triumphant war of the seventeenth century[37].

As mentioned previously, John was what was known as a 'tarpaulin' officer: someone who had worked his way up rather than a gentleman. Until the early 1640s, the majority of captains and lieutenants were appointed from aristocratic or gentry backgrounds,

but by the time John joined most captains of the fleets were drawn
from the ranks of warrant officers or were merchant owner-masters
like himself. Experienced, radical, merchant commanders like John
Lawson were just what the Rump needed, although it was not
always easy to lure them away from commercial activities[38].

The most important member of the admiralty committee was
Sir Henry Vane, who would play a critical role in shaping the
course of John Lawson's life over the next ten years. Vane had
been admiralty treasurer since 1642 and subsequently appointed
a commissioner. The three years Sir Henry spent in America in the
late 1630s had sharpened his puritan inclinations and he believed
in complete freedom of religious thought and that parliament
should be the only form of government. Vane actively recruited
such men, including Nehemiah Bourne and probably brought John
in too. As such, the new Commonwealth navy was a natural home
for John because most of the officers and men held similar political
and religious views and his certainly fitted with the new order[39].

John began his new career as the captain of a merchant ship
called *The Trade's Increase*. His former captain William Haddock
and John Bourne were assigned to the navy with their merchant
ships at the same time. Within six months, John Lawson was
appointed by Sir Henry Vane to captain the 34-gun frigate
*Centurion* in charge of 150 men to attend the army in Scotland.
One of the tasks he was trusted with was to transport money for
the army in Scotland.

John's employment at sea was not completely settled for several
months and the committee for state decided that this meant that
he should continue in command of his foot company as well. This
was to change when the naval commanders took the decision
to attack French shipping. The relationship between the two

countries was already poor when King Charles was sent to his death. His execution and the introduction of the Commonwealth deepened the rift between the two countries. The French banned trade with England, pledged financial aid towards the Stuarts' schemes for regaining their throne and turned a blind eye to privateers commissioned by Charles Stuart freely using French ports. The result was an increasing number of damaging attacks on English ships in the Mediterranean, with hundreds of thousands of pounds worth of ships and goods being lost. The import of French goods was banned first. Then, in the summer of 1650, naval commanders were ordered to attack French naval and merchant ships.

John Lawson was singled out for praise in scattering a large fishing fleet in Newfoundland in September and he joined the regular convoys protecting English merchant ships in the Straits of Gibraltar. In 1651 he followed Vice-Admiral William Penn to Portugal, then into the Mediterranean in command of the 36-gun ship the *Fairfax*. It can be safely assumed that John had completely given up his army command by now, as he was to spend many months in pursuit of Prince Rupert, the nephew of King Charles I and the admiral of the exiled royalists, who was successfully disrupting English trade[40].

John's new commander, William Penn, would become a lifelong friend, admirer and close neighbour. They had much in common although Penn was a few years younger than John. Like him, Penn was a merchant seaman by trade, having served an apprenticeship with his father. They shared political and religious sympathies, although Penn is perhaps better known today because of his son William who became a Quaker and oversaw the founding of Pennsylvania in America.

Despite failing to capture Prince Rupert, the two men spent fourteen months sailing as far east as Malta and taking many French and Portuguese prizes. John was formally recognised by the Council of State in the October of 1652 for his good service under Penn. Half the value of each warship captured would go to the captors, with the other half going to the relief fund for sick and wounded sailors, widows and dependents. Warships that were sunk in action were valued according to the number of guns they carried, with the crew receiving six pounds for each cannon. Proceeds from captured merchantmen and their cargoes were shared equally between the captors, the state and the relief fund[41].

Unfortunately, joining the navy changed little with respect to John's precarious finances. After fourteen months in the Straits of Gibraltar, off the coast of Portugal and in the Mediterranean, 'by reason of the treacheries and revolutions ashore and smallness of salary at sea', he and his family had received no maintenance from the public[42]. Nor, he told Sir Henry Vane in February 1653, had he 'used those ways of plundering that others have'[43] to make up the deficit. It is unclear whether this meant that John had not received the £60 of prize money awarded by the Council of State the previous October for his good service under Captain Penn, whether only part of it went to him personally, or if what he did get was simply not enough for his needs[44].

Either way, John resolved to leave his naval employment and find some other way to provide for his family. However, war had broken out with the Dutch over trade routes and he could not satisfy his conscience by leaving for the time being. He wrote to his Sir Henry Vane from onboard the *Fairfax* in February 1653 to say he was cheerfully convinced that committing to this service was by God's design and for the glory of Jesus Christ. Nevertheless, he was worried for the future of his family if he should die in battle[45]. Having suffered losses on land and at sea, John therefore implored Sir Henry to make provision for his wife and young children:

> If the Lord shall have appointed my course to be finished and shall take me to himself while I am in this employment (which at the appointed time I trust through his rich mercy and free grace in Jesus Christ he will do) that your honour will become instrumental that my wife and children may be considered in more than an ordinary manner, for they have suffered outwardly by my imbraicing this sea service last: my wife is dear to me, and I have good ground to believe she is dear to God. And therefore I assure myself your honour will be more willing in such a case to take the trouble upon you. I beg pardon for this presumption, beseeching the Lord to preserve your honour and all faithful ones at land, and that his presence may be with, and providence over us at sea. My most humble and bounden service presented, I crave leave to subscribe myself, Right Honourable, Your Honour's and the interest of God's peoples[46].

The war with the Dutch arose from commercial rivalry. All the fighting took place at sea. The Dutch had control of most of European trade through a mixture of aggressive – and some might say dubious – tactics, which drove the English (and others) out of the Far East, as well as a trade agreement that allowed them free movement in the Baltic without having to pay tolls[47]. This protectionism was anathema to John Lawson as a merchant seaman. He was not alone, then and for years afterwards, in believing that trade would be improved by removing excise duty, although in reality that seems to have been considered a one-way street, only to be applied to England being allowed to trade freely[48].

Tensions between the English and Dutch had ratcheted up after the execution of King Charles I, largely because Charles's daughter was married to William of Orange and Holland provided a safe haven to royalists fleeing England, including the two princes. As the Dutch had made peace with Spain the year before, they were now also able to move and trade more freely in their areas of interest. By the early 1650s, the Dutch were rapidly expanding into the Mediterranean and the West Indies. Moreover, there was a festering resentment against the Dutch, particularly among fishing folk, over the loss of profits from the enormous and highly profitable shoals of herring that hundreds of Dutch boats followed south each year from the Shetlands to the Thames estuary. Most if not all English people believed they were losing out on the financial benefits to be had from fish taken in their territorial waters and which had been claimed as such for England many years before by King James I[49].

The trigger for the final break between the two countries came in October 1651, when the Rump Parliament introduced an Act designed to limit the Dutch control of lucrative trade routes, by forbidding the import of goods unless they were carried by English vessels. Added to this was the claim of English sovereignty over the seas. Fighting began with a skirmish between the English Admiral Blake and the Dutch Admiral Maarten Tromp in May 1652, as the English fleet attempted to search the Dutch ships. War was declared in July and the first major battle occurred in September.

Two months later, John Lawson was one of the commanders who signed a petition sent by Admiral Robert Blake to the

General of State, asking for sixty men-of-war, each with no fewer than twenty-six guns topwards. Blake was keen that the whole fleet should be state ships. Nevertheless, he was obviously aware that he might need to compromise, as he agreed to accept some merchant ships as long as they numbered no more than one fifth of the total. However, they were to carry at least twenty-eight guns each and officers be put in by the state. Whatever force they had, Blake said, they would be ready to commit themselves to divine providence[50].

The day-to-day details of John's service on the *Fairfax* and later the *George* survive in a log book he kept from November 1652 until September the following year. Among mundane entries – which way the wind was blowing, where he anchored, how many men and boys were on board and repairs undertaken – are records of each engagement with the Dutch. In February 1653, John Lawson took part in a three-day battle, fighting under Admiral Blake, against the Dutch at the Battle of Portland close to Beachy Head[51]. 'The wind came westerley, fair weather stood to and again was thwart of Beachy'[52], wrote John after a council of flag officers in which they resolved to get there in expectation of meeting with the Dutch. Blake's squadron was vastly outnumbered. He was badly wounded and both his captain and master were killed, but it was victory for England. The next morning:

> About nine of the clock wee ingaiged them, and continued till sunset, the Tryumph and some others were forelorne that day wee had many men slaine and wounded, there was about 7 or 8 of there men of war taken suncke and burned, one of them taken was an East India Shipp, of 1200 tuns wee had one Flemish ship of 28 guns sunck, her name the *Sampson*, she was taken last year[53].

Admiral Tromp lost seventeen men-of-war and more than fifty merchant ships from his convoy on just the first day, while the English lost only ten ships. In the mêlée of the first day, John and his men accomplished the rescue of Admiral Blake's flagship when none of the rest of the fleet was able to approach as it came under prolonged volleys of shot to its hull. On the second day, his own ship sustained severe damage under heavy fire and John Lawson decided on an audacious tactic. About half an hour before sunset, he steered towards a Dutch man-of-war and 'came off with her'[54], forced the captured ship out of the Dutch line of battle and positioned her so that her guns could be used against her own side. This was a new manoeuvre, first recorded in this year, which had a significant role in the success of the English navy for centuries thereafter[55]. John believed he had escaped death through divine providence:

> I steared aboard one of the 38 guns, and came of with her, my selfe and company that had escaped being much spent, I had slaine both days 27 men and wounded 56, some of which are dismembered and will hardly escape besides my selfe and many others received blowes and bruses with splenters[56].

Although his bos'n was killed, John wrote in his ship's journal how God had 'proscribed the instruments of death flying very thick about us, on every side, yet had no commission to touch us, and the Lord kept upp our spirrits and struck terror to the harts of our enemyes for they runn'[57]. More was to come the next day. In another bold move, Captains Lawson, Marten and Graver chased the Dutch as they endeavoured to escape among the shallows, each managing to capture a man-of-war. John's ship the *Fairfax* was shattered. It was reported that many of his brass guns melted; probably distorted through repeated firing. A hundred of his men died and he nearly lost his own life.

Still, when the *Fairfax* put in to Dover port for repairs, John brought with him an enemy ship equipped with thirty-eight guns as well as others laden with salt, wine and other supplies. John had to transfer to the *George* while the *Fairfax* underwent repairs but requested to keep his own men rather than be given another crew and recommended his existing gunner, Richard Hodges, to be the master. Nevertheless, John really wanted to be back on the *Fairfax* as he believed he could do better service on it and kept a close eye on how its refitting was progressing[58].

The battle of Portland gave England command of the Channel and the Dutch were forced to take the long route round the north of Scotland. John Lawson was rewarded with the title of Rear-Admiral. When he received the news on 15 March that he was to become a rear admiral, he beseeched the Lord in his ship's journal to enable him to discharge this very high favour to God's glory and the comfort of his soul[59]. He reiterated these sentiments in a letter of appreciation that he wrote three days later to his friend Luke Robinson, the MP for Scarborough. It was, he said, 'a very high trust. I pray God enable me to discharge it; for of myself I am not able; it is too heavy'[60].

John was still worrying about his ability to fulfil what was expected of him in May, but accepted the honour with a grateful vow to the admiralty commissioners to serve the designs of God and the honest interest of England. It is hard to know if John's reaction just exposes a modest aspect of his character, a sense of unworthiness or real fears that he might not be able to fulfil his own or other people's expectations. Whichever it was, he obviously thought his new position was the will of God[61].

The rest of the spring and summer of 1653 was spent battling the Dutch and providing protective convoys against the 'rogues infesting the coast as Dutch men of war lying in wait took English ships daily'[62]. On just one day, John reported that three of them tried to capture an East India ship on its way from Newfoundland and how other ships coming in from the south chased a Virginia ship to St Ives, while the English merchant ships dared not move without a convoy. In between times, his duties took him home to Scarborough as the navy provided protection to the colliers trading in and out of the port[63].

Nothing is known of what John's wife Isabelle was doing while he was at sea, but their family was growing. They had been married for ten years by now and with a growing family of daughters it is likely she was based at their house in Scarborough. The burgesses of the town were still pursuing claims for compensation from the army and the residents did what they could to repair and rebuild damaged buildings and restore trade[64]. Elsewhere in England, there were inventions, omens and more social changes occurring. John Aubrey noted the invention of a machine to weigh grains by Christopher Wren, a terrible storm attending the execution of the preacher Christopher Love and the opening of the first coffee house in Cornhill in London[65].

John was away fighting the Dutch when Oliver Cromwell decimated the Rump Parliament by instigating a coup in April 1653. In an imitation of Pride's Purge five years before, Cromwell had nearly half the Rump MPs ejected from Westminster and army guards posted at the doors to stop them re-entering. Sir Philip Warwick later recalled how on that spring day, Oliver Cromwell, General John Lambert and Major-General Thomas Harrison entered the House of Commons and declared that its dissolution was a necessity. Moreover, their swordsmen would determine the question[66].

Three hundred soldiers stood at the door, in the hall and lobby as a file of musketeers marched into the House. Cromwell then bade the speaker come down out of the chair and accused MPs of being whoremasters, drunkards and corrupt and unjust men. It was not fit they should sit any longer, Cromwell said. He desired them to be gone, as the Lord had chosen another more worthy instruments for carrying on his work[67]. As Sir Peter Wentworth objected, Cromwell cried 'I will put an end to your prating... You are no parliament. I will put an end to your sitting. Call them in, call them in'[68]. More musketeers entered and Sir Henry Vane called out: 'This is not honest; it is against morality and common honesty'[69]. MPs in the House resisted being ejected. Then Major-General Thomas Harrison pulled the speaker out of the chair and Cromwell commanded the mace be carried away and the doors of the house shut up and guarded by soldiers. The Rump was finished. Parliament and the Commonwealth were reduced to the 'bare bones' of what they had been[70].

Shortly after dissolving the Rump, Cromwell established a new council of state known as the Nominated Parliament, or more commonly the 'Barebones Parliament'. This was after one of its members, the religious radical 'Praisegod Barebones', a leather seller by trade who had started a Baptist congregation in Fleet Street. The new body was an assembly of one hundred and forty representatives from England, Wales, Scotland and Ireland selected by the council and army. The Barebones Parliament began sitting in July.

It was God's will in order for them to put into effect good things, asserted Cromwell and his supporters. To him and his followers all forms of government were a means to the ends of godliness and justice. They had therefore been forced to take action because the Rump had failed to 'puritanise' the clergy, enable liberty of conscience and reform the legal system[71]. To this purpose, they had attempted to 'persuade and convince parliament men of their duty', but finding them slow had been compelled to find some more effectual method[72]. The MP Edmund Ludlow, who was one of the architects of the Rump's administrative body and Cromwell's second in command in the army, responded by accusing him of frustrating the intended reformation of parliament by aligning himself with corrupt lawyers and clergy[73]. Others such as Sir Philip Warwick found the 'new House of Commons of saints… so seraphical and notional, that they are much more troublesome than any former'[74].

In England, those supportive of the Rump were quick to respond with action and sympathetic printers turned out scores of pamphlets, broadsheets, ballads and cartoons. The satirical verses of *Parliament Routed or Here's A House to Be Let*, for instance, were accompanied by a note explaining they could be sung to the tune of 'Lucina, or, Merrily and Cherrily'[75], while a drawing on the same broadsheet portrayed the House and MPs upside down[76]. Exhorting its audience to cheer up, 'for the tempest is layd, and now we may hope for a good reformation' the ballad's refrain was 'twelve parliament men shall be sold for a peny'[77].

One objector, Robert Purnell, declared that 'self-seekers are self losers' and that 'no Member ought to feather his own nest'. 'Did you not', he challenged, 'know that the oppressions of the poor, which was so great in the midst of us, would pull down the judgments of God upon the heads of them that had power to relieve them, and would not'[78]. Others delightedly focused their protests on some of the hated acts by which the puritan leaders had reshaped their day-to-day lives, in particular the insistence on sombreness instead of mirth at Christmastime. One popular ballad, sung to the tune known as 'I tell thee Dick', summed it up for many:

> But such have been these times of late, that holidays are out of date, and holiness to boot; for they that do despise and scorn to keep the day that Christ was born, want holiness no doubt[79].

It finished with the hope that parliament would restore all that had undone before 'that we may Christians be'[80].

Cromwell's council attempted to quell public disturbances by issuing explanations and justifications. The government's own newspaper, *Mercurius Politicus,* reported that Cromwell only acted after parliament failed 'to give the people the harvest of all their labour, blood and treasure'[81]. This language of blood sacrifice and doing God's work resonated over and over again during the civil war and interregnum. It is hardly coincidental that John Lawson used almost exactly the same words six years later, when trying to force the restoration of the Rump Parliament. So much blood and treasure was sacrificed to establish the Commonwealth, he said. Now, at this moment in April 1653, the political embodiment of that sacrifice had been destroyed[82]. It was what John Lawson, Edmund Ludlow and other parliamentarian opponents of Cromwell would always call 'the interruption'. Eight months later, Cromwell was proclaimed Lord Protector.

Meanwhile the coup against the Rump had an immediate effect on the navy. Since the Commonwealth navy had been formed in 1650, the admiralty had worked hard to mould an officer corps loyal to parliament. Now, only months after John Lawson had entreated his friend the admiralty commissioner Sir Henry Vane to secure him a pension, Vane was singled out for attack by Cromwell and rapidly severed his connections with the navy. The navy's administration came close to total breakdown in the months that followed.

John was still at sea fighting the Dutch. When he and the other naval commanders first heard that parliament had been dissolved, they decided to see how matters played out. They carefully crafted a joint statement in which they declared their resolution to continue being faithful in discharging their trust at sea against the Dutch and all other enemies of the Commonwealth. When John wrote to the secretary of the admiralty Robert Blackborne about the great alteration in the affairs of state, he trusted these revolutions would bring 'glory to the Lord' and only good to his people.

John Lawson's position towards the new regime at first appears contradictory. He made his disgust clear at the overthrowing of the Rump in his writings and actions afterwards. When he declared for the republic, it was always for the Commonwealth formed in 1649. However, when John received the news of the coup, Blackborne's firm backing for the Barebones replacement seems to have allayed any fears he had. How much this was to do with Blackborne being sympathetic to religious radicals who believed that the Rump's fall could herald the start of a holy war can only be speculated upon. He was certainly linked to the Fifth Monarchists in the years to come[83].

Against this domestic background, the war at sea stuttered on and John Lawson continued fighting the Dutch. Amidst the losses and gains, the new rear-admiral played his part in even more notable victories. At the end of May, the Dutch Admiral

Tromp challenged the English fleet again, putting to sea with over a hundred ships. John recorded how on the morning of the second of June they discovered Tromp to the leeward of them, off the Gabbard shoal east of Harwich:

> About nine of the clocke he came within shott and presently after wee were ingaiged, but it fell almoste calme, my selfe and our squadron was on the left wing, and nearest, about noone it was very little winde, and came about to the N.E. soe Ruter and his squadron which was on their left wing taked upon us and weathered my squadron, most of which tacked soe all the Dutch fleet tacked, and soe bore up a little towards our owne fleete which was leewards and my vice Admirall and Rear Admirall came to mee, wee three fought alongst all the Dutch fleete being hotly ingaiged, yet it pleased the Lord miraculously to performe us[84].

The battle lasted four days. By the end, the enemy had lost around twenty warships and many of their crews. The English fleet lost no ships and few casualties. Despite the death of General Deane, John felt the fact that only one of his men was slain and another seriously wounded was due to the miraculous workings of the Lord[85]. The victory at Gabbard marked a major turning point. While Admiral Blake returned to England, General George Monck and the fleet were able to maintain an almost unassailable blockade along the enemy coast, bringing Dutch sea trade to a virtual standstill. The Dutch were anxious for a peace settlement and hoped the Rump's recent overthrow would make it easier to achieve. Unfortunately for them, the new Barebone's Parliament was opposed to it except on terms the Dutch were unwilling to accept[86].

Early one morning in late June 1653, the English fleet attacked the enemy. Leading the blue squadron, John Lawson 'charged through the Dutch fleet with forty ships'[87]. Engaging Admiral Tromp with the body of the fleet the fight continued until three in the afternoon – and the Dutch fled. The battle continued the next day as the English fleet went on the offensive with 'so much resolution, and put them in so great disorder, that tho' their admiral fired on them to rally them, he could not procure more than twenty ships of his whole fleet to stand by him'[88]. Sinking six of their best ships, blowing up two more and capturing eleven of the biggest ships as well as two smaller ones, the English fleet took thirteen hundred Dutch prisoners, including six of their chief captains. The officers and crew shared the prize money[89].

At the end of July, the new rear-admiral was with General Monck and Admiral Blake at the Battle of Texel as 'the smaller English fleet laid themselves alongside the Dutch ships and fought broadside to broadside'[90] for ten hours from five in the morning, until Tromp was felled by a musket ball. The Dutch lost thirty men-of-war and 1,600 sailors. The English lost half that number. Edmund Ludlow was just one who gloried in how by this point the English had taken, sunk or destroyed between fourteen and fifteen hundred Dutch ships since the beginning of the war[91].

In August, a gold chain worth £100 was the next mark of favour from the admiralty presented to John for his eminent service against the Dutch. His friend William Penn received another, while Blake and Monck were given chains worth £300 each. All the officers of the fleet were given medals as well, which cost the government £2,000. The same week that the Council of State voted to approve these gifts, they had more than one discussion over guarding John Lilburne and his trial. They also considered how to hinder the printing of abusive and scurrilous ballads and pamphlets and seditious books and papers. At the same time, the House expressed public thanks to the counties of Essex, Norfolk and Suffolk for the tender care and respect shown by them to sick and wounded soldiers and seamen put ashore in those counties. Among the parliamentary business dealt with a few days later, a letter in response from the new Rear-Admiral Lawson, General Monck and Vice-Admiral Penn from on board the *Resolution* was read out[92].

When General Monck returned to London in August, Oliver Cromwell held a dinner in his honour. Cromwell hung the chain around his neck personally and insisted that he wore it all evening. On it dangled a medal representing the sea fight[93]. Despite the appreciation of the council, William Penn and John Lawson were not feted in such a grand manner as Monck because they were lower in rank. Nevertheless, and whatever John Lawson thought of Cromwell and political events unfolding on land, he treasured the chain for the rest of his life. When he died, he bequeathed the 'gold chayne that was given mee in the Dutch warr' to his eldest daughter, Isabella[94].

# CHAPTER 3

# THESE FRENZIED-CONCEITED MEN

The 10th of April 1657: War hero John Lawson was under arrest for conspiring with 'these frenzy-conceited men of the Fifth Monarchy'[1] to assassinate Oliver Cromwell. In a double plot, trails of gunpowder ready to be ignited to blow up Whitehall had been discovered, hidden in the palace chapel. In another heinous design, desperadoes armed with a blunderbuss holding thirty or forty bullets were found hidden in a house overlooking the route Cromwell would take to Hampton Court, ready to shoot him as he passed by[2].

By now, John Lawson was in his early forties and had six young daughters with his wife Isabelle. Daring, brave and trustworthy, the last fifteen years had seen him rise from merchant captain to become a senior naval officer, fighting against royalist forces, the French and the Dutch. During that time he had witnessed the king's execution, the abolition of the bishops and the House of Lords and he had celebrated the establishment of what he believed to be a true and godly Commonwealth republic[3].

The roots of John's downfall had begun in the spring of 1653, after the dissolution of the Rump and its replacement by the Nominated Assembly, or Barebones Parliament as it was more commonly known. On the surface, John's star was in the ascendant. He had his gold chain, prize monies and promotions. Although the Battle of Texel in July marked the end of pitched battles between the English and the Dutch, there was still no let-up in minor skirmishes[4].

The carefully recorded entries of each encounter in the journal John kept onboard the *Fairfax* that year are almost too many to recount. In just one four-day period in August, less than three weeks after being honoured by Oliver Cromwell, John's fleet met some Dutch merchant ships, took five or six and sank two. That was not enough. He heard there were five Dutch East India ships at Copenhagen, waiting for their men-of-war to come and accompany them in convoy, as well as thirty Dutch men-of-war at the Fly and ten at the Texel[5]. Despite an ill wind and several of the ships under his command being damaged, he ordered the rest 'to ply northward, to find others which have been scattered' and 'annoy the enemy in their trade'[6]. In another encounter at the end of the month, he and his company took several Dutch vessels that came from Lisbon laden with salt, although one or two were sunk[7].

John spent the next few months chasing Dutch vessels, fighting and capturing ships, prisoners and goods[8]. Meanwhile back on land, the new Barebones Parliament was rapidly becoming the subject of ridicule and resentment amid accusations of being an army of usurpers. All criticisms were firmly rebutted by supporters, whose defence was always that parliament's own actions were responsible for it being dissolved. One favourable account in the government's weekly news magazine *Mercurius Politicus* ran to several pages while Cromwell felt the necessity to publish more than one defence of his actions[9].

The new body of state lasted only a few months as it became embroiled in conflict. First was the issue of tithes. Being compelled to contribute a percentage of income or goods to maintain Church of England clergymen was seen as an unfair relic of Roman Catholicism by all shades of religious dissenters and political groups, as well as by large sections of the army. Unfortunately, no agreement could be reached on how to replace the revenue the tithes generated. Few believed enough money would be raised to maintain ministers by voluntary contributions instead.

Further friction was caused by yet another trial of the Leveller John Lilburne, this time for agitating against the expulsion of the Rump. His subsequent imprisonment, despite being found not guilty, only raised tensions further. The third major area of disagreement was the reform of the legal system, with Fifth Monarchist MPs and their supporters wanting only to include laws that reflected scripture, while former members of the Rump Parliament pushed for progressive reform.

The Fifth Monarchy Men, Fifth Monarchists or Monarchy Men as they were variously called, were religious extremists who had emerged in 1649 with the aim of reforming the government in readiness for the imminent coming of Christ's kingdom on earth. During the early 1650s they were just one of several groups that attracted men and women who were turning away from trying to achieve a political solution to reforming government and the church. The Fifth Monarchists appealed to the religiously nonconformist and those in trade with, for some reason, a particularly large following among the cloth workers of London.

The movement had a strong millennial element, with many believing the end of the world was imminent. Their name came from a prophecy in the Old Testament Book of Daniel, which envisaged a total of five kingdoms or monarchies in the world's history. The fifth and everlasting kingdom would be established after the rise and fall of the first four great empires. Present day was interpreted as the fourth monarchy – and the fifth monarchy would be Christ's Kingdom on earth.

Those who believed that the end of the world was nigh were far from unique. But what made them stand out was the way in which they detailed how Christ's saints would govern this new kingdom on his behalf for 1,000 years, until he returned in person. This was based on the Old Testament description of a Sanhedrin of seventy selected godly men – known as saints – whose rule would accelerate the return of Christ in person. William Aspinwall, one of the movement's early promoters, envisaged that this kingdom under heaven would be given to the people, 'the saints of the most high'. Aspinwall's nine-page missive of 1653 concluded with a detailed prediction of the time when the fifth kingdom would begin[10].

For many Fifth Monarchists, the recent Anglo-Dutch War was seen as part of an inevitable process towards this fifth kingdom, which had begun with the civil wars. Once England had been converted to a theocracy, its army of saints would convert Europe and engulf the rest of the world. The solar eclipse of March 1652 had been a clear sign, especially for a sub-group within the movement who believed Christ would descend to earth in 1666. There were portents to reinforce their predictions: reports of bloody raindrops falling in several places in the town of Poole in Dorset one evening in June 1653; victories against rebels in

Ireland; riots and tumultuous meetings; the capturing of pirates and glorious victories over the Dutch at sea[11].

By 1653, there were three broad groupings within the Fifth Monarchist movement. The first was those who believed the new religious community of saints could only be achieved through prayer and setting a moral example for others to follow. A second faction thought it could be created through political influence and petitioned parliament periodically to implement their suggested reforms. A smaller, radical element that from this point became more vocal, believed that more decisive action was needed to help things along and advocated using force to accomplish their godly mission.

It is not clear which of these groups John Lawson was most closely aligned with, but he was arrested with the zealot, Major-General Thomas Harrison, who felt it was necessary to actively create the perfect circumstances for the kingdom on earth to occur. Like John, Thomas Harrison had volunteered for the parliamentary cause at the very beginning. He was MP for Wendover in Buckinghamshire and had fought under Fleetwood and Cromwell at Marston Moor, Naseby and elsewhere.

Harrison was a controversial figure from early on, falling into a religious rapture at the routing of royalists in battle and demonstrating a disturbing enthusiasm for the slaughter of Catholics when serving in Ireland. He had no doubt whatsoever that he was an instrument of God's will. One of those holy tasks was being appointed to the jury at the trial of Charles I and Harrison never regretted signing the death warrant that sent the king to the executioner's axe. So unwilling was he to compromise his beliefs that he never tried to escape the vengeance of Charles II after the restoration. His ending was to be hanged, drawn and quartered at Charing Cross in October 1660[12].

That was in the future. Within a couple of years of the Rump Parliament's formation, Harrison had grown increasingly hostile to it for not implementing radical reforms. After Cromwell's coup against the Rump, Harrison told Edmund Ludlow he was 'glad the thing was done, for I did see they did intend to perpetuate themselves, without doing those desirable things, which were expected and longed for by the Lord's people'[13]. The Rump's dissolution was an opportunity to push through more radical reforms, including the disestablishment of the State Church. Harrison's proposal was that the new ruling assembly should be based on Fifth Monarchist principles, with the number of MPs corresponding with the number of Old Testament saints. On the surface, Cromwell appeared to be conceding to the Fifth Monarchist's desire for a parliament of saints with a pledge to entrust government to the godly. However, the reality was a compromise between their demands and those of army leaders such as John Lambert, who wanted a council nominated by them to run government until a full republic could be established. In what was meant to be a temporary measure, the result was that 140 MPs were selected to take seats in the House. There were soon signs of more problems to come, as shortly after its first meeting the Assembly voted that it should become a parliament, against the wishes of Cromwell.

The royalist supporter Sir Philip Warwick was just one observer who suspected the Fifth Monarchists had baser motives. In his memoirs, he recalled that the officers of the army, especially Harrison and his fifth-monarchy men, pretended that only Christ would reign, with government being exercised on his behalf by saints. Warwick acidly pointed out that despite these holy ideals and higher purpose, the government would not trust the people with a representative of their own choice. Instead, new distinctions were created between 'the people of the land and the people of God'[14].

Huge numbers of people from across the political and religious spectrum found the ideas and influence of the Fifth Monarchists repugnant on more than one level. A wide range of pamphlets and broadsheets printed by their opponents emphasised the dangers of their beliefs to social order and even to people's souls. *The bloudy vision of John Farly* was one that refuted Aspinwall's vision and turned it on its head by stating the Fifth Monarchy would shortly be established under the reign of Charles Stuart. Others such as William Kaye, a minister from Yorkshire, later published their own warnings, which equated them with anarchy and popishness.

How much popular support the Fifth Monarchists had is questionable, as there were other groups agitating for religious and political reforms. The Quakers and Baptists were just as active in spreading propaganda and taking direct action. By this time, the Quakers in particular were vociferously campaigning for legislation in favour of liberty of conscience (although this did not usually extend to Roman Catholics), the abolition of tithes and for a godly government. They were frequently imprisoned for doing so.

In many respects the Fifth Monarchists were no more than just another vocal fringe group. Yet while it would be easy to overstate their influence and the number of their followers, they were seen as a serious threat to the state and generated enormous hostility and suspicion on all sides. Memories of how the civil wars had divided the country, friends and families were still very fresh. As such, the government could not afford to be complacent in case disaffected people who did not necessarily share the Fifth Monarchists' millennial ideology were pulled into their orbit and began to join in plots and protests[15].

By the winter of 1653, Oliver Cromwell was promoting policies that put him into direct conflict with Thomas Harrison and other MPs of his ilk, in particular over ending the Dutch War before it fulfilled its potential as a holy war[16]. On 2 December, John Lawson was promoted to vice-admiral, just ten days before the shreds of the Commonwealth Republic that he was so committed to were dismantled. For the Barebones Parliament, the end came on the twelfth. 'Very many persons came an hour and more sooner to the House than was usual,' wrote a witness. It 'was the first apprehension that was taken of any thing to be done; but by that, something more than ordinary was conceived'[17]. A few of the saints, as Warwick called those MPs who resisted the most, refused to leave the House on the grounds that they had been called to that place by God to promote the interest of Jesus Christ. They were driven out at musket point by Cromwell's soldiers[18].

Despite the protests and accusations that Cromwell had once again betrayed them to fulfil personal political ambitions, the Barebones Parliament was demolished exactly as the Rump had been just months before. A Council of State was established in its place, operating under a new written constitution entitled the Instrument of Government. The Lord Protector would hold executive powers, aided by a Council of State, a single chamber parliament of four hundred MPs from England and Wales and thirty representatives each from Ireland and Scotland. The property qualification was deliberately designed to exclude papists, royalists and all but a tiny percentage of men. As for religion, the Instrument declared in rather vague terms that there should be a national church professing sound doctrine. Cromwell justified the destruction of the Barebones by claiming that parliament had dissolved itself through failing to do what it had promised, but Harrison and the other saints were now his enemies[19].

Another person closely connected to John Lawson who broke with Cromwell at this point was Edmund Ludlow. He had been one of the chief supporters of Pride's Purge: another regicide who had backed Cromwell when he dissolved the Rump. This though was different. Ludlow accused Cromwell of being perfidious and forgetting his former vows as well as the blood and treasure that had been spent in this struggle. In Ludlow's view, Cromwell's mask had been removed and he was prepared to sacrifice all their victories for his own pride and ambition under the pretence of keeping the nation's peace.

Within days of the death of the Barebones Parliament, Oliver Cromwell was appointed His Highness, the Lord Protector. Edmund Ludlow subsequently claimed that the mayor and aldermen were tricked by Cromwell into taking part in the ceremony by being summoned to attend Whitehall in scarlet gowns, at which point they were informed of what was to take place. Whether this tale was true or not, city officials accompanied Cromwell on the procession to Westminster Hall. With them were judges, barons of the exchequer, the council of the Commonwealth and officers of the army, while Major-General Lambert carried a sword before him. There they heard the new Instrument of Government read and witnessed Cromwell's acceptance. Shortly after being anointed Lord Protector, Oliver Cromwell and his family took up residence at the royal apartments in Whitehall Palace. Edmund Ludlow took delight in recalling that Cromwell's wife Elizabeth was initially reluctant to move in, but soon became satisfied with her new grand surroundings. Cromwell's mother was, Ludlow noted, not so easily seduced[20].

Protests against the protectorate manifested in many forms. The Fifth Monarchist prophetess Anna Trapnel had a vision of Cromwell as a bull scattering cattle – the saints – the night before he was installed as Lord Protector. Trapnell travelled with the Welsh preacher Vavasour Powell to Whitehall three days later. Here, she fell into a trance, singing for hours. For twelve days afterwards, crowds of people flocked to see her as she lay in bed at her lodging house in the heart of city, eyes closed and a stream of prophecies issuing forth from her mouth. The attention that Anna received then and afterwards when she went on tour and even when imprisoned, was almost as worrying to the government as direct opposition[21].

Still, John Lawson did nothing overtly to challenge the government, although his name did appear on an unpublished declaration issued early in 1654 in the name of the navy generals and a number of other commanders. It began by flattering Cromwell, but contained a veiled threat of what the navy might do if he did not take enough notice of them. John's quietness may not have been purely strategic. Around the time that this declaration was written, both John and his wife had been suffering from ill health. John subsequently apologised to the commissioner Nehemiah Bourne (another enthusiastic puritan) for neglecting his duties.

John had, he said, been dull and indisposed, partly with a distemper of cold on himself and partly by being troubled 'to see my dear wife in such a great sickness'[22]. Isabelle had been struck down with a sore and violent fever, followed by an ague, possibly influenza, malaria or another illness that caused violent shivering. Given their health problems and what was going on politically, it is not too far-fetched to think of John's dull spirits as depression.

He trusted that the worst was over for Isabelle and rallied enough to tell Nehemiah that he looked forward to welcoming his commander's brother in law, Anthony Earning, to the fleet – where John would do everything in his power to ensure that he was welcomed and respected. He signed off by sending all his love and service to Nehemiah, his family and friends[23].

As protracted peace negotiations between the English and the Dutch got underway in February 1654, John confided in the secretary to the admiralty, Robert Blackborne, that he thought the chances of success were slim. Nevertheless, the treaty was signed in April and a day of national thanksgiving was ordered by Cromwell. John Lawson did not hear the news for several days, having sailed to the Fair Isles, then on to Brace Sound as he tried unsuccessfully to catch up with freebooters who had captured a ship called the *Raven*[24]. His report concluded:

Having taken in water and ballast, we sailed on the tenth and steered towards a fleet which we saw. It was De Witt, Rear-Admiral of Amsterdam, with three men-of-war, convoying seventy sail bound for Greenland. We consulted what to do, having heard at Leith that peace had been concluded, and resolved to demand nothing if he struck his flag, which he did; he gave us a salute, which we returned, and he submitted to a search, though he said it was not customary for men of war, and then they stood northward and we southward. Near the Orkneys I received a letter from Gen. Monk, with the proclamations of peace[25].

The Dutch had failed to achieve what they went to war over – the right of their ships to trade everywhere unhindered. Nevertheless, the two countries were finally at peace. Although there were reports of Hollanders still looking for English men-of-war, John Lawson felt satisfied that even Admiral de Witt was beginning to accede to the peace terms and show respect to English ships. Part of the agreement obliged the defeated Dutch to salute the English flag in territorial waters and pay compensation for loss of trade. When one group of merchantmen were seen to not just lower their flags, but let them fall all the way to the decks, then start dancing and flinging their caps into the air, it was reported as proof that most were willing to submit. A more cynical observer might ask if in fact their capering was simply mocking the terms imposed on them under the guise of compliance.

Despite achieving victory abroad, at home the political situation continued to deteriorate. The peace treaty was unpopular with large numbers of people who believed that perseverance would have forced the Dutch to accept even more stringent terms in favour of the English. Those Fifth Monarchists who had seen the war as another step towards creating Christ's kingdom on earth were among the most hostile towards the settlement, albeit for a different reason[26].

At first John seemed to have accepted the new regime. He continued on patrol as ordered. Provisions were scarce and he and other officers sent a stream of requests to naval officials on behalf of sailors who were sick and destitute, as well as for provisions for the ships. The only direct correspondence between John and Oliver Cromwell that seems to have survived occurs during this period. It is a short, rather mundane letter sent by John from the *Fairfax* while in the Downs on 15 June 1654, which simply reports on the disposition of parliament's ships, in particular the dispatch of the *Bristol* to Jersey and the *Maidstone* to Guernsey to relieve another ship that had run out of victuals[27].

In the summer and autumn of 1654, things began to change. Although John Lawson had served the government well he was now mixing in dangerous company and taking part in activities that began to make him suspect. As a ratepayer and member of the town council, he was entitled to vote in parliamentary elections in Scarborough. John had always openly supported the election of the republican puritan Luke Robinson as an MP. When Robinson had been expelled from the House of Commons for being against the Council of State the previous year, John had backed the outspoken former Leveller John Wildman to replace him.

In September, John attended a meeting between Wildman, the radical regicide Colonel John Okey and others, which was hosted at the house of merchant Mr Allen, in Birchen Lane in the city. They made plans to support and promote a petition drawn up by Wildman known as the 'Petition of the Three Colonels'. This denounced the new protectorate parliament as tyrannical and called for a return of justice and liberty under a free parliament. More meetings were held at later dates at Wildman's house, the Dolphin Tavern in Tower Street and elsewhere[28].

John Okey was another radical sectarian who had risen through the parliamentarian army. His dragoons played a crucial role at the battle of Naseby and he was one of the fifty-nine men who had signed the king's death warrant. His religious and political beliefs led him to oppose Cromwell becoming Lord Protector and he was more than willing to sign the three colonels' petition against Cromwell along with Thomas Sanders and Matthew Alured. They addressed Cromwell directly, pointing out the blood sacrifice made for the Commonwealth and arguing that Cromwell's rule was taking the country back to the tyranny of the 1640s[29].

John Lawson's position as Vice-Admiral meant that he was commanding the Channel forces with little supervision and he used Wildman's campaign to encourage unrest amongst the fleet. Officers in the navy were already aggrieved over the prize money still owed to them from their successes in the Dutch war[30]. The problems and discontent caused by not being paid were of course nothing new to John.

The sailors in William Penn's fleet presented their own petition in October and John backed it wholeheartedly. On 17 October 1654, John held a council of war at Spithead, where he persuaded his colleagues to approve the sailors' petition. Their demands were highly significant in political terms, as the sailors followed their demand to be paid more regularly with an appeal to parliament to end impressment. It was, they said, a form of bondage that no freeborn Englishman should endure. The sailors pointed to a number of army declarations on the same subject which reinforced their case, so had good grounds for expecting parliamentary agreement. One naval correspondent confided his fears that if the opportunity arose, three-quarters of the fleet would turn their guns against Cromwell and his government as willingly as they had against the king[31].

These stirrings threatened to undermine Cromwell's whole naval strategy. Since the execution of Charles I, the navy had been almost permanently occupied against royalists, the French and then the Dutch in guarding England against invasion, forcing other countries to recognise the Commonwealth and protecting and expanding trade routes. It was expected that it would continue to do so. After the Dutch War ended there was some initial dithering over whether to take action against France or Spain.

Conducting a war against either country had the benefit of keeping the navy in employment. Both countries were Catholic, so any move against them could be justified on religious grounds, which would be popular at home. Spain was the more appealing option. Appropriating some of their colonies would open up lucrative new trade opportunities, in particular silver mines. The result was the Western Design. It was a war in everything but name. Officially, it was about protecting trade routes and defending national security. The initial objective was to capture Hispaniola (now known as Haiti), although the commanders on the ground were allowed to vary their strategy if needed[32].

John was still a common tarpaulin at core. His tough actions and blunt speech over the sailors' petition undoubtedly stirred up existing prejudices against men like him who had migrated from the merchant service, as the long-standing preference for gentlemen officers had by no means died out. Nevertheless, his men appreciated it. Press ganging remained, but the men were placated by a generous distribution of money from the admiralty and William Penn was able to leave with his fleet for the Caribbean at the end of December 1654.

This was not the end for John. Around the same time he committed to a bold plot, concocted by Wildman against Cromwell, to restore England's liberties. The ex-Leveller Colonel Edmund Sexby was touring the country distributing copies of Wildman's petition when contact was made with General Monck's army in Scotland, who were there to counter the Highland rebellion. His soldiers were frustrated and angry, as their pay was regularly overdue; feelings that were exacerbated by being stuck in an unpopular posting. As a result, the plotters received a favourable response[33].

The conspirators were being spied upon and further details of John's involvement emerged a couple of years later from Samuel Dyer, a former servant of Sexby's. He witnessed John join with Wildman, Sexby and other well-known trouble makers at a number of venues, including John's house at Tower Hill and onboard his ship. During one of these clandestine meetings, Dyer overheard Wildman suggest that a tyrant such as Cromwell should not live. A couple of months afterwards, Dyer witnessed Colonel Sexby sending a hamper of arms and several boxes of propaganda material to collaborators at Hartley Row in Hampshire.

Dyer was later summoned to join Sexby on a mission to liaise with French, Belgian and Spanish sympathisers on the continent. In order to get out of England without detection, Dyer was instructed to liaise with John onboard his ship, which was moored at Deal in Kent. John warned Dyer that they must be careful as he was suspected of being a friend of Sexby and therefore being watched. He was also aware of troopers across the country searching for letters being sent to him. Despite the risks, John still arranged Dyer's transport to Ostend[34].

Eventually a grand scheme took shape. They would start a mutiny in the army, beginning with the regiments in Scotland, who it was believed would be most amenable. Plans were put in place to kidnap General Monck. Once he was out of the way, Major-General Robert Overton was to lead Monck's disaffected troops over the border to re-establish parliamentary rule. Overton was another Yorkshire-born radical and a distinguished soldier. He had replaced John Hotham as the governor of Hull when John was in exile there and passed on the order for John to lead a regiment in the successful 1648 siege against Scarborough castle. Like some of the other plotters, Overton had originally supported the dissolution of the Rump, but not that of the Barebones Parliament.

Secretary of the Council of State John Thurloe, who oversaw a network of spies and the gathering of intelligence, had no doubts that John Lawson had engaged with the other conspirators in this design. Thurloe wrote to Monck to inform him that John had been present at the first meeting and had pledged to take a squadron of the fleet to Scotland to assist with seizing Monck[35].

The mutiny and kidnapping plot was quashed, Overton and Wildman arrested and Sexby forced to flee abroad. Astonishingly, despite being questioned, John Lawson was allowed to resume his command. While this may simply have been because there was no direct evidence against him, there were many who were locked up or removed from their posts on little more than suspicion, or for uttering unwise words publicly. The spymaster Thurloe was certainly convinced of John's radical sympathies. Few firsthand accounts from crew members survive from this period, so only a partial picture emerges of how they felt about John. Nevertheless, those from other contemporaries leave no doubt that his background as an ordinary sailor and active efforts to secure their pay and better conditions made him hugely popular and influential. Therefore the only plausible explanation for how he escaped all punishment at this point, is that those in power believed it to be safer for the country if John kept his position (and was kept in sight), than to risk more protests or perhaps worse from the navy[36].

Meanwhile, Oliver Cromwell had been bitterly disappointed when the new parliament would not accept and implement the new Acts drafted by himself and the Council of State. His declared intention was that this parliament would heal and settle the nation's religious differences. Frustratingly, Cromwell could not convince enough of the other MPs, many of whom felt there had been too much toleration. Cromwell then tried to force the matter by making MPs sign an oath of loyalty to the protectorate. The hundred members who refused to sign were excluded from parliament. The MPs that did sign but still opposed him attempted to restrict Cromwell's powers through a new bill. In January 1655, Cromwell dissolved the first protectorate parliament.

Next, what is often described as effectively a military dictatorship was formalised, when the country was divided into eleven regions, each under the governance of a Major-General. Cromwell took further action against his opponents. The month after the dissolution of parliament, Thomas Harrison was among those summoned before the council and ordered to surrender their commissions because they refused an undertaking not to act against Cromwell[37]. Harrison was sent to the Isle of Wight, but eventually allowed to return to house arrest at his father-in-law's house at Highgate in London[38].

John Lawson, Thomas Harrison, John Okey and the others had rallied to restore what they called 'the good old cause'. They argued that loyalty should be to that and not to the protectorate. As such, it is improbable that they knew about Sexby's bizarre plans. After fleeing to the continent, Sexby offered to support restoring the king as long as Charles Stuart agreed to annual parliaments, one of the central demands of the Levellers. Sexby had letters from John, which he used to suggest that John might be willing to work with them[39].

John's discontent that autumn and winter of 1654–55 had been marked by royalist spies, who thought it could be used to their benefit. Around the same time, they instigated a number of plans that were designed to overthrow the protectorate. Then, in February 1655, Charles Stuart wrote to John in secret in an attempt to induce him to change sides. In return, he was promised a pardon and reward[40].

Sexby and the royalists completely misjudged John Lawson. However mistrustful he was of Cromwell and appalled at what he had done, John was devoted to republicanism and resolute in his belief that destroying royalists was God's will[41]. He was almost gleeful the following month, when he heard how 'the Lord has broken and dispersed the malicious and desperate crew of cavaliers at Salisbury, which is a signal testimony of God's displeasure against that wicked interest'[42].

On shore, there was still much dissent against parliament and copies of Wildman's petition on the lawfulness of taking up arms against a tyrant were widely circulated, as were other treasonous writings denouncing the protectorate for creating a new bondage for English folk. Cromwell had good reason to be worried about his personal safety as well as attempts to overthrow his government. His intelligence gathering revealed almost continual plots against his life. In response, Cromwell significantly increased the numbers of lifeguards protecting him and, by February 1656, had almost doubled the previous cost of his own protection to £14,089. It did not do much to reduce the number of people wishing him dead[43].

The Fifth Monarchists and other disaffected groups were still being spied upon. In one of his reports, the spymaster Secretary Thurloe observed that the house that Harrison was staying in was renowned as a meeting place for those with the same principles and he spoke his mind freely to all those who visited[44].

Soon, John's circumstances mirrored political events and his world turned upside down. This was how many of his contemporaries had described the turmoil of the 1640s in protest ballads, broadsheets and political speeches. It was just as apposite now. In the same month that Cromwell increased his personal security and pledged, it seemed, to all but destroy the Commonwealth except in name, John Lawson suddenly resigned[45].

Why now? John had been appointed vice-admiral of the fleet preparing against Spain just a few weeks earlier. Admiral Blake was to lead the expedition, with Edward Montagu sharing the command as General at Sea. Montagu's appointment was political, in that he could be trusted to watch Lawson and hopefully, curb his influence. Cromwell had no intentions of allowing Lawson to assume command if Blake should die during the course of the expedition and Montagu provided a safe alternative. It also meant that John would have no independent command – and less opportunity to influence his men than before[46].

John received the last of his navy pay and his reimbursements for entertainment and retained the gold chain worth £100 that had been bestowed on him by Cromwell. Accounts in government and newspaper reports and letters between royalist spies vary and are sketchy on the details. Some claimed that the vice-admiral refused to go to Spain because he was required to act under sealed orders. At least one suggested he was arrested. Other claims appeared that his commission was taken from him, having refused 'to go to sea till he knows the design'[47].

Some of John's fellow captains expressed sympathy. Captain Hatsell felt he 'cannot help but admire Capt. Lawson's actings, seeing he went so far and then retreated; [but] fears he has been biased by those who do not wish well to the present public transactions'[48]. Whereas Captain Frances Willoughby was 'sorry Vice Admiral Lawson has deserted the service, being troubled when honest men leave it'[49]. One of the government's informers reported that there were many Anabaptists in the fleet, aggressive in their beliefs and opinions, who spoke out admiringly on behalf of what John had done, especially Captain Newbury of the *Portland* frigate and Captain Martiall. To the writer's dismay, these men and their crews were liaising with men in the army of a similar disposition[50].

Another captain recounted how John's departure 'caused some disturbance in the fleet, but it was soon remedied by Badiley's appearance in his stead, and by the generals going abroad'[51]. Royalists were delighted and focussed on how the potential repercussions might be turned to their advantage. A month after John's resignation, Edward Nicholas, Secretary of State to Charles Stuart's court in exile, reported:

> The fleet in the Downs is very mutinous. Blake and Montague were sent by Cromwell to pacify the seamen, who are angry because Lawson is not Vice-Admiral. Cromwell took his commission from him suspecting him to have had a hand in last year's mutiny. Badiley takes his place, but is not so well beloved as the other. The discontent among seamen is so general that, if they had known they would have security in the King of Spain's ports, by his having made a fast conjunction with our King, many, nay most of the fleet would have abandoned Cromwell, who is said to be most odious amongst seamen[52].

The repercussions continued to be felt in the fleet. Reports sent to Thurloe throughout the following year drew attention to there being many Anabaptists in the fleet 'that doe in their speeches justifie admiral Lawson's late actings, that he was questioned for'[53]. Some of his officers resigned and others were dismissed.

One can only speculate as to whether his resignation was part of a bigger plan to scupper the Western Design expedition. The sailors' disquiet at John's departure does indeed say much about the esteem in which he was held and their appreciation for his efforts in trying to make sure they were paid. It was, after all, not so long since he himself had been in the same position as them[54].

At this time, France and Spain were at war with one another and Cromwell eventually decided to form an alliance with France, despite enmity over the execution of King Charles I[55]. Meanwhile, increasing numbers of people with opposing views to the government were being imprisoned or exiled, including the former Lord High Admiral, Sir Henry Vane. Unlike Thomas Harrison, Robert Overton and Edmund Ludlow, Sir Henry Vane had objected to the dissolution of the Rump Parliament in no uncertain terms. This had soured his relationship with Cromwell and he spent much of the next three years working on a religious treatise and giving private lectures that criticised the new government[56].

By 1656, many of John Lawson's friends and colleagues had been dismissed from their posts or imprisoned for various acts seen to be against the protectorate. Among the political dissidents and religious ideologues was Admiral William Penn, who ended up in the Tower of London after his return from the controversial Western Design expedition. His arrest was however a punishment for the dismal failure to take Hispaniola from the Spanish, despite the fleet having over 9,000 sailors and soldiers committed to the endeavour. In an attempt to come away with something, Penn and his companions turned their attention to the Isle of Jamaica. Even though it had not been considered important enough to include in their original plan, it was seen as an easy target and the English fleet sailed west to annex it.

Although William Penn's fleet successfully took the island, little was done to safeguard it or ensure a permanent settlement. Half the force died from dysentery and starvation. Morale among the survivors was so low that most just wanted to return home. Jamaica was not the prize Cromwell had hoped for and the consequence of the whole expedition was a formal declaration of war by Spain in 1656. In June, Penn effectively deserted by sailing for England without orders. Although a grovelling apology to Cromwell secured his release from prison, the humiliation and frustration it caused the Lord Protector meant that Penn never again held a position in Cromwell's navy[57].

Meanwhile in England, the political situation had begun to disintegrate even further. Sir Henry Vane's writings and actions made Thurloe and others suspect him of using Quaker agitators, the Fifth Monarchists and other fanatics for his own designs. Vane's book *A Healing Question* proposed a new government of the people. In July 1656, being summoned before the Council of State to answer accusations of criticising the protectorate in his book, he was then imprisoned for three months in solitary confinement at Carisbrooke Castle on the Isle of Wight.

There is little sign of what John Lawson did to make a living after his resignation. What is certain is that he kept in touch with former comrades who shared his ideals – and he was still being spied upon. He became actively involved in trying to build an alliance with a group of supporters of the Commonwealth and Fifth Monarchists. They did not necessarily all share the same ideals, but had a common goal in wanting to overthrow the protectorate. This group included some of John's former naval colleagues: Colonel Okey, representing the army and the Fifth Monarchist preacher Thomas Venner, whose congregation met in the upstairs room of an inn at Swan Alley, off Coleman Street. This became one of their regular meeting places. It is unclear whether Thurloe and Cromwell were more disturbed by their alliance – or by the fact that Vane's book was passed to them days before it was even published, with Lawson, Okey, Venner and the others in the room reading it at the first of their gatherings[58].

Just after Vane was arrested, John Lawson and other Commonwealth men congregated to see how they might influence the forthcoming parliamentary elections. On the same day, a group of Fifth Monarchy Men met separately, where they agreed that the time had come for 'destroying and pulling down Babylon'[59]. Acting on intelligence, troops broke up the meetings and John was among those taken in for questioning. The following month John Thurloe sent a report to the Major-General of the army in Ireland. First, he mentioned Vane's book and how it had led to him being called before the council. Thurloe ordered proceedings to be taken against Okey, Lawson, Rich, Ludlow and those called 'saint monarchy men' who had raised disturbances. Thurloe's opinion carried weight. His position as secretary to the council meant he was rarely apart from Cromwell and was believed to wield considerable influence over policy-making.

John was quickly released, but spies and informants continued to pass on numerous reports of disaffection in the navy, army and civilian population throughout the summer. One crew member on the *Adventure* reported his captain, John Best, to the admiralty commissioners in August for being a great enemy of the state. One of those he named was the wife of Robert Overton. The other was John Harrison, a neighbour of John Lawson's from Scarborough, who was among the few who had gone with him into exile in Hull when Scarborough was taken by the royalists in the 1640s. The informer elaborated on his complaint by stating that the captain had libellous books that accused Cromwell of knavery and that he had been heard to say that the king had lost his head over ship-money, but things were now ten times worse.

Pamphlets were widely distributed as a means of influencing the elections and stirring up discontent. Thousands of subversive papers were found onboard merchant ships carrying supplies to the fleet off Spain and packets that had got through were seized onboard navy ships. Among them were multiple copies of a popular treatise entitled *England's Remembrancers,* which had also been widely circulated at Venner's meeting house. This made an eloquent and emotional appeal directly to sailors, as well as denouncing Cromwell and encouraging people to choose MPs who would rescue their liberties. A lengthy section decried the sad plight of the seamen, who were forced from their wives and children just to serve Cromwell's personal ambitions, evidenced by the debacle over Jamaica[60].

Both moderates and conservatives within government grew increasingly frustrated with the extremists. In September 1656, the second Protectorate Parliament began its sittings. The elections were not entirely approved of by the protector and 140 MPs were refused admittance to the House. In response to their objections, Cromwell gave a three-hour speech that roused support. At the beginning of 1657, some of Cromwell's supporters implored him to become king. Although the offer was intended to curb his power not extend it, many parliamentarians were appalled that it should even be considered and urgently petitioned him to refuse it. Again, printers went into action and Samuel Butler's popular verse was just one of the scores of protest ballads and broadsheets mocking the proposal:

> As close as a goose
> Sat to the parliament-house,
> To hatch the royal gull;
> After much fiddle-faddle
> The egg proved addle,
> And Oliver came forth – Noll[61].

On 9 April 1657, three hundred Fifth Monarchy Men formed a design to depose Cromwell. According to Edmund Ludlow they were mostly tradesmen, united in a desire to give their judgement on the laws and government. In expectation of receiving extraordinary assistance from heaven, they gathered with swords in hands. A crouching red lion could be seen on their flag fluttering high above the heads of the crowd. It was emblazoned with the words 'who shall rouse him up'. Unfortunately for the would-be revolutionaries, there were spies within the movement. Cromwell had suffered them to continue with their plans until the night before their rendezvous, when around fifty of their most prominent members were seized by the Lord Mayor's officers as they came out of their meeting place on Coleman Street[62].

One of these 'malcontented persons' who desperately dared to 'throw down and oppose all, both government and governors'[63] was John Lawson, who had, just two years before, been rewarded for his honourable service in the Dutch War. As nearly three hundred plotters were rounded up at their Mile-End rendezvous point, John and the ringleaders, Major General Thomas Harrison, the preacher Thomas Venner, Colonel Rich and the Baptist

Colonel Henry Danvers, were held in custody by Westminster's sergeant-at-arms[64].

Their suspected co-conspirators, Richard Martin, William Kirkby, Samuel Morris, Thomas Bernard and their scribe, William Madey, were variously imprisoned in the Tower, Lambert House and the Gatehouse prison. Later that week, the *Publick Intelligencer* newspaper hoped that that the full extent of the business would soon be brought to light, while the suspicion was voiced more than once that the chief conspirators were Anabaptists and Quakers[65]. When John Thurloe made his report to Oliver Cromwell, he stated that they were 'were truly very inconsiderable and indeed despicable', and led by Venner, a 'desperate and bloudy spirit'[66]. Thurloe was publicly thanked in parliament for his care in discovering the plot[67].

A young man called Day was among those arrested. He was fined £500 and imprisoned for twelve months for calling Cromwell a rogue and traitor. Day's unsuccessful defence in court was typical. Cromwell had, he said, publicly promised on many occasions the people should have the liberty to say he was those things if he ever oppressed the conscientious, betrayed the liberties of the people, or failed to remove tithes by a certain time – long past. Day's statement was worthy of note in official reports that were compiled afterwards, as he named John Lawson as one of the rebel sympathisers in his public address.

Royalist spies and informers were quick to pass on details of the designs of these wild and dangerous people. One wrote of how the Protector was taking his time to give an answer on whether he could accept the proposal to become king. This issue was the only one that parliament had concerned itself with since Easter and they would not consider anything else until the matter was decided. The agent thought that Cromwell was wary of agreeing to kingship because the Major-General and much of the army were against it. A tone of satisfaction seems to seep out of the page, as the writer continued by elaborating on Cromwell's reluctance being exacerbated by the arrival of the Fifth Monarchy Men 'to dethrone him as an antichrist, and Gideon-like, doubted not to do it with such a number that one should chase 1000'[68].

That day, as John was held under guard, hundreds of people pressed into the banqueting hall inside the Palace of Whitehall to cheer Oliver Cromwell's escape. The palladian-style hall, designed by Inigo Jones and once used for royal receptions, ceremonies and entertainment, had a symbolic resonance. The ceiling was commissioned in honour of Charles's father, King James I. Golden cherubs and enormous biblical scenes in vivid colours celebrated virtues over vices and the union of England and Scotland. In the centre, James I is raised aloft towards heaven by the figure of justice to represent wise government and the divine right of kings. The hall was a very public reminder of how England had descended into civil war, as by the time it was complete, King Charles' profligacy had nearly bankrupted the nation. The painted image of his father ascending to heaven was one of the last things he saw, as he was led out of the long window from the gallery onto the scaffold on that bitterly cold January morning in 1649. Following his execution, the palace remained virtually deserted until Oliver Cromwell became Lord Protector and made it his London home.

Under the magnificent ceiling, painted by Rubens twenty-one years earlier, the crowds grew larger. Eagerly pushing up onto the gallery at the top of the stairs where the public used to watch the king dine, the stairs collapsed under their weight. One hundred people were injured, among them twenty Members of Parliament, including Cromwell's son Richard[69].

After the attempt to blow up parliament and then later to shoot Cromwell in April 1657, men and women going to work, church, pubs and market heard of the arrest of discontented army officers and armed Fifth Monarchy Men who sought 'to involve these nations again in bloud and misery'[70]. News 'of plots and treasons, yea, of gunpowder treasons, which would have sent the Protector to heaven in a fiery chariot'[71] reached royalists in Paris from spies and intercepted correspondence on its way to the French Ambassador. It had been a year in which the cavaliers had struggled to keep up with intelligence from England and had held little hope of overcoming their enemies. Now they greeted the reports of parliamentarians turning against Cromwell with glee, reinvigorated by the opportunities it might create[72].

The former Vice-Admiral Lawson, Major-General Harrison and Colonel Danvers were still under arrest two weeks later. Eight of the men held at Lambeth House were removed to the Gatehouse Prison in June after one unsuccessfully attempted to escape[73]. The Tower was still a castle with no purpose-built cells and prisoners kept there tended to be of a higher social status. They were allowed to make life more comfortable by buying food and other provisions through the Lieutenant. Walter Raleigh spent so long in the prison in the early 1600s that his accommodation was altered to accommodate his growing family as his wife chose to join him there. She was not unique in moving into prison quarters to be with her husband. When the Leveller leader John Lilburne named one of his daughters 'Tower' it was not only a physical reminder of his lengthy incarceration, but also illustrated how common it was for spouses to visit or even live in the prison.

Those incarcerated elsewhere were less fortunate. Fifth Monarchist leaders who were carried to the Gatehouse 'lay long in a miserable condition'[74] and the prospect of a lengthy imprisonment, torture or even execution for John Lawson was very real. One can only wonder if he spent his time in prayer or, as so many did, by organising petitions for his release or writing letters or poems to his loved ones[75]. When the cavalier poet Richard Lovelace was imprisoned at the beginning of the civil war, he wrote to his beloved the famous lines that 'stone walls doe not a prison make, nor iron bars a cage'[76]. Perhaps John's faith and fondness for his wife and children transcended his surroundings to give him similar comfort.

The Fifth Monarchists and their attempt to overthrow government appear to have had little general support, even among those hostile to Cromwell and the government. Perhaps they were felt to be too extreme, or there was fear for what further disturbances could degenerate into. For many parliamentarians another coup or war carried the all too real risk of restoring the monarchy.

There was, as might be expected, an outpouring of propaganda in broadsheets and the official newspaper. One report from Launceston in Cornwall in the *Publick Intelligencer* less than a month after the attempt on Cromwell's life is typical. Fifth Monarchists from their area and Plymouth had gone to a rendezvous in the town of Chard. The writer wondered what had made them so 'high and threatening in their language, as they were of late, but the discovery of their design hath satisfied us sufficiently'. The insurrectionists were, they said, 'exceedingly degenerate, and both impared [sic] and corrupted in morals, intellectuals and spirituals'[77]. Such hostility is perhaps not surprising from the government-controlled *Intelligencer* newspapers, but there were plenty of dissident publications still being printed that were not much warmer towards the rebels.

Political and religious agitators of all kinds did however continue to spread their views very easily. In May, a notice was read in parliament of 'the dispersing of divers abominable desperate pamphlets up and down, many of them being sealed in brown paper covers, laid in the streets, and scattered in the Mews by Charing-Cross, and other places in about the City, striking at the honor and safety of His Highness'. Further discoveries of parcels of pamphlets made up like bales of silk were discovered hidden near the Tower and an Anabaptist publisher was arrested in June[78].

On 8 May 1657, less than two weeks after the Fifth Monarchists tried to kill him and usher in a true parliament of saints, Cromwell met with his MPs in the painted chamber of the banqueting hall at Westminster. There he told them he could not 'undertake this government with the title of king'[79]. Instead he agreed to a new constitution, which included a second chamber with a power of veto, to replace the old House of Lords. On 26 June 1657, a large platform was raised at the upper end of Westminster Hall under the great window, for Oliver Cromwell's second investiture as 'His Highness Lord Protector'[80].

In a kingly ceremony a 'rich cloth estate set up, and under it a chair of state placed upon an ascent of two degrees, covered with carpets'[81]. On either side of the platform, richly covered seats for the MPs were raised one above the other[82]. At two o'clock, Cromwell arrived at Whitehall by water, landing at the parliament stairs, from where he went inside. Reverend Edward Fraser of Scotland recorded how, after signing some bills, the company progressed in stately order to Westminster Hall with the greatest pomp and magnificence[83].

Three trumpeters marched with banners and the coats of arms of the three nations and His Highness, as Cromwell was now to be known, were carried behind. Commanders, officers and troops then more trumpeters followed, as did the sword-bearer, attended by the mayor of the city and his aldermen on horseback, two by two and all dressed in scarlet and purple. The lifeguard marched at distance, followed by the officers of state and their attendants.

Adorned in princely state, Cromwell received the four emblems of government. He sat with a golden sceptre in one hand and a bible studded with gold in the other, as the Earl of Warwick draped a purple velvet robe lined with ermine around his shoulders and the speaker delivered a sword and sceptre to him. Once girded, he took the oath to preserve the protestant religion. The proclamation was read out by the mayor and his entourage at the castle gate, bridge gate, the corn market and elsewhere, with trumpets sounding three times at each place. According to the government's own newspaper, the streets rang with the joy of all kinds of people, the noise of bells ringing and volleys of muskets firing. This version was in marked contrast to the observations of the Venetian diplomat Francesco Giavarina, who witnessed the spectacle. He thought it a funereal atmosphere, seeing few guns being discharged as the new protector of the country returned to Whitehall after the ceremony was over. The few shouts of joy, were, he said paid for.

Celebrations occurred across the country. Those that took place in Norwich were typical. The mayor and his brethren dressed in scarlet and two companies of volunteers gathered at the market cross to hear the petition read. The city waits – public entertainers commissioned by the council – played, trumpets were sounded before the dignitaries and two companies processed to several more places, stopping to read the proclamation at each one. Bells rang out throughout the day and the festivities finished with a noble dinner[84].

What now would rouse John Lawson once more?

# CHAPTER 4

# SUCH PERNICIOUS DESIGNS

For a year or more John Lawson disappeared from public sight. At some point before the end of 1657 he was released from the Tower of London, although it is not known exactly when. There are gaps in the official state papers and no trace of any appeals to the government from friends or relatives for John's release. His name is not among the surviving lists of prisoners released to their hometowns on financial bonds that pledged they would not act against Cromwell or the State. Neither did he appear in the official records of people ordered to leave England altogether. A little can be surmised from newspaper reports: one that mentions John still in custody a month after the insurrection and another a year later, that refers to his being lately imprisoned and cashiered. Exactly how recently was not stated[1].

John and Isabelle Lawson had been married for seventeen years. They and their six daughters Abigail, Mary, Sarah, Isabella, Elizabeth and Anna probably took refuge in Scarborough. The eldest of the girls was approaching marriageable age. They still had property, friends and family there – and no good reason to be in

London. Despite being among the few who had overtly supported the parliamentarians whenever Scarborough fell into royalist hands, John never seemed to experience any problems in fitting back in when political allegiances changed again. This time though, he did not play any part in public life as he had done before. He dutifully paid his rent for the Garlands fields on the edge of town to the burgesses and bailiffs of the corporation, but, despite still having a position on the council he no longer attended meetings[2].

One of the clerks to the collector of customs was trying to locate John in February 1658 over a bill. His complaint to the corporation that John was not at the address they had given him raises the question of whether John really was absent, or if the Scarborians were trying to protect him. If John, Isabelle and their girls did spend their exile in Scarborough, for the first time ever recorded, John was not being responsible or considerate to his neighbours. Twice he was noted in the town records for not maintaining his property and the area around it, something that had never happened before. Yet, despite his resignation from the navy and the arrests for conspiracy, the town officials still signified their respect by calling John a vice-admiral – even as they fined him in October 1657 for 'his door not being drist', and again the following April for 'not drusing the chenill beforr his door'[3].

At the beginning of September in 1658, ministers and others assembled in a room at Whitehall to pray for Oliver Cromwell. His end was near, but Edmund Ludlow claimed that even now Cromwell still showed little remorse at having sacrificed their cause to his own ambition. After his death on 3 September, the contrasting scenes of mourning and celebration mirrored the divisions between roundheads and cavaliers, as well as between those at loggerheads on the parliamentarian side.

A leading statesman of France rushed to congratulate Charles I's widow Henrietta Maria and there was dancing in the streets of Amsterdam[4].

There was little rejoicing, however, when the proclamation appointing Oliver's son Richard as the next protector of the Commonwealth was published in Westminster, Temple Bar and the Old Exchange. Meanwhile Cromwell's body lay in state at Somerset House until All Souls Day, the apartment draped in black, illuminated only by the light from wax tapers. From there, his embalmed body was carried into the great hall and laid alongside a life-size effigy on a bed of crimson velvet, which was dressed in a gown of the same colour with a sceptre in hand and crown on its head. When the funeral eventually took place several weeks later, the city of London came to a standstill as drummers and trumpeters heralded the lavish procession towards Westminster Abbey. Despite many genuine outpourings of grief, there was more than a hint of smugness among those with no liking for Cromwell who thought the number of people dancing, singing and raising toasts made it a most joyful occasion[5].

John Lawson stayed quiet. One can wonder how he felt about the death of Oliver Cromwell. Was he able to honour Cromwell for the beliefs they had once shared? Or, as was more likely, did John unhesitatingly condemn Cromwell as much a traitor to the cause as Hugh Cholmley, John Hotham and Matthew Boynton had been when they changed sides?

Once Oliver Cromwell's son Richard succeeded him, the fault-lines between his civilian supporters and military opponents immediately opened. Revolutionary ideas were abroad again. Unlike his father, Richard Cromwell was unable to balance the demands of the army, religious radicals and conservatives. The protectorship was dependent on the support of the army to survive, but the exchequer was empty and little could be done to provide the months of back pay owed to the troops. Protests by the army triggered accusations that they were giving weapons to the Anabaptists. Again, the term was being used generically along with 'sectaries' to describe all the religious radicals who were highly critical of the government, vehemently against any church state and opposed to the enforced payment of tithes. More bizarre to modern eyes, which associate them with pacifism, are the stories of the army giving guns and swords to Quakers. A palpable sense of alarm spread across the country as support for Richard rapidly evaporated[6].

At first, John Lawson could only witness the power play from a distance. There is however one tantalising clue that he may have been readying himself for further political change. He appears to have stood unsuccessfully for parliamentary election in Scarborough in January 1659, as a covering letter with a writ naming him for the election survives in the corporation records[7]. He did not have long to wait. By May, after less than nine months as protector, a faction of republican army leaders had forced Richard Cromwell out of power and the army was in control.

There was no clear plan as to what would replace the protectorate. The militia were divided in loyalties and demands for a free parliament began to be heard. This could not be countenanced by army chiefs such as Fleetwood and Lambert, as it would alter the balance of power by allowing royalist MPs back in. They would form a majority and almost certainly force a vote on restoring the monarchy. The solution was the installation of a new version of the Rump Parliament. Once done, the Rump declared it would re-establish a Commonwealth without a single ruler. The six-year interruption of the good old cause was over. John's sacrifices had not been in vain.

For the first half of May 1659, John remained in Scarborough. Political chaos precipitated a dramatic increase in agitation by royalists who did not believe the Rump would sit for long. One of their targets was Edward Montagu, who they approached in the hopes that he would support the restoration of the monarchy. Montagu was in a precarious position. He had only returned to parliament in 1653 after breaking with his army colleagues over the execution of Charles I (employing his kinsman Samuel Pepys shortly afterwards). He had been appointed General-at-Sea within a couple of years, and, like Monck, transferred his allegiance to Richard Cromwell after Oliver's death. Through political canniness and good connections, Montagu held on to his position after Richard Cromwell was removed and was sent to the Baltic to aid the Swedes against the Danes in keeping trade routes open. Although at this time Montagu rebuffed the royalist overtures, rumours spread and leading political figures such as Edmund Ludlow suspected he might no longer be a friend to the Commonwealth.

To counter Montagu's potential influence, the restored Rump brought John back from exile towards the end of May in 1659 and reinstated him as vice-admiral. According to Edmund Ludlow, John's primary task was to repel any invasion from Flanders and gather intelligence against the cavalier party. His overt and unswerving republicanism meant he was a trustworthy balance against potential royalist adherents such as Montagu. John's regeneration had begun[8].

John took to being back in command with enthusiasm. The next few months were spent on patrol off the Flanders coast, from where he passed on any news about the Spanish and French, questioning passengers who might be royalist supporters travelling to England and finding most to be merchants on lawful business or English soldiers who had been left behind in Flanders when sick. Unfortunately for John and all the others who had welcomed the Commonwealth's rebirth, the new regime faced as much chaos as the one it replaced. Frictions emerged, as the MPs of the second Rump tried to reassert its parliament's constitutional legitimacy and denounced the army's interference in political affairs. But still the army went unpaid. Charles Stuart and his royalist agents seized the opportunity to fuel further dissent, in the belief that the dissolving of Richard Cromwell's parliament provided a just reason for people to take up arms to defend themselves until some form of government was settled.

Sir Edward Hyde, chief advisor to the exiled Charles Stuart, was a key figure in channelling intelligence to and from Charles and his supporters. He carried on doing so, even after responding to overtures from parliament after the death of Oliver Cromwell and taking the post of Lord Chancellor. Hyde was delighted to be able to pass on news from his informers that the common soldiers felt worse off under this parliament than they were before. Even more pleasing was the sentiment that if it was necessary to have a single ruler, then Charles Stuart would do the most for their interests. Added to the mix were rumours of what the fleet might do, including one unconfirmed account of a mutiny in Dunkirk. Protests and riots, even by those who were not on their side, undoubtedly had the potential to bring down the government. But the royalists still needed to actively win people over. Although he was optimistic, Hyde still cautioned that much work needed to be done before an invasion or internal rising should be attempted.

In July, royalist rebels attempted a rising against the Rump. Charles Stuart's friends in England were heartened by reports of thousands of London apprentices joining with them. Cheerful news kept coming, as five hundred cavalier soldiers entered Bristol ready to fight with groups who had already gathered artillery, arms and other necessaries for a war. In Gloucester the mayor backed the royalist plans and they now believed that Bridgewater and Taunton could be secured, along with other areas of England including Lynn in Norfolk. The plot against the Rump was uncovered. John's squadron was kept off Ostend in order to prevent any invasion as one of the counter measures successfully taken to quash it. But there was much more to come.

Thomas Rugge was a contemporary of John's who kept a diary at the time – his diurnial. Throughout the summer and into the autumn, he noted calls for a free parliament in places such as Shropshire, Cheshire, Kent, Sussex and London. In London everyone was full of expectations and the sword cutlers, gunsmiths and armour makers were busy making instruments of war. Suspected sympathisers were interrogated and people's homes searched. Although Charles Stuart's advisors continued to warn him against moving too soon, the immense hostility provoked among the general population by the government's actions was an asset to them. It meant they had great hopes of gaining an advantage with those who had completely lost hope for their Commonwealth[9].

While John Lawson was back in favour, Edward Montagu was still dogged by stories that he was in contact with royalist supporters and even that he had secretly met with Charles. When Montagu returned to England in August, he was stripped of his peerage, his colonelcy and his place on the council. His lodgings at Whitehall were reclaimed and private papers seized. He was fortunate to be allowed to retire safely to his estate in Hinchingbrooke.

John Lawson meantime was entrusted with overall command of the fleet. The circumstances in which he now found himself must surely have brought back unhappy memories of the financial problems he had endured during his earlier years as a merchant seaman, then in the army and the navy. The Rump continued to face major monetary crises, with not enough money available to pay the army and navy and no more crown or church lands to plunder. This was compounded by a fractious relationship with the army, whose leaders were disinclined to take orders from the Rump even though they had helped bring it back into being.

In October 1659, John Lawson's world tilted once more. On the twelfth, he was at the naval base at Rye in Sussex when, after months of conflict, the Rump attempted to limit the power of the army. The next day, in an echo of the events of 1648 and 1653, the army in London, under Colonel John Lambert's command, took control of parliament. The MP for Leicester, Arthur Hasilrigg (or Haselrig as it was often spelt) called for Lambert to be arrested. Lambert's reaction was to throw a guard around the Palace of Westminster, who prevented the MPs assembling and dissolved the council. A new scheme of government was proposed by the Committee of Safety with a parliament, senate and council of state. However, it was to be controlled by the army. The coup had been formalised[10].

Perhaps the army leaders should have anticipated the response that came from large sections of the populace, who refused to accept the dissolving of parliament by the army. For as Rugge put it, much as parliament was unbeloved 'they liked any government better than rule by sword'[11]. 'Anger began to boil to an exceeding great height' reported the *Monthly Intelligencer*[12]. What kind of government we shall get is unknown, wrote the royalist agent Mr Samborne to Hyde. He and other agitators could barely contain their delight at the possible advantages of parliament being dissolved once again[13].

Hasilrigg was one of nine members who refused to accept the army coup and appealed for support from General George Monck, who maintained control of the army in Scotland. Monck was John's former General-at-Sea –and the man he had not so long before been suspected of plotting to kidnap. For over a decade, he had led parliamentary forces at some of the most vicious battles fought on land in Ireland and Scotland and at sea against the Dutch. Although Monck had declared allegiance to Richard Cromwell after his father's death, he did not intervene when Richard was ousted. Instead, Monck pledged support to the Rump. When the Rump was overturned he continued to declare for parliament, but made no direct move and no one was quite sure what he would do. Soon Monck would play a crucial part in John's future - and England's.

John's known republican beliefs and history made him an obvious threat to the army leaders who led the coup. Moreover, he was in command of large numbers of officers and crew who shared his revulsion over what had happened. An admiralty officer was very quickly sent to the Downs on behalf of the army to try and convince John and other senior officers that the coup was justified. The fact that his former patron Sir Henry Vane had accepted the new order may have influenced him, but he was still a down-to-earth Yorkshireman who had by now seen a lot of pledges made, numerous promises broken and people he trusted and served under turn traitor. For now, there was no obvious sign of him making any mutinous moves against the generals.

The attempts to placate John did not work for long. Although another executive body, still called the Committee of Safety, was quickly established by the army, the seamen and troops remained unpaid. John made repeated appeals to the admiralty over the next few weeks for victuals, equipment and pay on behalf of his captains and their crews. Concern for the well being of his men seems to have been his main preoccupation at this time – at least publicly. The flood of complaints included John's fears at the end of the month that the port of Dover would be unable to supply the ships there and that the state's surgeon at Deal reported great discontentment in the town, due to a lack of money to care for the fleet's sick and wounded.

Matters deteriorated. In November, a remonstrance against the enslavement of the nation was published, signed by over four hundred and fifty people from parishes in London and Westminster and beyond, including Vice-Admiral Lawson, other naval officers, the mayor of London, many councillors and senior figures in the army. In the same month, John was invited to help choose the navy's representatives on the Committee of Safety, but he refused. He was never going to accept the military having rights over and above parliament, least of all to create or dispose of it. But otherwise he was silent for a little longer.

December 1659 was marked by riots in London between the soldiers and apprentices. The rest of the country was in turmoil too. In the first week of the month, Arthur Hasilrigg went to Portsmouth to secure the town for parliament. Several companies of foot marched into the town, drums beating and colours flying, to issue a declaration that called for the restoration of parliament and the people to their ancient rights and liberties. They now had a garrisoned base. Almost predictably, John Lawson gave his public support to Hasilrigg from his own base in the Downs, which made John and his fleet even more of a potential threat to the army junta.

Would John and his men join Hasilrigg? That was the fear driving the Committee of Safety and the admiralty, as they desperately tried to stop the rebels gaining control of naval ships based at Portsmouth. Attempts were made to keep the mutinous sailors loyal, with promises of being paid immediately and by luring them to London. How successful this was is unclear. At the same time, representatives and numerous letters promising supplies and assurances that parliamentary rule would be restored were sent to John, to persuade him to support the junta instead. Just in case that failed, the Committee of Safety ordered a squadron of ten ships to be sent out, ostensibly to give work to unemployed sailors who might otherwise be tempted to join the royalists, but in reality as a deterrent and, if necessary, to be used against John if their blandishments failed. John firmly insisted that the only solution was to recall the Rump[14].

Other areas of the country soon followed Portsmouth and the junta forces sent to retake the town were easily persuaded to join the protestors. Afterwards, Hasilrigg was able to boast of how the siege was lifted without a drop of blood being shed. Hasilrigg's advance was a trigger point for John. He was also mixing closely with old friends, puritan-minded navy comrades and political associates again. The commander of the defecting troops in Portsmouth was Colonel Nathaniel Rich, who just happened to have been one of the Fifth Monarchist Men imprisoned with John in the Tower in 1657. Shortly afterwards, their fellow prisoner

John Okey sought refuge with John's fleet after a failed attempt to seize the Tower of London in the name of the Rump. Another fruitless appeal was made to John by Lord Fleetwood on the twenty first, but the army grandees still refused to allow parliament to return.

Now John Lawson declared himself.

On 13 December, John led his fleet of twenty-three men-of-war from the Downs and anchored at Gravesend at the mouth of the River Thames. John and his fleet were ready to fight and die for the Commonwealth as he demanded the recall of parliament. While Rugge thought there were only sixteen or seventeen frigates there, John was reported to have another three thousand sailors in reserve that could be spared and were willing to fight on land[15].

The 350,000 Londoners crowded into rows, alleys, streets and squares were hugely dependent on the river for trade and transport. In particular, any blockade would inflict serious coal shortages and deprive most city dwellers of the means to cook and keep warm. Londoners boarded up their shops and homes or fled to the shires for safety.

John wrote to the Lord Mayor, aldermen and councilmen of London the same day and sent a copy to Lord Fleetwood:

We have been necessitated, according to our judgement and consciences, to declare to the world, that we apprehend the only visible means of healing our breaches, and settling us again in peace, is, that there might be all Christian waies and means used to reconcile the differences betwixt the parliament (interrupted the 13th of October last), and the officers of the English army; which we earnestly intreat your Lordship, with your honourable brethren, the aldermen and common-council, to you use your utmost for the procuring and accomplishing of; and that the force, that's now put upon parliament, may be taken off, that they may return with freedom  to the exercise of their trusts: But if it cannot be done by Christian and friendly means, we are resolved, according to our declaration inclosed (through the Lord's assistance) to use our utmost endeavour for the removal of that force, in which we earnestly desire your assistance and which we doubt not will be to the glory of God, and the reviving the decaying trade of your city in particular, and the nation in generall.[16]

The accompanying declaration addressed to the mayor and London corporation members was even more emphatic. It described how Lord Fleetwood had written to him a few days before asking for his thoughts. John's response then, as it was now, was to entreat the army as servants of the Commonwealth to allow parliament to sit again. If necessary he and his men were prepared to give their lives to ensure it. The army could not be allowed to rule government. The Rump must be allowed to sit again. John's public declaration stated we serve only the interest of Christ. In a call to arms across the country he invited his brethren in the churches, army, navy, and militia who professed to love God and his people to join with them.

John was not content just to see parliament re-established. He had firm ideas on how the nation's prosperity and spiritual wellbeing could be enhanced. He followed his demand for the restoration of parliament with another eight demands. The first was a simple request that all who had been involved in 'the late unhappy differences desist and place no more obstructions in restoration of trust between the army and parliament'[17]. Next, he wished for something that was for many worryingly reminiscent of the Barebones Parliament and Fifth Monarchists. This was for the government to be settled on godly grounds and the repeal of all laws that were not agreeable to the word of God.

John then made a case for liberty of worship for every person without any prejudice to others. This tolerance only went so far. He was specific in saying religious worship in the way of Jesus Christ so it obviously did not apply to non-Christians. It is highly doubtful if John meant it to include Roman Catholics either, as he was quite explicit that superstition and idolatry should not be allowed in worship, which automatically excluded the Catholic Church whose practices were believed to facilitate both and were therefore repellent to puritans such as John[18].

The contentious issue of tithes was addressed too. Here, John demanded that a way to support pious and godly ministers without using tithes to pay for it must be found. The decaying state of trade was of equal importance and John proposed ending excise duties. Next, he tackled the issue of impressment, He did not go quite as far as calling for a total ban, but did suggest that no one should be forced to serve in the army or navy unless it was in defence of the nation. Linked with this was the demand that sailors should not wait for more than ten or twelve months at the most to be paid. John's next proposition was for proper provision to be made out of the sea chest or prize money for the care of disabled sailors and their widows or orphans. This was, he said, 'the price of their blood'[19]. His final point addressed the need to find some way to employ the able-bodied poor and maintain the impotent and lame[20]. By this of course he meant only the deserving poor, the 'can't works' rather than those who could, but would not: a distinction first enshrined in law more than a hundred years before.

Terrified of John Lawson's power to paralyse the city of London, his former mentor Sir Henry Vane was dispatched down river to 'stroke' him[21]. Vane's role at this time was to liaise between the army and Westminster and to negotiate with those opposing the dissolution of parliament. Henry Vane's close relationship with John made him an obvious choice. Harry, as he was more commonly known, had secured John's first position in the navy. Then there was their shared ideology. Vane was a revolutionary. He believed in complete freedom of religious thought and that parliament should be the only form of government[22]. Though only a few of John's written words on politics and religion survive, the language he used bore strong similarities to Vane's.

Henry Vane had opposed the military takeover of parliament that occurred in 1649 and subsequently broken with Oliver Cromwell over his military dictatorship, which he despised. Somehow, after the death of Oliver Cromwell, he had become caught between the army and parliament as the governance of England plunged into chaos. Vane now found himself in the unenviable position of believing the military should be subservient to the representatives of the people, while trying to limit that control so that it did not cause the officers to revolt. While Penn described Vane as trying to infect John with his poisoned and jesuited breath, no one can know exactly what John Lawson thought of Vane doing the bidding of army leaders. This was not what they had both fought for over nearly two decades. In so many ways the internal conflict, shifting allegiances, political accommodations and broken loyalties these two men experienced at this time encapsulate national and familial divisions across England[23].

A satirical eight-page account of their meeting entitled *Sir Henry Vane's last sigh for the Committee of Safety* was published almost immediately. While the content of their negotiations was essentially the same as John's own narrative and those of others who were there, the tone is undoubtedly critical. Vane is represented as heartbroken, mourning John's ingratitude to those who had aided his career. In it, Vane bemoans how he had suckled the innocent young Lawson with 'the sweet milk of state policy' when he had known nothing of mischief. Having brought John into employment and taught him to 'climb the shouds [sic] of preferment' he had placed him where he was hoping that he would prove an instrument of salvation. The seriousness of the situation did not prevent the anonymous satirist having some fun with wordplay as they created an image of Vane lamenting the vice-admiral having left them 'in the suds'[24].

There was a great deal of truth in this. Vane had indeed secured John's first naval commission and aided his promotions. They had worked together against Cromwell's usurpation of the Rump and were both arrested on suspicion of being involved in plotting against Oliver Cromwell. Nevertheless, John still rejected Sir Henry's overtures. He passionately believed that both the Rump parliaments had done everything possible 'to shake off the yoke of the army' and set 'the nation upon the path towards a 'just and honourable basis of true freedom'[25]. As a result, John was truly appalled by the tyrannical mischief-makers in the army, who he saw as undermining this ideal. At the same time he condemned those who advocated a free parliament. This, he felt, was simply a ploy to deflect attention from the present emergency and destroy the Commonwealth.

In vain, the mediators argued with John that the army had to take control in order to preserve what all republicans had fought so hard for. John's response was that England could only be free with a constitutional government. This then, was the crux. Lawson and these men had fought on the same side. They had helped bring into being the Commonwealth that John still swore to protect. Both sides believed (or claimed) that they were protecting the republic. Now his former comrades in arms had swept it away. The only thing they still agreed on was that there should be no monarchy[26].

John was adamant that parliament must adhere to the public interest and should not be controlled by the army or any single person. He believed the only means to keep out the royalists and protect everything they had fought for was to reinstate the Rump and bring the army back under control. If the army and the Committee of Safety did not comply, then his forces would 'bring them to account for all their horrid perjuries, breach of trust, blasting, and abusing of the nation'[27]. He was declaring for the Commonwealth republic as created in 1649.

There was panic. All sides scurried around frantically over the next few days. The forces in Ireland announced their solidarity with the Rump. The city apprentices were, as usual, restless and making plans for a rising. The Committee of Safety responded by ordering everyone who had ever served the late king or his sons, plus all papists, to leave London within twenty-four hours and to stay away for five weeks. Rugge wrote of how one desperate man who had stayed longer than allowed escaped by hiding inside a bundle of straw carried down the river on a boat[28].

Hasilrigg's three regiments began marching on the capital to force the Rump's reinstatement, while rumours spread that John was ready to send his 3,000 sailors ashore to join them. In his own account, Hasilrigg praised God for sending parliament such able, honest and honourable deliverers on land and sea as Vice Admiral Lawson, General Monck and Colonel Whetham, the governor of Portsmouth[29]. They had, Hasilrigg said, absolutely checked 'the exorbitances of such who have betrayed their trust and walked contrary to the light of knowledge'[30]. John and his fleet were singled out for their determination to restore parliament.

On 21 December 1659, John made a second declaration followed the next day by the publication of an eight page narrative of the proceedings of the fleet. It was, John said, 'the duty of every man to oppose and hinder the carrying on of any such pernicious designs, which tended to nothing less than converting the supreme power of the nation into the hands of the army'. The Committee of Safety, which only received its power from the army and not the people, should have nothing to do with making the laws of the nation. As becomes Englishmen his whole fleet would pursue the restoration of those liberties with their lives and fortunes[31]. The Lord Mayor and council officers of London held meetings to decide how to respond and acknowledged the meaning and substance of John Lawson and Arthur Hasilrigg's letters and declarations. In doing so, they agreed that people's dissatisfactions would not be allayed without those freedoms and their lost trade being restored. On Christmas Eve, London's councillors appealed once more to General Monck, Commander-in-Chief of the Army in Scotland, to support parliament.

This letter, along with John Lawson's letters and declaration in defence of the Rump, had been printed onto broadsheets. They were handed out in market places, pinned to church doors and other public buildings, read out in inns, people's homes and workplaces to those who could not read themselves, reaching large numbers of people from all social classes. Now the ordinary soldiers of the London regiments turned against their commanders and began protesting outside Whitehall in favour of parliament[32].

John Lawson broke the heart and will of the Committee of Safety, said Edward Hyde and Edmund Ludlow afterwards. Army rule collapsed and on Boxing Day the Rump was restored. The speaker and MPs walked together to parliament to applause and shouts from the soldiers who, just days before, had kept them from sitting[33]. John's daring, decisive – even stubborn – actions had such an important impact that Samuel Pepys was moved to mention him in the very first entry of his journal, begun on 1 January 1660: 'The Rump, after being disturbed by my Lord Lambert, was lately forced to sit again. The officers of the army all forced to yield. Lawson lies still in the river'[34].

While the publication of John's' statements and demands cannot be claimed to have directly changed the course of history, there is no doubt that they played a crucial part in forcing the army to accede to his demands. There had been a flood of printed pamphlets from all sides on the political spectrum since Oliver Cromwell's death. By making his declaration and letters public, John was simply putting into practice propaganda techniques that the Levellers and Quakers had previously refined.

Print, politics and religion were inextricably linked. As different forms of parliament were set up, dissolved and overthrown, royalist plotting escalated and riots became a regular occurrence, pamphlets, broadsheets and newsbooks promoted political and religious solutions through the dissemination of news, deliberate attempts to form opinions, scaremongering and appeals to conscience. Material that first appeared in pamphlets was often reproduced in newsbooks with a commentary, while pamphleteers used news reports as fuel for further debate. Eyewitness accounts of events were interspersed with reports of crime, unusual weather, bizarre deaths and witchcraft and tragedies signifying God's disapproval. Fake news and satirical accounts that twisted real conversations and meetings were popular techniques used to portray opponents in a bad light, as happened with *Vane's last sigh* over John and Henry Vane's meeting.

This distribution of news was not confined to print. A Turkish drink called coffee had recently begun to be sold on almost every street, while china tea and a hearty liquid chocolate were being tried for the first time. The new coffee houses that had opened up to serve these delights provided another forum for the exchange of ideas and debates on events of national importance and how they might be resolved[35].

John's warships lay in the Thames ready for action for several more weeks. Despite the army giving way, the crisis was clearly not over and this show of force ensured the Rump's survival. More and more protestors took to the streets. General Monck began to move his troops south. As his 5,000 men crossed into England, how the country would be governed in the future hung on whether he would support the Rump, insist on re-admitting only the members ejected over a decade before, or call for a free parliament[36]. The latter is what the republicans feared, as the first full parliament to sit since 1648 would open the way for the return of the monarchy. Those 213 MPs who had been shut out during previous coups were mainly royalist, or at least moderate. Once they were allowed to take their seats again, any free vote proposed in favour of restoration would be carried by a majority.

Snow fell hard and the city froze as Monck and his army continued slowly south. Pepys enjoyed meals of steak, rabbit and goose and turkey pies, with games of cards and much discourse with friends and colleagues on the political situation.

John Lawson and General Monck were elected to the new Common Council of State by the restored Rump, even though Monck had not yet reached London. Two days later, John attended Whitehall to be thanked publicly[37]. The House being informed that the vice-admiral was at the door, he was called in:

> And being come as far as the Bar of the House, and standing there, Mr Speaker did acquaint him, that the parliament took notice of the great and eminent services done by him since the late Interruption of the parliament; and of his constant fidelity to the parliament[38].

Parliament then granted John and his heirs a pension of five hundred pounds a year, half of what was given to General Monck. John was given Lambert's quarters in Whitehall and had his position as commander of the fleet confirmed. There were inevitably some who were unappreciative of what John had done, including royalist sympathisers who accused him of being untrustworthy and a violent Anabaptist who had declared for Gog and Magog – the apocalyptic battle at the end of the world predicted in the Old Testament. This was surely a barbed reference to his rumoured links to his religious leanings and involvement with the Fifth Monarchists[39].

Engraved portrait of Sir John Lawson (1615–1665) by Robert Cooper. (Courtesy of Fairclough Collection, Special Collections Online, Leicester University)

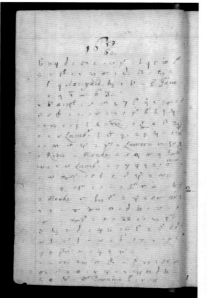

*Above left*: 'Lawson lies still in the river,' wrote Samuel Pepys on 1 January 1660. (Pepys Diary, page 1. By permission of Pepys Library, Magdalen College, Cambridge)

*Above right*: The ruins of Scarborough Castle. One of the greatest fortresses in England, badly damaged in the siege of 1645 and besieged by John Lawson in 1648. (Author)

*Below*: The view over the north bay from Scarborough Castle; crucial to trade and defence of the town. (Author)

*Above*: A view of Scarborough Castle from the grounds of St Mary's Church and St Thomas' Chapel; all severely damaged during the civil wars. (Author)

*Right*: St Mary's Church, Scarborough; commandeered by Parliamentarians during the 1645 siege. (Author)

A merchant's house in Scarborough town close to where John Lawson lived, and similar to his home. (Author)

Portrait of John Lawson. Line engraving, late 17th to early 18th century, by unknown artist. (Courtesy of National Portrait Gallery, London)

'Allegory on Oliver Cromwell' by Crispin van de Passe (II), 1652. Oliver Cromwell is shown as a tyrant, oppressing the French, Dutch, Irish and Scots. The depiction of him being crowned by a griffin – a mythological winged beast – producing gold coins from its backside mocks him as having a love of money. (Courtesy of the Rijksmuseum)

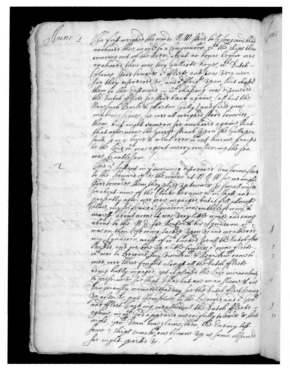

John Lawson's journal aboard the *Fairfax* and *George*, 1 and 2 July 1653. (Courtesy of Lilly Library, Bloomington, Indiana, USA)

This Helmet was a Crown by Revelation
This Halbert was a Scepter for the Nation
So the Fifth-Monarchy anew is grac'd
King Venner next to John a Leyden plac'd

'So the Fifth-Monarchy anew is graced.' Portrait of Fifth Monarchist preacher Thomas Venner. (Public domain)

*Above*: Battle of Texel, 1653. (Courtesy of the Rijksmuseum)

*Right*: King Charles II as a child in 1630 by Wenceslaus Hollar. (Yale Center for British Art)

King Charles II enters London in 1660: *Restoration* by William Hogarth.
(Yale Center for British Art)

Prospect of Tangier from the east. (Library of Congress)

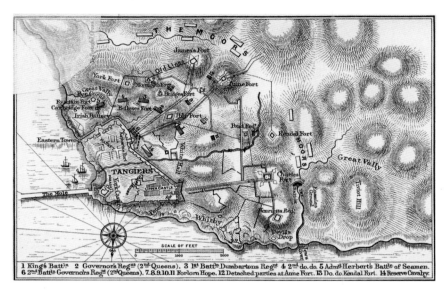

Map of Tangier showing the ill-fated mole. (Library of Congress)

Tangier Regiment – the 2nd (Queen's Royal) Regiment of Foot – battle honours. The Tangier regiment is second in seniority only to the 1st (Royal) Regiment of Foot. Although the battle honours 'Tangier 1662–1680' and 'Tangier 1680' are the oldest, they were actually only awarded in 1909, 229 years after the occupation of the port. (Library of Congress)

A Moorish standard captured by the Tangier Horse at the Battle of Tangier, 4 May 1664. This is an unlikely scene. Governor Andrew Rutherford, 1st Earl of Teviot, led 500 men into a trap. Only 30 escaped and he was not amongst them. (Public domain)

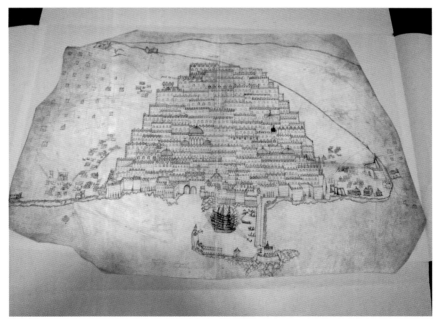

A plan or bird's-eye view of Algiers *circa* 1661, presented to the Duke of York by Sir John Lawson. (K.Top.117.73b © The British Library Board)

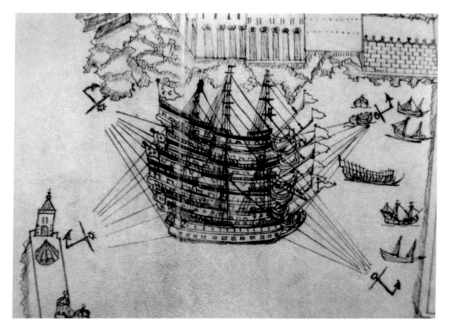

Seven men-of-war moored abreast in Algiers harbour, probably including John Lawson's flagship. (Detail, K.Top.117.73b © The British Library Board)

17th-century illustration of Algiers. Lawson's gunboat diplomacy there in 1661 did not subdue the inhabitants. (LoC)

Battle of Lowestoft, 1665, by Petrus Johannes Schotel. (Courtesy of the Rijksmuseum)

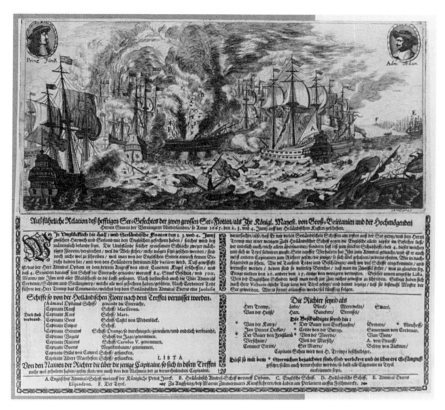

'The violent sea battle between the two great sea fleets of His Royal Majesty of Great Britain and the highly regarded Lord of the state of the United Netherlands, 2–4 June 1665 off the Dutch coast.' Engraving by Georg Wolfgang, Augsburg. 'Prinz Jorck', top left, is James, Duke of York, later James II. (LoC)

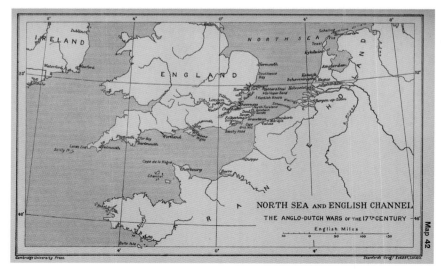

Map of the North Sea and English Channel during the Anglo-Dutch Wars. (Courtesy Perry-Castaneda Library Map collection, from the Cambridge Modern History Atlas 1912)

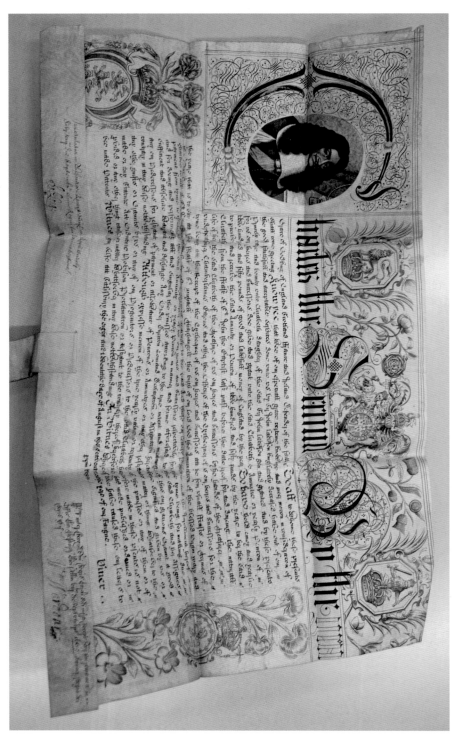

Grant of half of John Lawson's annuity to his daughter Elizabeth after his death in 1665. (Lincolnshire Archives, 1-Dixon/1/E/93)

The burial place of John Lawson, St Dunstan in the East Church in London.
(Author)

SIR JOHN LAWSON.                                                LELY.

Posthumous portrait of Sir John Lawson by Sir Peter Lely. (Royal Collection Trust / © Her Majesty Queen Elizabeth II 2017)

As the restored Rump began purging those who had who had led the coup and co-operated with it, John unsuccessfully petitioned to have Henry Vane readmitted to the House. It may simply have been an attempt at peace making, but it is hard to imagine that John had lost all vestiges of loyalty to someone who had helped and influenced him in the past. After all, they were still both republicans. Nevertheless, defending a collaborator created suspicion among some Rump MPs about where John's sympathies lay, despite his own actions and could have cost him his position in the navy.

The royalists also paid attention when one of Hyde's royalist informers accused John of conspiring with Vane and Lambert to start another rebellion. Others considered how John's actions could be used to their advantage, but only one seems to have considered whether he might be persuaded to the cavalier cause. That notion was completely rejected. Mr Samborne was forceful in telling Hyde that John was little better than a fisherman and violent Anabaptist. As his captains were of a similar stamp, no good could be done with any of them[40].

Around this time John visited his friends who were held in the Tower. They were comfortable enough for him to be able to dine with them. Which friends he saw is not recorded, but several former commanders and crewmen had ended up imprisoned during the latest upheaval. 'At his departure' wrote Rugge, 'their ware severall great games played from of the Tower, [its] towers and flankers'[41]. Perhaps John was too sober and serious a companion for the fun to begin while he was still there.

During the month it took Monck and his men to march from Scotland, the population grew increasingly dispirited. Parliament and the army were equally derided in countless broadsheets, speeches, verse and song. Across the country citizens prepared themselves for further conflict. Chains and posts were put up and gentry went well-armed. Pragmatic royalist supporters were delighted by the potential to advance their enterprise, with many suggesting an invasion attempt should be made from abroad while the navy was preoccupied with the situation at home. Few believed the status quo could continue. The council sent to General Monck with their desires for a free and full parliament. These were, they said, the desires of all[42].

As the future of the republic looked increasingly bleak, a barrage of public appeals were made in print by the army, parliamentarians and royalists to General George Monck and other key figures. As Monck continued moving southwards to intervene in the political turmoil, the letters exchanged between him and the mayor and aldermen of London, the speaker of parliament and prominent army officers were widely reproduced as broadsheets. Pamphlets such as *Glory of the West* and *Heroick champion* proclaimed Monck as England's hero. He was, they said, a man of valour and prudence who would ensure the country's ancient liberties were restored and bring great joy to the nation by calling for a full and free parliament. Others elaborated on the betrayal of men such as army leader John Lambert. Instructions as to which tune any verses included should be sung to were helpfully included[43].

These publications were not just designed to pass on information. They tested people's allegiance and applied pressure. The letters first appeared as pamphlets and were then printed as supplementary documents to weekly newsbooks and parliamentary speeches in the *Weekly Intelligencer,* which communicated the affairs of Europe by order or parliament. Hyde explicitly recommended getting pamphlets printed on at least one occasion in order to inform the populace of their folly.[44]

When General Monck finally arrived in the city in the first week of February 1660, there were no cheers of welcome. Instead, he was besieged by people calling for a new and free parliament. At the same time John's support for the Rump made him a direct target for satirical broadsheets, pamphlets and songs. A picture was hung at the Exchange, wrote Pepys, 'of a great pair of buttocks shitting of a turd into Lawson's mouth, and over it was writ "The Thanks of the House." Boys do now cry "kiss my parliament" instead of "kiss my arse" so great and general a contempt is the Rump come to among all men, good and bad'[45].

Reports were passed to the royalists about the city's almost daily troubles and the ill effect it had on trade. Despite being hailed as a potential saviour, Monck almost immediately managed to alienate the city's residents by following the Rump's orders to pull down the city gates and burn them. Although he would apologise for this the troops already quartered in London were further incensed when they were moved out to make space for Monck's. The soldiers responded by refusing to accept their new officers, creating havoc in the streets at night and calling for their pay and a free parliament. Civilians joined in, cramming Threadneedle Street where the cries of the crowd could be heard all day long. London was, wrote one royalist, like a widow in mourning[46].

Despite the army mutineers being paid with borrowed money, the troops continued to be highly discontented and had no love or trust for their masters[47]. Still no one was quite certain where General Monck's allegiance lay. John Lawson and Edmund Ludlow set out to court Monck by visiting him in his rooms at the Palace of Westminster. There, they pleaded with him to assist in settling the government onto just foundations[48]. Receiving them courteously, Monck zealously reassured them that he would live and die for the Commonwealth. Ludlow recalled that the vice-admiral was so satisfied afterwards that he quoted the parable of the Good Samaritan. As the Levite and the priest had already passed by without giving aid, John was optimistic that in Monck they had found their Samaritan[49].

Others were less trusting of Monck, with Pepys noting how his employer Montagu worried right up until March 1660 that the general wanted power for himself[50]. There were three factions in parliament now, observed Rugge: One for a single ruler, one for a Commonwealth and the other in between, ready to side with the strongest. Royalist supporters began to work upon John, hoping to move him away from his rigid stance in favour of a Commonwealth and the Rump. Although they were unsuccessful they were hopeful of finding him more amenable in future[51].

The turning point for both John and the country came on 11 February, when Monck surprised them all by moving against the Rump. Insisting it was unrepresentative, he called for a free election and recommended the Commonwealth, while still maintaining that he was against a monarchy. The Rump Parliament finally broke. One correspondent compared the jollities in the city to a brisk and sprightly bride-to-be rushing to her wedding hand in hand with her sweetheart. Pepys joined the crowds at Chancery Row rushing towards Westminster that evening, as the news spread that the excluded MPs were going to reclaim their seats. Bells rang out. Bonfires lit up the sky from one end of the city to the other. Rumps of mutton and even good beef were hung from little gibbets and burnt over bonfires to symbolise the end[52].

One intelligence report claimed that John was so angry at the news that he threatened to take his ships up to the Tower. But another reported how the twenty ships John had moored at Tilbury Hope were not fit to go to sea again. They lay in much disorder without any commanders and barely enough stores. Whatever the cause, the crews were unwilling to set sail without being paid their arrears. Another six or eight of John's ships were in the Downes and the same number in the west.

John's old friend Nathaniel Rich tried to start another military rising: Ludlow attempted to organise a general revolt that he hoped the fleet would support and Robert Overton, the governor of Hull, declared for the republic. There were more whispers, this time that John had taken his ships to join Overton, but nothing came of it and John swore he would stand by Monck.

John seems to have believed that the republican cause could still be saved. The new parliament was still committed to overseeing a Commonwealth without a king or House of Lords. Equally, feelings of omnipotence may have played a part in his decision to do nothing. He had after all successfully forced the army to cede and there was a real possibility of a mutiny in the navy if he was removed as commander of the fleet[53].

However, there was no holding back the momentum for further change and within weeks there was much noise among the populace for having a single ruler. It was thought by some cynics at the time that having made himself odious to the people by burning the city gates, this was the moment when Monck made up his mind that Charles Stuart should become king. Whereas

William Penn claimed in his memoirs it was evident that once the people had the free parliamentary representation they so desired, a mutual attraction would spring up between them and the king that would end his exile. Based on this analysis, Monck was merely bowing to the inevitable, while Penn was of course writing with the benefit of hindsight[54].

Could John Lawson be turned for the king now? The first hint that he might be moved lies in a letter dated 17 February, when the royalist spy John Heath told Sir Edward Hyde that there was good hope of John Lawson for the king. A Dover merchant called Arnold Braems was chosen to liaise with John. He had obviously known John for some time, possibly dating back to John's days as a merchant seaman when Braems also traded in coal with Newcastle and Scarborough. Braems started by writing to John and then visited him in London. Although John was obstinately loyal to the republic and resisted financial inducements, Braems believed his efforts with the vice-admiral eventually helped prevail on him for the king[55].

While the royalists were leaning on John, comrades such as Ludlow continued to express full confidence in his faithfulness[56]. Nevertheless, when a new council of state was elected, it would seem the new regime still mistrusted John as he was no longer a member. Whatever the reason, he retained his position as vice-admiral, but was removed as commander-in-chief of the navy and replaced by Montagu. It was a wise move for Monck and Montagu to try and persuade parliament to increase John's salary by a pound a day and John diplomatically thanked them for this when congratulating them on their new positions. He was, however, still actively working for the old cause. He was still held in high regard in Scarborough and his active support for the re-election of republican and former Leveller Luke Robinson when elections for the Convention Parliament took place helped ensure Robinson's success.

Samborne warned Hyde early in March that John was endeavouring to stir up a mutiny in the navy. Despite this ostensibly alarming possibility, Samborne felt there was no real danger and they should concentrate on Montagu instead. A week later, Montagu had committed to the king's cause as long as certain conditions were met[57].

Then the incredible happened. John Lawson made his submission. A few words in two coded letters, dated 16 March and sent between royalists the same day that parliament was dissolved. John had turned and chose to enable the return of the king. It was so unexpected that Samborne hastily sent an addendum to the report he had written to Hyde earlier the same day, in which he claimed that John was just waiting to show his teeth. John received assurances five days later and both he and Edward Montagu swore publicly to serve Charles Stuart with all their might, thus reassuring him of the loyalty of the fleet. Almost simultaneously, Lawson publicly declared his commitment to a free parliament and appealed to all other naval officers to follow in his wake. All his captains except one followed him[58].

It took less than a month, maybe as little as a week. We can only imagine how, step by step, inch by inch, John Lawson was converted.

Was it conviction, a road to Damascus conversion, a leap of faith, or pragmatism? Did he really, as some have claimed, simply want to save his own skin or name his own price as offered by Charles Stuart via Braems? There was after all his age and position to consider. Despite all his sacrifices, could this have been the moment at which John chose financial security over conviction? No doubt he prayed for guidance.

He left no words of his own to explain. Yet the suggestion that John simply followed the lead of Montagu and Monck or changed tack purely to keep his command ignores the kind of a person he was. In every word and deed for eighteen years, he demonstrated his fervent belief that fighting for parliamentarianism was doing God's work. Throughout, John had unwaveringly risked his life and freedom over and over again.

Faith, love for his country and a duty of care for his sailors measured against the alternative – a modified monarchy and a stable government? Loyalty and strength of faith are the abiding characteristics that can be gleaned from the actions John took during his life. For him, religion and politics were inseparable. Above all else, John Lawson had fought for a just, honourable and godly government.

The continuing fragmentation of government and resulting social chaos left few options. His background as a collier and closeness to his grocer and merchant kinsfolk meant he was fully aware of how much the prosperity of the country depended on good trading conditions. Without that there could be no political stability. In turn, without a stable political system, it was difficult for trade to prosper. His Commonwealth cause was irrevocably lost. The country he loved was on the brink of financial disaster. There was a very real possibility of another civil war or military coup. Ultimately, given John Lawson's character and beliefs, these was more than enough to transform him into a loyal subject of the king[59].

Years later, John's friend William Penn would claim that John regretted the part he played against the royalists during the civil wars and interregnum. If true, this shift came later as John never showed any sign in words or deeds before 1660 that he could ever lose faith. Even when he acceded to the demands of a free parliament, it was a simple statement of acceptance. His unwavering devotion makes it almost incomprehensible that he could turn away from his cause so completely. Yet, once John changed sides, he swore to keep the letter of assurances for his future from Charles next to his heart and never demonstrated any wavering or regret. He would be as devoted to the king as he had once been to the republic[60].

John Lawson, Edward Montagu and George Monck had all performed an historically significant volte-face and ensured the return of the king. Strangely, other than in local and naval histories, little is said of John in most accounts of the Commonwealth's end. Rather, it is General Monck who takes centre stage. His character and motives in bringing his troops to London have inspired much controversy and vitriolic debate. Yet it was John's decisive action in positioning his fleet in the Thames that forced the army to yield in 1659, while Monck was still hundreds of miles away. While the domino effect this created was not something that John ever wanted or anticipated, he was ultimately as responsible for the restoration as the other lead actors whose names are heard in ballads, appear on plaques at historical sites or have road names or statues dedicated to them. Being indisposed to playing political games for the sake of personal advancement, unlike those more charismatic (or rather, perhaps, self-publicising) personalities, John Lawson's name has faded into the backdrop of history.

Understandably, John's conversion did not escape scepticism, hostility and accusations of treachery. Some would never forgive him. During a long conversation with Samuel Pepys three years later, Robert Blackborne, who had been very close to John when he was secretary to the admiralty, could not contain the bitterness he still felt towards him, or to Monck. In Blackborne's eyes, General Moncke was perfidious as he had helped to ensure that there were no limitations placed on the power of the king at his restoration. John Lawson was rather sneeringly condemned as nothing more than an ordinary seaman: stout but false and 'the greatest hypocrite in the world'[61].

At least one of Hyde's correspondents felt that John was presenting a fair face but was sure to rejoin any group of zealots that tried to rise up again. There was never any sign that he did. Although he seems to have dissociated himself from those who continued to put up resistance, John still took care of those towards whom he felt a personal loyalty. Only three days after the news of his submission, he wrote from onboard his ship the *James* to the mayor and council officers of Rye in Sussex to recommend William Penn as their candidate for the election that had just been announced as taking place in April. Penn was, he assured them, a man of worth who would be more than able to serve the town. John's squadron joined Montagu's on 23 March and Pepys commented on how respectful he was. A few days later, John and his frigates saluted Montagu's ship so vigorously and with such an 'abundance of guns' that they broke the windows of Pepys's cabin[62].

As negotiations for the restoration went on, Pepys excitedly recorded each piece of news. At the end of March, as new representations of the king were being made to be put up in the exchange, there were whisperings about whether John's men were really planning to oppose Monck. John of course denied such claims completely and reasserted his intention to stand by the general. Despite this, some of his captains were soon relieved of their commissions. Sadly for John, this included one of his favourites, Deakins, who was suspected by Montagu of being an Anabaptist and sent off on convoy duty to the Straits to keep him from stirring up mischief, rather than being appointed a rear-admiral, as John had wanted. A couple of days later, Pepys recorded his satisfaction at being able to make the vice-admiral welcome onboard by giving him a bottle of wine[63].

In the spring of 1660, the twenty-nine-year-old Charles Stuart was in Breda in Holland, at the court of his sister Mary, the widow of William II of Orange. He had always been addressed as King Charles II at friendly foreign courts and by his supporters in England. Now, the government was willing formally to recognise him as such. From Breda on 4 April he issued a declaration, which was seized upon by parliament as offering terms for his return. Charles Stuart promised a full pardon to all who appealed within forty days – except those who had signed his father's death warrant – liberty of conscience and to pay the arrears owed to the army. On the same day, Charles wrote an appeasing but bold letter to the Speaker at the House of Commons. In it, he took a stance that would have been beyond his father's comprehension by asserting that the liberties of king and parliament were dependent upon each other. The son and heir of King Charles I had ceded one of the principal tenets that had led to civil war.

Once the news was relayed, there was a rush to strip public buildings of all signs of the Commonwealth, much as churches had been vandalised and scoured in the name of the godly parliamentarians not so long before. On 11 April, 'the Skinners

Company when entertaining General Monck in their hall took down parliament's coat of arms in their hall and set up the king's'. Throughout this time, John went about his business as usual and Pepys was moved to note after one merry dinner with some of the other commanders on board what a very good-natured man John was. In the third week of that month, Pepys was delighted when Montagu instructed him to personally convey to John Lawson the order for his restored commission as vice-admiral[64].

The restoration of the monarchy was formally agreed by parliament on 25 April and John wrote to Charles to assure him of his loyalty in all actions. One wonders what he thought as Luke Robinson, his old republican comrade from Scarborough, stood up immediately after the letter from Charles was read in parliament to make a tearful and abject recantation of everything he had done and expressed his willingness to submit to imprisonment[65].

In May, John Lawson and Edward Montagu were able to publicly demonstrate their new allegiance, when they were dispatched to Holland to bring the king in waiting home. As Montagu's secretary, Samuel Pepys accompanied them. John was in command of *The London*, a 76-gun, three-decked ship only four years old. The welcoming flotilla was gaily decked out with silk flags and the captains were accompanied by trumpeters and fiddlers. On the very first evening that they set sail, John joined Pepys, Montagu and other commanders in the great cabin. Calling for a bottle of wine, he commanded them to drink a health to the king[66].

Meanwhile there had been a rounding up of people who would not accept the full parliament or rebelled against the prospect of restoring the monarch. The prisons now held men who had only a few months before been fighting and disputing with each other. Among them was the leader of the army coup against the

Rump, John Lambert. He managed to make a daring escape from the Tower in April 'by which he slided down and in each hand he had a handkerchief. Upon his descent six men were ready to receive him who had a barge ready to hasten away'[67]. Lambert was not at liberty for long and other former comrades such as Arthur Hasilrigg and Thomas Harrison soon joined him in prison[68].

In London there was a growing air of expectation over the return of His Majesty and the dukes. The masters of each guildhall ordered new liveries for their footmen. Ready to express their joy, thousands of citizens built great bonfires on street corners up to two or three storeys high, with pitched barrels or streamers depicting a crown or the king set on top. The bonfire at Southwark was bigger than any house, wrote Rugge, while many more 'stately' ones appeared in the Liberty of Westminster and smaller ones everywhere next to taverns that had space. The celebratory atmosphere continued on land and at sea. As John and the rest of the welcome party landed in Holland the shore looked black, it was so full of people waiting to greet them. The guns were fired twice, the first time Charles had been saluted as king by the English navy[69]. 'With a fresh gale and most happy weather we set sail for England', confided Pepys to his journal[70].

Samuel Pepys worried for John's future. On the journey home from Holland he noted that Montagu dined with the vice-admiral today and that John was 'as officious a poor man, as any spaniel can be'[71]. But the diarist confided his belief that it would serve no purpose, for he did not think the vice-admiral would keep his position. He may have also feared for John's liberty and life. For, despite the pardons promised, there was no absolute certainty that those who switched sides would escape the retribution sworn by Charles Stuart against those responsible for his father's death. The Duke of York (later James II) was accommodated on board the *London*. As John and the rest of the royal party sailed into Dover, an enormous crowd of citizens, horsemen and nobles greeted them with shouts of joy beyond description[72]. As Charles Stuart was escorted onto shore with John's fleet in attendance, it is hard to imagine that the vice-admiral felt truly triumphant.

The republican dream was dead and John Lawson was a turncoat. On 29 May 1660, he witnessed King Charles II making his way to London. People came from thirty miles around or more, hedging the road on both sides while the trees overlooking the road were full of those scrambling for a good vantage point. Shouts and loud acclamations filled the air. Coming into Dartford in Kent with General Monck riding at his right-hand, a hundred maids all dressed in white made a gallant show, strewing his path with lilies and roses.

King Charles II entered London to cries of indescribable joy from the 2,000 troops on horse and foot who were brandishing swords. As the procession reached St George in the Fields, the mayor and aldermen received the royal party. After a hurried meal they set forth for Whitehall along streets hung with rich tapestries and balconies and windows filled with spectators. Thomas Rugge positioned himself on the Strand, where he observed General Brown's troops marching past first, all dressed in silver doublets, followed by 'a most noble troop of Londoners all young men in buff coats with laced sleeves and green scarves'. It seemed as if the procession passing him by was an endless sea of liverymen, footmen and troops in lace-fringed velvet coats with gold chains in colours of purple, sea green, blues, silver, pinks, yellow, white, red, gold and black, sky colours and more. After them came kettle drums, the great streamers, twelve ministers, the Spanish merchants, city merchants and waits, the officers, sheriffs and aldermen in scarlet gowns[73]. My heart was uplifted, wrote the diarist John Evelyn:

The way strewn with flowers, the bells ringing, the streets hung with tapestry, fountaines running with wine... All this without one drop of blood shed, and by that very army, which rebelled against him[74].

# CHAPTER 5

# A HEALTH TO THE KING

'A health to the king', toasted John Lawson on the journey to escort King Charles II home to England[1]. Five months later, on 24 September 1660, he was knighted for his part in restoring the monarchy, when he would have knelt before the king and sworn allegiance to the crown. Only nine months had passed since John took his fleet into the River Thames in defence of the republic and forced the army to yield. He adopted the redundant coat of arms of the Lawson family of Longhirst in Northumberland, despite there being no evidence to link him to that family.

No description of the ceremony survives, although Pepys made a note of it in his journal along with the news that he had tried his first cup of china tea and enjoyed a good dinner at the Globe theatre. Another navy officer, Richard Stayner, was re-knighted on the same day, (having originally been knighted by Cromwell some years before). John Lawson, former collier, tarpaulin captain and Commonwealth ideologue, had after eighteen years not only become a royalist, but an ennobled one[2].

One of the first Acts implemented by Charles II was the Act of Indemnity and Pardon, in August 1660. It formalised the pledge made at Breda for reconciliation. Forgiveness for past actions during the wars and interregnum was granted to all apart from those classed as regicides. These were the people who had presided over the trial of Charles I and signed his death warrant. Abjurers – those who continued to refuse to recognise the crown – were exiled, imprisoned or had their lands confiscated. A law was also passed to recover all crown lands, although for the time being those seized from private owners were left untouched.

Despite the personal promise given to him by King Charles, John's fears for his future after he changed sides were well founded. Shortly after the restoration, he came perilously close to suffering the same fate as the regicides. According to Ludlow, John's name was read out in parliament on the list of those excluded from the pardon. Fortunately, there were some MPs present, including Mr Clergies, Monck's brother-in-law, willing to intervene vigorously on his behalf[3].

John's troubles were not over. A couple of months after being knighted, the king confirmed the £500 pension originally granted to him by the Rump Parliament, plus a further allowance. At this point, John's enemies, old and new, saw another opportunity. When the petition was presented to parliament for confirmation, a group of royalist MPs denounced him as a traitor amid calls from other MPs that he get the reward he truly deserved.

Despite testimony of John's fidelity to Charles from Braems, the MP Sir William Wylde argued that his abjuring the royal family and assisting the Committee of Safety meant he deserved nothing, while Mr Prynne claimed that any pension granted by the Rump was invalid. The satisfaction they took in successfully blocking the payments to John was noticeable, commented Penn. It took another seven months before he received the promised gift of £1,000 (nearly £77,000 at modern rates), which the king ordered to come out of the proceeds from the first sale of decayed naval stores. It was another year before his pension was approved by parliament[4].

Following his triumphant return, Charles II unsurprisingly had a number of complicated administrative and structural problems to deal with. The Commonwealth government and armed forces needed to be transformed into royalist organisations, which would take time and money. The navy had benefitted from Cromwell's investment in it and there was now a fleet of 157 ships. However, Charles' return meant the end of the war with Spain and parliament was unwilling to vote extra money towards the navy in peacetime. This aroused hostility in a fighting force whose personnel at all levels were still primarily republican in their sympathies.

A Navy Board was set up in July 1660 under James, Duke of York as Lord High Admiral, to replace the admiralty and navy commissioners. Edward Montagu was now a Knight of the Garter, the 1st Earl of Sandwich and Vice-Admiral. His influence also ensured Samuel Pepys became a senior officer with a new position as Clerk of Acts to the Navy Board and another as one of Montagu's deputies at the Privy Seal. The board dealt with all the civil administration, including provisions and ship repairs. As a result, both Pepys and Montagu would continue to work closely with John Lawson[5].

Edward Montagu was ordered to undertake a thorough purge of the officer corps to rid it of republican radicals. In theory, every level was to be scoured out. In practice, removing every republican sympathiser would have left an unworkable shell, so compromises were made. Most of the officers identified as problematic who were not pushed out were demoted or assigned to unattractive postings, often at a considerable distance from England's shores. Few of the captains who had helped John restore the Rump in 1659 were kept on or given good positions.

The whole navy was compelled to take the oaths of supremacy and allegiance of loyalty to the Church of England and the Crown. As the oaths were processed throughout the summer and autumn, there was a small percentage who refused on religious or political grounds, but far more who simply paid lip service to Anglicanism and the monarchy. Most of the former parliamentary officials were, at least on the surface, conciliatory. Some who were unwilling to accept the changes, such as Nehemiah Bourne, left the navy altogether while Robert Blackborne was not alone in remaining but expressing deep bitterness at those who had betrayed the cause[6].

Apart from those who had indispensible skills, crew members, carpenters, dockers, rope makers and other shoreside personnel who identified as Anabaptists were quickly removed, along with Quakers. Even those who were not Quakers themselves, but had wives who might corrupt them with their ideas, were ejected. It may be simply coincidence, but one of those who survived the cull was Sage Lawson of Scarborough, who was still a ship's master in 1665. It is not certain whether he was a Quaker himself, but his widow Jane was noted as one when she died some decades later; and there had been a small Quaker community in the Scarborough from as early as 1651[7].

John Lawson was not ousted or demoted. This was in large part due to the promise made to him by Charles II when he submitted to supporting the restoration. He was also helped by Edward Montagu, who respected his sea faring experience. John was appointed as a commissioner and treasurer-at-war, which meant that he was directly involved in the process of paying off the sailors. Who better to help weed out those still hankering for the good old cause? His friend William Penn, who had already been brought out of retirement and back into the navy as an admiral by Monck, kept his position too[8].

In contrast, most of the radicals that John was once aligned with did not do so well. Luke Robinson's tearful recantation and promise to be a loyal subject to the king may have saved him from worse punishment. He spent a month in prison after a humiliating expulsion from parliament as MP for Scarborough. Edmund Ludlow was arrested, but escaped from the Tower and had a £300 reward put on his head[9].

The first bloodshed in revenge for the killing of Charles I took place on 13 October 1660, just three weeks after John was knighted. Great shouts of joy could be heard from the crowds of people, as a man was dragged on a hurdle to his place of execution at Charing Cross. It was John's Fifth Monarchist collaborator Thomas Harrison. As Harrison was taken from the Tower to Charing Cross, he called out to the crowd that his death was for the most glorious cause ever. He was hanged, cut down alive and his heart and bowels ripped out before being burnt before his face. Among those watching was Pepys, who remarked that Harrison looked as cheerful as anyone could be in that condition[10].

Arthur Hasilrigg, who had played such a vital role alongside John in overturning the army coup in 1659, was also a victim, even though he had played no direct part in the king's trial. His history of opposition to the restoration meant that his life was in danger until Monck interceded on his behalf. His life was spared, but he was imprisoned in the Tower in May 1660, where he died the following January before coming to trial. There were undoubtedly many who saw little difference between Hasilrigg and John's actions and felt that he too should have been included in the pardon. For Hasilrigg's family, there was at least no ignominious traitor's burial in unconsecrated ground, as Charles permitted them to take his body home to Leicestershire[11].

Another of John's former comrades-in-arms who suffered the consequences in this year was Robert Overton. Rumours of a great plot against the king and government emerged in December and Overton was arrested as a suspect. One popular broadsheet entitled *Hell's Master Piece* named him as one of the inveterate enemies of the king and God, linking him directly with the Fifth Monarchist saints and cheerily exhorting its readers to sing the verses describing the plot to the tune of 'Summer Time'. Like Robinson, Overton at least escaped with his life, but his continued activism meant he spent most of the next eleven years in prison for seditious practices[12].

The practical process of transforming the country back into a royalist state continued slowly. While the army was almost completely disbanded by the end of the 1660, only a small number of naval ships had been paid off and John began warning parliament of growing resentment among the men. Pepys was concerned too, describing how navy officials were frightened of leaving their offices because of the sailors' anger.

Over the next few months, as the Commonwealth navy was gradually dismantled, John spent much of his time at sea. On one occasion in June, the vice-admiral brought a canoe from Greenland that measured around eighteen or nineteen feet which he wanted

Montague to see. It was closed in on top apart from a round hole in the cover, which one person could sit in and paddle. When on land in between voyages there are glimpses of John dining and drinking with Pepys and Montagu and other naval officers[13].

There was time for all sailors to socialise when off duty, both onboard and ashore. Accounts of convivial meals, drinking, smoking, dancing, singing and gambling appear from those who travelled or served with the fleet; as do fights and sexual encounters. It is hard to know exactly what John thought of such activities. His royalist conversion was unlikely to have undone a lifetime of political and religious leanings towards puritanism. His notorious suggestion of restricting men's shore pay during the 1650s so that they would not spend it on prostitutes certainly hints at disapproval, or at least concern for sailors' wives and families. If he abstained from the delights of visiting brothels himself he was obviously in a minority, as evidenced when in Lisbon the following year, thirty-seven men out of three hundred on one ship in Montagu's fleet succumbed to venereal disease[14].

More rebellions and plots were to come. A year had passed since Pepys wrote of John's fleet lying in the River Thames, when on 6 January 1661 the Fifth Monarchists rose up again. Their leader was the preacher Thomas Venner, who had been imprisoned for two years after he and John were arrested for plotting against Cromwell in 1657. Unlike John, Venner was not willing to make any accommodation with the new regime. Instead, he saw it as a test of faith, while Harrison's defiance when executed and the other radicals he witnessed imprisoned, hanged and tortured for their cause only inspired him further.

Around forty armed fanatics grouped near Venner's meeting house in Colman Street and fifty or more broke into Saint Paul's

Cathedral. Around three hundred rebels in small bands broke through the city gates. When confronted by soldiers, they declared that they were for King Jesus. At the corner of Wood Street nine of the king's lifeguard, commanded by Colonel Corbett, charged them but were forced to run. As more skirmishes took place on the ninth and again on the eleventh, over twenty people died. Eventually the Fifth Monarchists were overwhelmed and many taken prisoner. The women involved in the movement attracted particular vitriol in reports of Fifth Monarchists' activities at this time. Stories of promiscuity and refusal to enter a state of slavery by marrying circulated widely. Such dangerous independence was seen as indicative of the saints' wider rebellion against social and political order.

This time John was not involved. By now the only ties he seems to have retained with his past were with other turncoats. He had good reason to firmly dissociate himself. Just over two weeks after this rising was foiled, Thomas Venner, Giles Pritchard, William Oxman and Roger Hodgkin were dragged on sledges to their place of execution. Venner and Pritchard were hanged, drawn and quartered, while Oxman and Pritchard were hanged and beheaded in Wood Street. Two days later another nine rebels met their end in the same manner[15].

On 30 January 1661, the twelfth anniversary of the execution of Charles I, a strange and terrible sight was seen. The dead bodies of leading parliamentarians Oliver Cromwell, Henry Ireton, John Bradshaw and Thomas Pride were disinterred from their graves. As the coffins were carried before the public, Cromwell's was noticeable for its rich gilded hinges and nails. They were taken to Tyburn on the edge of London, where several criminals could be hanged simultaneously on the triple tree gallows. There, the embalmed corpses of the regicides were symbolically executed, dangling in chains on a gibbet from morning until sundown. Pride's body was too decayed for the order to be carried out on his. Once the others were taken down from the gallows, their heads were crudely hacked off and the loathsome remains of their bodies buried in a common grave underneath the gallows[16].

Charles II was more than aware of the symbolic resonance of the date. His revenge on his father's killers was far from over. The heads of Cromwell, Bradshaw and Ireton were displayed on spikes at the south end of Westminster Hall. Bradshaw's was placed in the middle over the very spot where he had presided over the king's trial. Their heads would remain in place at the hall for twenty-five years or more. Cromwell's ended up in private hands, until after nearly four hundred years it was buried at his former college, Sidney Sussex College in Cambridge. The execution episode was glorified in a popular seventeenth century song that gradually became corrupted into a nursery rhyme, beginning:

> Oliver Cromwell lay buried and dead,
> hee-haw, buried and dead,
> there grew an apple tree over his head,
> hee-haw, over his head.[17]

Over many years to come, Charles II's agents went to enormous lengths to track down the twenty survivors of those who had played a part in the trial and execution of his father, including the poet and propagandist John Milton. The hunt spread as far as Germany, the Netherlands, Spain, Switzerland and America, where those located were ambushed and killed on the spot, or brought back to England for trial. Those that were captured endured public humiliations, some abasing themselves tearfully before the House while Milton's books were burned by the common hangman.

Just over a year after Venner's uprising, John Lawson's fellow Fifth Monarchist co-conspirator, John Okey, was kidnapped in the Low Countries and executed for having signed the king's death warrant. In a last letter written beforehand, Okey showed no sorrow for his actions, only total acceptance that for the last time he was about to seal his commitment to the cause in blood. Among the twenty regicides that went into hiding abroad, Edmund Ludlow fled across France before taking refuge in a small town on the shores of Lake Geneva, in Switzerland. He was joined there by John Lisle and William Cawley. Despite the protection given to them, Lisle was assassinated but Ludlow survived, despite several attempts on his life[18].

In May 1661, Charles II announced to parliament that a marriage had been agreed between him and the Portuguese princess, Catherine of Braganza. The news was greeted in Portugal with bonfires and an extraordinary display of fireworks, while their ambassador in Holland caused two fountains to run with wine and threw 400 florins out of his window as a gift to the crowd massed below. Catherine's magnificent dowry included England's newest colony of Tangier and first African possession, along with Bombay in India.

Tangier's acquisition gave England a strategic foothold in the Mediterranean, from Gibraltar in the west to the Levant in the far east, from which to develop trade prospects. Tangier also had a ready-made market place where English merchants could sell goods and stock up on provisions. In return, England would help to protect Portugal from Spain. John Lawson was about to play a vital vole in ensuring that English merchant ships could pass freely through the Ottoman Empire and way beyond and, in the long run, ensuring England's successful empire building. No ship could pass through the Straits of Gibraltar during daylight hours without being seen from Tangier and patrols by men-of-war could intercept those who tried at night[19].

Founded by the Carthaginians, Tangier had been ruled by the Romans, the Vandals and the Byzantine Empire before coming under the control of the Portuguese in 1471. Its position on the Moroccan coast commanded entry into the western entrance of the Straits and gave access to the Mediterranean, making it a principal commercial centre on the North West coast of Africa. It also provided a protective base against Barbary pirates operating in the region – and a crucial observation point over Spanish enclaves in the area.

After being occupied by Spanish troops and merchants when the Spanish and Portuguese crowns were united between 1580 and 1640, Tangier was reluctantly returned to Portugal in 1648. By the time the marriage was arranged between Charles II and Catherine of Braganza, conflict between the two countries and other threats to the Portuguese meant it was increasingly difficult for them to hold. They were therefore willing to trade it for the strong alliance with England that this marriage would bring[20].

For the next few years, John was to patrol the waters of the Mediterranean between Portugal and Tangier and the Mediterranean ports of Algiers, Tunis and Tripoli. The task assigned to him and other naval commanders was to protect British ships passing through from pirates and hostile states. The East India Company had been formed in 1600 to pursue trade in the region (and ended up effectively ruling large areas of India).

Their ships and the merchants that passed through the Straits of Gibraltar on their way back from the Near East were particularly vulnerable to piracy, even from as far away as Algiers.

Piracy was big business. Although it had been outlawed in England by James I, it was still an international trade. The Barbary pirates, or Barbarians as they were also known, took their name from the Barbers who inhabited the coastal regions of North Africa. They roamed over one million square miles, stretching from the Straits of Gibraltar in the west to the Holy Land in the east: plundering merchant ships, buying and selling stolen goods and taking Christians captive and selling them into slavery.

The dominant power in the region was the Ottoman Empire, a conglomerate of principalities and vassal states who frequently went to war with each other as well as against Christendom. To Europeans, the Barbarians were all one and the same – cruel and immoral Muslim infidels – and it was a Christian's duty to fight them. This holy war against Islam had long roots and lasted for centuries. It began with the Catholic powers based in the Mediterranean then spread into northern Europe and the protestant nations. Fighting the forces of the devil on behalf of God also conveniently gave European countries a justification for attacking Muslim shipping.

By the beginning of the seventeenth century, the three Barbary States of Tunis, Tripoli and Algiers owed allegiance to Istanbul. The fourth major presence was the independent state of Morocco, with Spain and Portugal holding some bases, including Tangier on the North African side of the Straits. France, Venice, Holland and England all made a number of trade treaties with the Empire throughout the 1500s and 1600s, known as articles of capitulation. These agreements were intended to guarantee the rights and liberties of the citizens of those countries, including freedom of religion and free passage throughout the Empire by land and sea, a limit on the duty that merchants had to pay in its ports and protection from pirates.

The English Ambassador to the region was appointed by the king, but the post was paid for by the London-based Levant Company, which held a monopoly on English trade with the Empire. By the 1620s its merchants were sending over £250,000 worth of goods to Turkey each year. Over the next few decades this grew to half of all English exports. Such riches attracted English pirates too. Those prepared to concentrate their activities against the Muslims were given sanctuary in Majorca, Sardinia, Malta and Genoa, while protestant zealots had the opportunity to fight against Spain and popery[21].

Trade interests and political and religious alliances meant that the marriage between Charles II and Catherine of Braganza caused another rift with Spain. The Dutch were equally anxious that England should not make an alliance with Portugal. Ongoing disputes over freedom of the seas resulted in Edward Montagu, the Earl of Sandwich and his protégé Samuel Pepys being appointed to the Tangier Committee set up by the king to run the new colony. It would be formally surrendered to Montagu in January 1662. Montagu had previously suggested Tangier as a suitable base in the region after surveying it for Oliver Cromwell, despite it being surrounded by lands occupied by hostile Muslim tribes.

Montagu was also appointed ambassador to Portugal. Sixteen warships commanded by Montagu, along with John Lawson, left England in June 1661. Their mission was to subdue the Barbary corsairs, secure England's new acquisition of Tangier and negotiate treaties with Algiers, Tunis and Tripoli that would allow English ships passage through their territory without being molested. There were two general groupings of Barbary pirates to deal with: Turks who were part of the Ottoman Empire and Moors who lived in or came from Morocco. By the time they arrived in Algiers, the navy board had completed their reorganisation. The navy they served was now fully royalist and all shreds of the Commonwealth service that John originally joined had disappeared[22].

While John was en route to Algiers tragedy hit his family. Abigail, the eldest of his six daughters was struck down by a fever. This was probably the spotted fever – typhus or cerebrospinal fever, meningitis – that killed 3,490 people in London that year. Thousands more, including General Monck, became seriously ill but survived. Samuel Pepys' wife Elizabeth and Lady Batten, wife of the navy's surveyor, attended Abigail's funeral on 3 July at Saint Dunstan in the East Church, where they received mourning rings for themselves and their husbands to remember her by. Such tokens were commonly given to chief mourners.

Abigail's sisters Mary and Sarah died of the same fever very soon afterwards and were buried on the fifteenth. Pepys had a death in his own family and was out of town when their interment took place, so made no mention of Mary and Sarah's deaths in his journal. The three girls were laid to rest together in the great aisle of the church, lamented, said William Penn, by all who knew them for their inner and outward accomplishments[23].

Knowing the depth of John's love and tenderness towards their children, Isabelle wanted her husband to be prepared for the shock. She wrote to John with the mournful news and sent it via Penn in one of the packets of letters that were carried to overseas ports on men-of-war or merchant ships. Isabelle asked Penn to forward her letter to Montagu first, beseeching the earl not to let John be surprised by the news. A few words from Montagu before he opened the letter, would, she felt, much avail[24].

John Lawson and Edward Montagu sailed south past the coasts of France, then Spain and Portugal. They then turned eastwards and passed through the Straits of Gibraltar into the Mediterranean, before turning northwards. They stopped briefly to revictual at the Spanish port of Alicante. John's ship the *Swiftsure* and the rest of this fleet weighed anchor out of Alicante on 23 July and arrived in Algiers on the North African coast six days later.

The report from John of what happened next did not reach London for two months. As the English fleet steered into the bay at Algiers, the general, admiral and rear-admiral all saluted the town with a volley of gunfire. The general sent his boats ashore with the flag of truce and the Algerian consul returned with a present of a young lion and some provisions from their chief. This warm welcome was very brief, as the Algerians refused to accept the treaty and their chief almost immediately proclaimed war.

For two days there was an uneasy lull as negotiations continued. Suddenly, while the general and all the commanders of the fleet were on board together at about one or two o'clock, a volley of shots came from the pirates' ships as well as the forts and castles overlooking the bay. Fewer than eighteen sailors were killed or hurt on this occasion, but a series of short sea battles commenced.

The Venetian Resident (consul) in England was pleased to report that John Lawson, a brave soldier, experienced in both the military arts and in navigation, was left to blockade Algiers while Montagu left for Lisbon to make arrangements for the royal marriage between Charles II and Catherine of Braganza. From there, Montagu went on to Tangier to oversee the evacuation of the Portuguese[25].

In the meantime, John kept sending news to England of the various skirmishes with the Algerians. In one episode, a small boat hailed Captain Blake, pretending that they were slaves seeking freedom. His suspicions aroused, Blake refused to let them board, at which point the brigands began firing. Despite being wounded in the shoulder, Blake and his men forced them off the side with small shot and pikes.

In another dramatic incident, John was on patrol hunting for Barbary corsairs while the rest of his fleet continued bombarding Algiers when he captured two enemy ships and freed another from Genoa laden with oil, which the Barbary pirates had taken. One of the vessels was commanded by a renegade; a European who had joined the pirates and converted to Islam. John and his crew made slaves of the 125 captives they took, but released over 30 Christians from different countries who were being held. Slaves taken by John and his fleet were sold to the Spanish while they executed those renegade Christians who had given up their religion and become Muslims[26].

As reports of the continued hostilities against Algiers filtered back home, Rugge noted how Sir John Lawson had become a great power there. It was a great comfort, wrote one of Montagu's correspondents in Alicante, to know that John's squadron was in the seas there to protect the merchant ships. At some point in between patrols and exchanging gunfire with the Algerians, John had a detailed map drawn up of Algiers and its bay to present to the Duke of York. On it, a number of ships can be seen in the harbour. What stands out is a group of seven men-of-war moored abreast in the centre of the harbour. One can assume that John's is amongst them[27]

At home in England during the winter of 1661, people marvelled at a female Egyptian mummy decorated with hieroglyphics and escutcheons, which had been brought out of the Libyan desert from near the ruins of the city of Memphis to be presented to his majesty. And yet another pernicious and horrid plot by Commonwealth men and Anabaptists against the king was uncovered[28].

On this occasion John's squadron was unsuccessful in subduing Algiers and he and his five hundred crewmen travelled the five hundred miles to join Montagu in Tangier in January 1662. Leaving from Cape Trafalgar on the European side of the Strait of Gibraltar, they crossed to the Coast of Africa at the point where the Mediterranean Sea meets the Atlantic Ocean. As they sailed into the four-mile-wide bay, they could see the sea washing the walls of the city towering high above[29].

They arrived to a colony under attack. While John was still engaged at Algiers, the first conflict occurred at Tangier. Montagu had been welcomed warmly by the inhabitants when he first arrived. As a result he was able to report success in making an arrangement with the king who commanded the Moors in the area, so that the English could move around freely and engage in commerce.

But this was not to last. The first land attack occurred on 14 January. A group of Montagu's men ventured out of the city and beyond the safe Portuguese area on a cattle raid, kidnapping thirty-five native women and girls as well. As the captives were being taken towards the city to sell into slavery, their menfolk tracked them down and attacked in return. Accounts of the number injured and killed vary, but it was to be the first of many lightning strikes by natives on the town and garrison.

The city gates were kept almost permanently shut for protection, with the result that the inhabitants were almost completely powerless to stop the Moors seizing their cattle, which grazed outside the city walls. At the same time the English had to contend with the Spanish at sea, who were actively trying to extend their own African territories and so made life as difficult as possible for the English naval and merchant ships, which had to pass through areas they controlled[30].

Once John and his fleet arrived in Tangier later that month, Montagu returned to Lisbon to continue the marriage contract negotiations before escorting Catherine of Braganza to England for the royal wedding, which was to take place in May. John Lawson's former parliamentarian comrade and rear-admiral, Sir Richard Stayner, took temporary command until the arrival of the new governor, Henry Mordaunt, Earl of Peterborough. Stayner stayed on in the fleet under John, but was taken fatally ill a few months later.

Sir Henry had briefly served in the parliamentary army during the early years of the first civil war, but had quickly switched to supporting the king. The new governor arrived at the end of January 1662, bringing with him a specially raised regiment of foot known as the Tangier Regiment. The troops were essential to combating the constant threat on land from the Moors as well as the dangers at sea from pirates[31].

When surveyor Hugh Cholmley arrived in Tangier the following year, he thought that the city's exposure to two seas gave it a pleasant and healthy air, even in summer. Many years later, Cholmley still marvelled at the exquisite fresh water from its springs and fountains and excellent tasting fish in the sea, believing the wonderfully rich soil to be the reason that every family had an abundance of bread, herbs and fruit. Perhaps more importantly, the engineer was delighted to find that no ships could be hidden from view as they passed by along its beautiful coastline.

When the English took over Tangier, it had about five hundred houses, a handsome parish church and a Christian convent belonging to the order of the Austin Friars, plus nine other chapels and places of religious worship. Cholmley estimated the population to be between 4,000 and 5,000, although many of the original inhabitants chose to leave rather than adjust to English rule. There was also a thriving and highly profitable trade in slavery, in which an 'average' man or woman sold at market fetched about twenty pounds.

The city began to be rebuilt and expanded and John Lawson, Richard Stayner and Edward Montagu were among those honoured when the existing streets, posts and gates in Tangier were renamed. Others were named King, Queen and Duke of York, while the later naming of York Castle and Whitby Fort was reputedly after Yorkshire-born Cholmley and the team of workers he brought with him[32].

On-site in the garrison was the governor, a sergeant-major and two aid-majors. Each company of foot was commanded by captains, ensigns, sergeants and corporals and the army received an allowance from the king. Foot soldiers were given around a bushel and a half of wheat plus nine testones – worth ninety English pence – but two-thirds of this allowance was given in cloth rather than cash. The higher the rank, the more they received, with a captain being given fifty-six testones and five times as much wheat. The horsemen brought their own horses and arms and received an allowance towards the upkeep of the horses. These allowances tended to be passed on from father to son and to the widows and children of those killed by the Moors.

Theft, wastage and disobedience among the troops were common. One survey of the stores early in 1662 found a significant portion of the items brought over for the garrison had been embezzled, including spades, shovels and pickaxes as well as wheelbarrows, bills and hatchets. With no easy means of replacing such essential supplies, the earl resorted to issuing a proclamation ordering their return within forty-eight hours upon pain of death.

The commander and his officers also discovered that, despite almost hourly commands to the contrary, ammunition was being unnecessarily wasted by soldiers shooting pistols, carbines and muskets within the garrison. Along with the temporary amnesty for the stolen goods, Mordaunt declared that if any soldier fired within the garrison walls or on a march without permission, he would die without mercy[33].

The Earl of Peterborough's tenure as governor did not last long. He managed to conclude a treaty with the Moors in April 1662, but his men were ill equipped and roundly defeated in a skirmish the following month. He returned to England for supplies and reinforcements very soon after this. However his second stay in Tangier was equally brief and he was replaced by Andrew Rutherford, Earl of Teviot, in December 1663[34].

John's next task was to work with the surveyor Hugh Cholmley on overseeing the building of a defensive mole (from the Latin word *moles,* meaning a giant heap). This was a fortified harbour that would provide a secure place for ships to anchor all year round. Cholmley had already gained a reputation for his construction of a mole at Whitby in Yorkshire, where he had an estate. The Whitby Mole was exposed to the sea on all sides for about two hundred yards, so several new techniques were invented in order to make it secure and which Cholmley was able to subsequently apply in Tangier[35].

The vice-admiral and Hugh Cholmley signed the agreement to build the 1,436 feet high mole on 30 March 1662, at a cost of £340,000. Work would begin the following year at the foot of Tangier's York Castle, extending hundreds of yards in each direction in order to enclose the harbour so that ships could 'ride in five fathoms at low water defended from the violence of the sea'[36]. A partly paved parapet, crowned for all sorts of carriages to travel on, was to be built over the first 400 yards, with two-foot-high steps leading to it[37].

The two men were aware that it would take several years to complete and predicted that the first stage would be finished before the end of June 1664. The original contract allowed thirteen shillings per cubic yard for the mole, parapet and any other structures on it, to be paid in half-yearly instalments beginning the following April. Having worked on the Whitby Mole in his home town, Cholmley brought the first miners out from Yorkshire. Stone was brought from quarries opened up near the cliffs, which the English miners soon named Whitby.

When Cholmley wrote his account of the building of the mole some years later, he recalled concerns over the scale of the project and how long it would take to finish, as it would be greater than any built before. There were not enough quarries in the region to supply it and it was the first to be built in deep and flowing water[38]. In the long run, the lack of shelter in Tangier meant the notion of using the colony as a major naval base came to nothing. Thirty years later Tangier was abandoned by the English, who blew up the mole as they withdrew[39].

John's relationship with Hugh Cholmley is intriguing. Cholmley's father, also called Hugh, had been the turncoat governor of Scarborough Castle whose actions in joining the royalists during the civil war had first forced John into exile. John had subsequently displayed an unforgiving attitude to those who had betrayed that cause. Now he was to work closely with the son of a man he had once thought treacherous.

Despite this, they obviously grew to like and respect each other. In the letters that Cholmley wrote to John, he confided his good opinion of some of the workmen and other people they knew. More significantly, he signed himself 'your faithful friend and humble servant'. While 'servant' and 'obedient' were common conventions, designating himself as an affectionate friend signified more[40]. When Cholmley heard of John's death he felt a great discouragement. It was, he said, a great loss to the nation, but also to himself of a powerful, intelligent and worthy partner in their endeavour, and his dear friend[41].

While preparations for work on the mole got underway, John continued to be deployed at sea protecting merchant ships from pirates. In 1662 he was sent to command another expedition against the Moors of Algiers. This time there was a favourable result. On 23 April 1662, John Lawson concluded a peace treaty between Charles II and the City and Kingdom of Algiers and its territories, with copies published in England[42].

Each side promised to treat the other with respect and friendship and offer no offence or injury. Most important was the clause that British ships could pass through Algerian dominions unmolested and exempt from search. In addition to which, all ships 'belonging to the King of Britain or any of his subjects may freely come to the port of Algiers and buy and sell as in former times and also unto any port that belongs to the government of Algiers paying the custom of ten per cent as in former times'[43].

The wording on the treaty caused some friction between John Lawson and Edward Montagu, as Montagu's name was omitted. The Duke of York's was added, even though he had not contributed one word to it. John told Montagu afterwards that the council of war had decided to include the Duke's name. However, Pepys noted that the Duke had in turn proposed that John's name should be added[44].

Following the ratification of the treaty with Algiers, John moved on to Tripoli and Tunis. However a month later, the deputy governor of Tangier sent urgent word to John that he was needed. Intelligence had been received of a planned attack on the settlement by Spanish forces that had joined forces with the Moors. John had to leave his business with Tripoli and Tunis unfinished as preparations rapidly got underway to organise Tangier's defences. Under Sir Henry, the English garrison at Tangier suffered serious losses in a sortie against the Moors. In a further attempt to disrupt the settlement, the Spanish spread rumours there was plague in the city[45].

In June 1662, Sir Henry Mordaunt left Tangier for London with a few officers to report to the king about garrison affairs. The fleet also arrived from Lisbon. Their visit coincided with the trials of Henry Vane and John Lambert. Charles II remitted the death sentence of John Lambert, who had led the army coup in 1659, although Lambert was kept in captivity until his death more than twenty years later.

Sir Henry Vane was not so fortunate. No one knows what John thought when he was brought to trial for regicide. Unlike the other regicides executed and hunted down, Vane had not signed King Charles I's death warrant or presided over his trial and execution. The former naval commissioner had many enemies and had refused to submit to the king after the restoration. Instead, Henry Vane's signature on a Navy Committee letter written on the day of Charles I's execution was claimed as proof that he had not opposed it, for otherwise he would have stayed away from work[46].

In what can only be described as a strange coincidence, John was still working with Hugh Cholmley, whose father he had condemned so bitterly for his treachery in a letter to Henry Vane only eight years before. Vane's death was deliberately scheduled to take place on Tower Hill on 14 June, the anniversary of the battle of Naseby. Rugge and Pepys wrote in their diaries of seeing him drawn from the Tower upon a sledge to the place of execution. Rugge thought Vane was still a very handsome and portly man, who remained fresh complexioned up to the minute he died.

As Vane spoke his last words, the attending soldiers were ordered to beat their drums loudly and trumpets were brought underneath the scaffold so that the crowd could not hear. Like Harrison, Henry Vane proclaimed before he died that he would never give up the good old cause – the Commonwealth. Parliament's cause was God's cause. Former friends and colleagues such as Pepys and Montagu thought him courageous and wise right up to the end[47].

The consequences of Vane's continued loyalty to a cause that had once been John's had a horrible irony that could hardly have been lost on him or on others who now served the king. After all, John's rift with Henry in 1659 had been over the attempt by the army to supersede the Rump Parliament. At that time, John had threatened to hold London hostage on the principle that no one should have authority over parliament, while Henry had accepted the army coup. Now Henry Vane paid the price for beliefs they had both shared with an agonising death, while John Lawson was now as wholeheartedly committed to the monarchy as he had once been to the Commonwealth – and well rewarded for it.

John's reputation was enhanced further when he negotiated favourable peace treaties with Tunis and Tripoli, after capturing several enemy ships, releasing a couple of hundred of their captives and selling as many Moors into slavery. The treaty with Tunis was concluded in October 1662, with John as the signatory for the crown. It allowed ships from both countries who displayed their colours to enter any port or river in their respective dominions, without molestation and only paying duties on what they sold. Both sides were sworn to protect each others' goods and passengers when they were on their own ships.

There was a clause guaranteeing the freedom of any castaways: their goods would not be taken from them but no one from either dominion would be abused with or otherwise mistreated. There were still problems with the Algerians, who were reported not to be keeping to the terms agreed. Nevertheless, when Pepys heard the news, he thought that John's continued success would see him highly honoured once he returned home[48].

At the beginning of December 1662, John set sail for England to spend the winter at home. At the end of the month his lifetime pension of £500 a year was finally reinstated in honour of his services. Pepys thought that John's service in the straits meant that was now held in great renown by all, including at court. Although there would be some who cast doubt on John's achievements, they were very much in the minority. When he and John met again the following month, Pepys thought it worth noting that the vice-admiral was still the same, plain man he had always been, despite his success[49].

In around 1663, John decided he needed a new base close to naval headquarters in England for his family, which he could return to when on leave. He bought Warren House and an adjacent plot of land, close to the church in the tiny village of Alresford, near Colchester in Essex. The land was purchased in June 1663 and he almost certainly bought the house at the same time or before, although no specific record of this transaction survives. Unlike the land, which was copyhold and therefore appears in the manor court records, the house was freehold so there was no requirement for its sale to be recorded.

The house was next to a tributary leading the River Colne and came with its own ballast quay, which meant that John had easy access to the river and the sea. It was soon renamed Alresford Lodge and would stay in the family for many decades to come. At around the same time, John purchased land and houses in the nearby parish of Wanstead, where his friend William Penn already owned property. The county of Essex also attracted a number of John's mariner, merchant and grocer relatives, who migrated to Wanstead and Bocking in the mid to late sixteen hundreds[50].

One can only speculate as to whether or not John was troubled by news from Yorkshire throughout this period. He was surely aware of the levels of dissent and unhappiness there, as he still had strong ties to the county, through people who had served with him in the navy and before that, from his time spent in the army, as well as still owning a house and lands in Scarborough. Yorkshire had always been one of the most mutinous counties throughout the civil wars. It had elected agitators and had strong connections with the radicals in the New Model Army. Although it could never be said that the people in such a large and diverse region had homogenous views or reactions, in general, the restoration had been far from wholeheartedly welcomed. The plot by Robert Overton, which took place very shortly after the return of the king, was just one case in point. Then came the mass ejections of clergy that accompanied the Act of Uniformity in 1662, leading to further unrest. Yorkshire suffered fifty-two dismissals, although this did not put an end to seditious preaching[51].

A series of uprisings against the restoration occurred in the north of Yorkshire in the autumn of 1663. Many of the plotters were nonconformist. Their fears and objections included seeing an increase in the numbers of Roman Catholics and the government's tolerance of blasphemy, adultery, drunkenness, swearing, the staging of plays and idolatry. The banning of public meetings of Quakers and Anabaptists had begun and former parliamentarians were being removed from municipal offices in favour of royalists.

These Yorkshire risings failed and twenty-six rebels were condemned to death in October 1663. Sixteen were hanged, drawn and quartered on the same day in the city of York. Nearly all those executed came from an area steeped in support of the parliamentarian cause during the civil wars, twenty-one from the West Riding. Many had served the Fairfaxes in the northern army and believed they would be supported by former allies among the nobility and gentry. Although this plot was foiled, it was far from the end of anti-royalism in Yorkshire[52].

Over the next year or so, John spent most of his time patrolling the waters close to Algiers and Tunisia, interspersed with trips home and liaising with the new governor of Tangier and Hugh Cholmley to arrange for more material for the mole. He sent regular reports of his work back to the navy board in England and to Montagu. There was news of negotiations with foreign states over passage through their waters and a number of disputes when his fleet anchored in Cadiz in Spain, the Bay of Bulls in Newfoundland, Malaga and elsewhere. In Portugal in 1663, another gold chain was given to him in honour of his services. This one was as equally treasured as the one received during the Dutch war, and would be left to his daughter Elizabeth[53].

There continued to be conflicts with Spain as well as encounters with pirates. During every journey he made, John was always concerned with upholding the honour of the English nation and its flag. It was just as important to him now as it was when he had fought the Dutch for the Commonwealth in the 1650s. He cared deeply that the correct etiquette should be observed on both sides. The correct gun salute was expected when encountering foreign vessels and when entering a port. Officers were very quick to take umbrage if not enough guns were fired, or if the salute was lacking in some other way[54].

John's sense of honour over any lack of respect for the English flag came to the fore in March 1664, no doubt involving a Spanish official. On the fourteenth, he wrote a vociferous letter of complaint to the English ambassador in Cordova about the governor in Alicante. Having arrived in Alicante on their way to Algiers a few days before, with a squadron of eleven frigates and a ketch, they were treated uncivilly by the governor in what John saw as a calculated slight to his Majesty's subjects.

In contrast to the politeness they had had received at Cadiz and Malaga, the governor of Alicante refused to honour their arrival by answering their salute gun for gun. Such a lacklustre and insufficient number of gun volleys fired on arrival was as provocative as if no greeting had been made at all. John therefore felt it his duty to protect the honour due to the king's flag, and in a tit for tat response, refused to make any salute to the Spanish at all. This of course displeased the Alicante governor.

John asserted that the governor was obliged to show the proper forms of respect to the King of England regardless of his own status. Even the king's brother, the Duke of York and High Admiral did so. Anything less from any another admiral, king or in any port would have a detrimental impact on discipline and cohesion in their own ranks, as minor officers in the English fleet would feel no need to salute either. The insult from the governor was, in John's view, compounded by his having previously ordered formal gun salutes to be made to the private frigates and men-of-war belonging to other nations that arrived in their ports. Yet the Spanish still refused to show equivalent or greater respect to the King of Great Britain's flag[55].

The refusal by the Spanish governor to observe the rather elaborate code of honour expected between the representatives of the two countries was merely a reflection of their rather fractious relationship. The takeover of Tangier and the successful treaties John Lawson helped to negotiate in the region only exacerbated those tensions.

The incident of the gun salute would not be the only bone of contention. Enclosed with John's letter of complaint were three depositions about a dispute between Captain Beach of the *Leopard* and the governor of Alicante. The accounts of exactly what happened and who was to blame vary, but according to Beach his ship had been attacked by Turkish pirates under the pretence of being in distress. Two of his men were wounded, one mortally. The English sailors managed to fight the pirates off and rescue some Moors, renegadoes and Christians who were being held by the Turks. However, Beach received orders from the governor in Alicante that as they were in Spanish waters, they must hand over the captives to him. When Beach refused and tried to leave, he was imprisoned by the governor until he agreed. The governor of Alicante's view of what occurred naturally differed[56].

By this time Tangier was a free port and construction of the mole was underway. Over the four years, John had been responsible for negotiating and enforcing peace treaties with three out of the four Barbary States. The mole was less of a success, not least financially. The Tangier accounts were mismanaged by Thomas Povey, the treasurer of the committee. Pepys complained more than once about the strange and irregular accounts relating to Tangier, stating that he did not understand the mole contract and the sums involved. He would eventually replace Povey as treasurer in 1665. The same year, Cholmley regretted ever engaging in the business, with the monies he was owed negatively affecting his relationship with the Lawson family[57].

Rutherford lasted even less time as a governor of Tangier than Sir Henry Mordaunt. On 4 May 1664, he marched into a wood around two miles from Tangier. With him there were around five hundred men, including his principal officers. Caught there in an ambush by the Moors, he along with nineteen officers and nearly all the soldiers were killed. His replacement was Colonel Henry Norwood[58].

A month later, John Lawson was pleased to report from Tangier that the building works for the mole were still going on vigorously and courageously since that recent disaster. 'I am sailing for England today,' he wrote[59].

# CHAPTER 6

# INCOMPARABLY THE MODESTEST
# AND THE WISEST MAN

On 25 February 1665 John Lawson signed away more than half of his fortune. It was a dowry of eight hundred pounds per year, up to a total of six thousand, for his eldest surviving daughter Isabella's marriage to Daniel Norton, of Southwick in Hampshire. The marriage took place the following day. Pepys, who had an eye for attractive women, admired Isabelle Lawson's prettiness and good deportment and thought that they made a fine-looking couple. However, that did not prevent him from condemning Norton as a melancholy, ungenerous, bad-natured fellow who had negotiated for Isabella as if he were buying a horse[1].

This type of prenuptial agreement was common, in an era when married women had no rights over their property unless a contract was drawn up beforehand. Without one, anything she owned or inherited automatically belonged to her husband. Such legal arrangements usually included a clause allowing a portion of the woman's inheritance or dowry to be retained for her own use. This would pass directly to her children after her death, although her husband may have been granted the interest or income from investments and rents. Another was a guarantee that the wife could draw up a will to dispose of these assets, something that a married woman could not do without her husband's permission until the late nineteenth century.

The amount given for Isabella's dowry was, thought Pepys, an act of great rashness. He obviously believed it to be over-generous, especially as a proposal from Sir William Berkeley had already been refused by the family, even though Berkeley would have accepted a much lower dowry of two thousand pounds. Berkeley had served under John in the Mediterranean, and recently been promoted to rear-admiral. He was one of the king's favourites, and particularly close to the Duke of York. As such he would have helped Isabella's two little sisters at court, whereas Norton's tyrannous, ill-natured father was never content with the arrangement – or with the amount agreed[2]. As for John, there was a consensus among Pepys and others who knew him that he could ill afford it and was extremely foolish for 'breeding up his daughter so high and proud'[3].

As well as his salary, John Lawson had made a great deal of money from his share of prizes from captured Barbary ships and the sale of slaves taken from the pirates and Moors. Like most people of his time, he seems to have little or no hesitation over being involved in the buying and selling of human beings. No doubt the majority being Muslim and non-white assuaged any pangs of conscience. There were, however, a remarkable number who had been Christian before being captured from merchant ships and coastal villages and towns, even as far as Ireland to the west and Iceland in the north-west. Many of these European, white slaves had converted to Islam, most often as a survival tactic. Those willing to return to Christianity would be released, but not otherwise. Unlike the Fifth Monarchist women who drew a correlation between marriage and slavery, John seems to have had no such thoughts when it came to using profits from human trafficking when bartering his daughter[4].

John had been recalled to England in the autumn of 1664, as preparations for war against the Dutch got underway. When John arrived in Portsmouth on 11 October, he brought news that the previous month the Dutch Admiral De Ruyter had taken a great supply of victuals from Spain and they were heading for the Guinea Coast[5]. On 4 March 1665, a procession of his Majesty's heralds wearing tabards decorated with the king's coat of arms, carrying maces and accompanied by four servants at arms and trumpeters, arrived outside Whitehall Gate. There they publicly proclaimed that hostilities had begun before going on to do the same at the Temple, where they were received by the Lord Mayor of London, aldermen and sheriffs, then on to Cheapside and the Royal Exchange[6].

This was the second war to be fought against the Dutch over control of trade routes. Despite an uneasy ten-year peace, major tensions had arisen between the two countries since the restoration. Tensions were exacerbated by the number of MPs and political agitators who had been unable to accept the new regime, or feared for their lives under it and had fled to exile in Holland. As disputes over shipping routes escalated, so did fears of a Dutch invasion and that it could be accompanied by an uprising in England among those still sympathetic to the old parliamentarian cause and against the revival of the monarchy.

In England, merchants were increasingly convinced that going to war against the Dutch again was the only way to save their overseas investments and trade, while those who had fought against them in the first Dutch war believed they could be equally successful. In April 1664 the merchants of London had complained to parliament about injuries done to them by the Dutch over the previous thirty years. The East India Company claimed they had lost over two hundred thousand pounds in that period, while the total from traders to the Levant, Portugal, Africa and other regions came to five hundred thousand. The Dutch were, understandably, hardly falling over themselves to reimburse[7].

King Charles began to build up the fleet in anticipation of war and outlying squadrons, including John's, were called home. Subsequent negotiations over a settlement between the two countries over the next few months broke down. The final trigger was the result of England's friendly relationship with Portugal since the marriage of Charles II, which meant that when Portugal and Holland came into conflict over Dutch colonies on the Guinea coast that Portugal had seized, the Dutch treated England as equally culpable. It was not yet full-scale war, but with Holland planning to expel the English from Guinea and England driving the Dutch out of Tobago and New Amsterdam, the increasing number of stand-offs – and pressure from merchants whose trade was adversely affected – meant it would not be long.

John Lawson was among those who sincerely believed that the king of England would overcome the Dutch as long as God was on his side. Whether it was true or not, Pepys felt that John had influenced the king to throw the nation into this war, with his confidence that England had never failed to beat the Dutch even with fewer numbers: sixty vessels would be as effective as one hundred[8].

By the early 1660s, John's relative Samuel Lawson was acting as his attorney. Samuel was the son of John's cousin, also called

John, a grocer who lived on Lyme Street in London. Unlike John, both men were Londoners born and bred. Like John however, they were deeply rooted in trade, although the father's was on land rather than sea. They earned the right to be admitted as freemen of the city. Samuel served an apprenticeship with his father. By the time he started signing legal documents on John's behalf, he was a merchant and at some point joined the East India Company. When the vice-admiral was in Tangier, Samuel met with Pepys on his behalf to arrange for bills to be paid and organise supplies. Samuel's father also became involved in John's overseas business from at least the autumn after John's return from Tangier[9].

John Lawson and Sir William Penn became the chief advisers to the Duke of York (later James II). John was already vice-admiral of the red squadron and a fleet of 100 ships manned by up to 30,000 men, with thirty more on convoy and coastguard duties, all approved for the 1665 campaign.

The navy was concentrated at the Thames and Medway dockyards. Chatham in Kent was the largest, serving as a major refitting yard and shipbuilding centre. John's 76-gun second-rate flagship the *London* was put into Chatham Docks in readiness and had over eighty pieces of brass ordnance in place when she set out. First launched in 1656, the *London* was one of the ships that had escorted Charles II back to England at the restoration. The king's brother James, Duke of York and later James II, had his quarters on board during the journey. Samuel Pepys observed that the ship's state room was bigger than on the *Naseby*, which had carried the king, but was not so richly decorated[10].

It was bitterly cold on 7 March 1665, as John Lawson's 'good ship'[11] the *London* set out from Chatham. She was one of the largest ships in the navy and was to join the rest of his fleet at its new berth: sailing towards the Hope, a stretch of the Thames named after the Hope stream, which was used as one of the main anchorages when the fleet assembled.

John Lawson was not on board, but over three hundred of his men were. They were joined by around thirty women and children who had come to take leave of their husbands and fathers before they went to war. The civilians were to disembark once they arrived at the Hope and make their own way home again, catching a lift with any other vessels heading their way if possible, but straggling back on foot and hoping to catch a ride on a passing cart if need be.

At about nine o'clock in the morning, the *London* was approximately ten miles from her destination. As she came within half a league – a mile or two at the most – of Leigh Road, a shipping channel close to Southend in Essex at the mouth of the Thames estuary, a fire took hold in the powder in the gun room. It was so sudden that before anyone could quench it the *London* blew. A sound like a thunderbolt from heaven was reportedly heard in Holland.

The front half of the ship was propelled over four hundred yards westwards by the force of the blast. Most of the central part of the vessel was totally destroyed and the ship sank a short distance from where Southend pier stands today. More than three hundred men, women and children onboard were killed. As the blast threw timbers into the air, another man on the *Monleague* which was sailing by was killed by a flying splinter[12].

So it was, John Evelyn said, that one of the bravest ships in Europe had perished. News of John's great loss reached Samuel Pepys and others the following day and was taken much to heart at the Exchange and elsewhere. Among the dead were a large number of John Lawson's relatives, with Rugge putting the figure as high as twenty-one. Scarcely any of the names of the hundreds killed and maimed have entered the annals of history.

John Evelyn was one of the commissioners appointed to make arrangements for the expected sick and wounded victims of the war. Those from the fleet that needed hospital treatment would be transported to Saint Thomas' Hospital in London, where half the building was set aside for them. The day after the *London* disaster, he went to receive the 'poor burnt creatures' that were saved and assisted with plans to help the women and orphans. He counted fifty widows, forty-five of whom were pregnant[13]. The twenty-five recorded survivors – twenty-four men and one woman – were rescued because they were travelling in the roundhouse and the coach, the only sections to remain above water after the rest of the ship shattered[14]. These were a suite of rooms – usually the most important cabins – high up on the stern of the ship.

In warships the size of the *London,* there were usually two powder magazines. The main one was located in the hold towards the bow and the much smaller magazine towards the stern, close to the base of the rearmost mast of the vessel. There was also a filling room directly connected to the main magazine. Powder was transported from the main magazine to the filling room, where it was loaded into cartridges to be ferried up to the guns.

The risk of fire was always a great worry, and responsible captains took what steps they could to minimise the possibility. John's own report to the navy board after the event was that two weeks beforehand he had discovered a large quantity of wood and empty casks lying about the ship, which he ordered the purser to remove or he would throw them overboard. His purser, Mr Dam, confirmed that there were 21,000 billets of wood, eighty

dozen candles and some empty water casks, iron hoops and bags
on board when the ship blew up. Whether this was considered a
contributory factor is not clear. Gossip in the coffee houses blamed
the explosion on captains having easy access to cheap gunpowder
of poorer quality, which somehow exploded. Such accidents were
known occurrences, where one careless spark in an enclosed space
packed with unstable explosive matter could be all it took[15].

On 11 March, Pepys reported the result of an inspection of
the wreck. They believed the brass guns might be rescued, but
the hull was of course completely lost. Within a week of this the
Mayor and Aldermen of London offered to build a replacement
for the king and to support three ships in the fleet at their own
expense. The eighty-gun, three-decked *Loyal London* was begun
at Deptford immediately and would cost £18,355. City companies,
the corporation of London and merchants, aldermen and others
donated more than £16,000 towards the costs.[16]

John spent one pound and nineteen shillings on employing
Mr Borrough, a gun founder, to remove whatever guns that could
be salvaged[17]. There were not many. The value of those that could
not be retrieved was such that for decades afterwards there would
be many attempts to recover them.

Just over a year after the *London* was destroyed, its replacement
the *Loyal London* was launched as 'the phoenix daughter of the
vanished old'[18]. It was a celebratory occasion with the admiralty
lending a sergeant-trumpeter, eight naval trumpeters and a kettle
drummer for a fee of twenty-seven pounds[19]. John would never
command her.

Just a few weeks after the sinking of the *London,* the first signs
of plague arrived in the city of London. At first only five or six
houses were affected. By the end of the month, Rugge noted that

seventeen had died in a week, alongside the exciting news of a 'black moor' girl being baptised into the Church of England at Convent Garden. And war was getting closer[20].

Perhaps the spread of plague and preparations for war against the Dutch meant that John already planned to write or update his will. Or maybe the loss of his ship and so many relatives influenced him. Whatever the reason, John wrote his will on 19 April 1665. As well as bequests to his family, he left five pounds each to the two William Lawsons serving on board another warship, the *Royal Oak*[21]. If indeed they were his relatives and among those who survived the *London* disaster, then one of them may have been the cousin of that name identified through relatives' wills[22].

Maybe, as Lord Clarendon suggested, John had a foreboding of what was to come. Either way he also took further steps to protect his wife and other unmarried daughters financially. He approached the treasurer and chancellor to alter the terms of his pension, which only covered him during his lifetime, so that should he die, his unmarried daughters would benefit after his death. While he hoped that God would protect him, he was, he said, to embark on an expedition from which many honest men would not return. John felt they should know that while he was generally considered to be wealthy, this was not so. He asked for £200 a year for his wife during her lifetime, but desired nothing if he lived and needed no security other than the king's word[23]. The king was more generous. Isabelle would receive her annuity and the original pension was revised, so that their daughter Anna would receive the full £500 a year. John then made an arrangement in his will for it to be shared equally between Anna and her sister Elizabeth[24].

The first engagement by the royal fleet against the Dutch took place on the first day of June 1665 at the Texel, the site of one of

John's glorious victories in the first Dutch war. Two days later, the English and Dutch fleets came within sight of each other off the east coast close to Lowestoft in Suffolk. John was in command of thirteen men-of-war under the Duke of York, whose own ship *The Royal Charles* was the largest and grandest in the world. They encountered the Dutch fleet numbering 120 vessels, including 10 fireships, off Lowestoft.

A fierce battle commenced very early in the morning, with the English having the wind in their favour. The noise from thousands of cannons firing for over eight hours could be heard 120 miles away in London, while in Dunkirk the reverberation was so great that it shattered window panes and there were reports of houses collapsing. As Pepys enjoyed a meal of fowl and tansy, he received the good news that the Dutch fleet was losing.

News quickly reached London that the Dutch flagship with Admiral Cornelius Tromp on board had blown up and that he had fled. Cornelius Tromp was the son of Admiral Maarten Tromp, the man John had fought and helped to defeat in 1653. Tromp survived to cover the retreat, but three or four of his vice-admirals were slain, twenty-four ships taken or sunk and the Dutch fleet defeated with a loss of 8,000 to 10,000 lives. The English side claimed to have lost less than five hundred. In one notable incident, three men were killed simultaneously by one cannon ball, their blood and brains flying into the Duke of York's face. It was the greatest victory known to the world, thought Pepys[25].

In the middle of the battle, Vice-Admiral John Lawson was hit in the kneecap by a musket ball. Falling to the deck in agony and unable to stand, he sent word to the Duke of York immediately that he should bring over another commander from the *Royal Oak*. The knee was almost certainly badly fractured. A surgeon was sent for the same day and operated to remove the damaged part of the bone (or several bones if what Pepys heard was correct). There was a danger of infection if any fragments of shot remained inside the body. To check and remove them, a metal probe was inserted to feel for other metal and, if necessary, could be used to expand the wound to assist in taking them out.

It was believed at first that John would recover. But more than a week later John's wound was not healing well and he was hastily taken to Greenwich for treatment. His friends began to worry as a rash appeared and he started to hiccup. John had gangrene. The wound was inflamed and the flesh and muscles beginning to rot. As the infection took hold, the colour of his skin would have begun to change and a foul-smelling pus start to seep from the wound. The worst cases would lead to septic shock.

John's body began to shut down as the infection spread to vital organs. The hiccups indicated that it had reached his lungs. The next day, William Penn and Samuel Pepys visited him and found him apparently better, but still poorly. His hiccups meant he had difficulty talking so they were unable to have much conversation together[26]. Mr Clarke, the apothecary, was sent for, which cost the family seventeen pounds and eighteen shillings; around one and a half thousand pounds in modern terms. This was almost certainly the royal physician, Timothy Clarke, a founder of the Royal Society and celebrated anatomist, who was commissioned to treat the sick and wounded from the war. But for John, it was to no avail[27].

As John's condition deteriorated, a day of thanksgiving was held on 20 June for the great victory over the Dutch. Persons of quality arrived in London from the fleet, great bonfires were lit across the country and the sound of bells ringing out and guns firing could be heard all over the city[28]. On Sunday 25 June, twenty-two days after John was wounded, Pepys took a boat from Whitehall to Greenwich to visit him once more. When he arrived, he found to his astonishment that John Lawson had died that morning. 'The nation hath a great loss', he said[29].

Pepys rather spoilt the tribute by going on to say that, 'I cannot without dissembling, say that I am not sorry for it, for he was man never kind to me at all'[30]. This sour note and another a few days afterwards on how John had never obliged Pepys by word or deed, is at variance with most other opinions Pepys had expressed about John over the years. They can probably be partially explained by his frustrations over the financial muddle in the Tangier accounts and John's unwillingness to do Pepys any financial favours in these dealings. The other major factor was Pepys' loyalty to his mentor and employer Edward Montagu, who had become jealous at the respect shown to John and his influence at court[31]. And then perhaps it should come as no surprise that the bibulous, scandal-mongering, acquisitive man of letters was not over-generous in his final assessment of the god-fearing, unsophisticated John Lawson.

John's body was brought up river from Greenwich to St Dunstan in the East Church, close to the Tower. There was no guard of honour or crowds of people lining the route to see it arrive. Ten pounds eighteen shillings and four pence was paid out to the sextons to prepare the gravesite in the chancel and for the minister to perform the service. Then, late at night on 1 July, in the almost empty church with no company to pay their last respects, the grave diggers lowered John into the ground[32]. As he requested, John Lawson was buried 'without noise' – no pomp or ceremony – and with his beloved daughters, Abigail, Mary and Sarah in the great aisle of the church[33].

This brave seaman who had risen to such a high position was lowered into the ground with none of his family present. His daughter Isabella was in Hampshire with her new husband, while his wife and daughters Anna and Elizabeth undoubtedly stayed away out of fear of the plague, which had in that week alone swept away 267 people in London.

No memorial tablet or stone ever marked his resting place and the plain entry which records his name and the date in the burial register gives no indication of his extraordinary life[34].

It is appropriate for the last word on his character to go to Edward Hyde, Earl of Clarendon. Unlike John, he had always been royalist in his sympathies and actively gathered intelligence on John and other republicans before the restoration. Somehow John had not only survived his change of allegiance with his reputation more or less intact, carrying many others with him, he had earned the admiration, friendship and respect of many of those – like Clarendon – that he had once fought against.

The death of a man of such eminent skill and admirable conduct as John Lawson was an irreparable loss said Clarendon, because his measured analysis in debates carried weight and even the greatest seamen were willing to take his advice. John died courageously, said Clarendon, at the very last professing his duty and fidelity to the king:

> He was indeed of all men of that time, and of that extraction and education, incomparably the modestest and the wisest man.[35]

# EPILOGUE

There was a public tribute of sorts for John. The Duke of York commissioned a series of paintings of the officers – the flagmen – who had vanquished the Dutch at the battle of Lowestoft. John's posthumous painting by Sir Peter Lely shows him wearing a generic, one size fits all type of outfit: a buff coat, sash and breast plate. At his side is a sword. In one hand he carries a baton of command, leaning on a cannon with the other.

John Lawson appears to have left his family in a precarious financial situation. Pepys certainly believed that his foolishness over his daughter Isabella's dowry meant that little was left for his wife and other daughters., Pepys claimed that it was the inheritance that Isabella received on the death of her husband Daniel Norton that saved her mother and sisters from penury[1].

It is far from clear whether this account of the Lawson's financial circumstances after John's death is accurate. Daniel Norton did die in 1668 leaving his wife with a two-year old son and a very large inheritance. It is also certain that John's widow Isabella faced some financial and legal problems in the years to come. However, John did leave property and land in Essex and Yorkshire. The pension to his widow was approved, and the agreement relating to the other half was revised by King Charles and the treasury so that it would be divided equally between his daughters Anna and Elizabeth. They and their mother continued to receive annual payments until their deaths, although, as had so often happened before with John, there was more than one occasion when the women had to petition the treasury as the money was overdue[2].

John left his house in Alresford in Essex, together with the farm and ballast quay that belonged to it and all profits from the estate for his wife to enjoy during her natural life. Isabelle would later move to Wanstead, living there until at least 1693. Unfortunately, where and when she died is unknown. It is likely she died in Wanstead, but there are gaps in the registers. Or she may have moved to be near another family member[3].

The two William Lawsons serving on the *Royal Oak* received five pounds each. His daughter Isabella was to have the chain given to him in the Dutch war in 1653 for her first-born son, but if she had no son, then it would go to the eldest daughter. As Isabella already had a dowry, her gift was personal: two of John's best silver dishes and six silver plates. John was evidently fond of her husband Daniel, as he left him all his guns, pistols, scimitars and swords that were onboard ship. Daughter Elizabeth had the other gold chain that had been given to him in Portugal in 1663, to be passed on to her eldest son or daughter. She shared the rest of the gold plate and money with her sister Anna, along with the house in Scarborough and three closes of land there[4].

John's cousin John, the grocer of Lyme Street in London, was given his new black velvet coat and a 'flea bitten gelding'. This was not some mangy creature, but a white or grey horse with very small darker spots[5]. Cousin John's son Samuel was gifted a long gun that had been given to John by Mr Henry Crane and his best silver-hilted rapier. John requested that the father and son assist his widow Isabelle in her duties as executrix by being overseers of his will. John did not forget his hometown either. He left one hundred pounds 'to the poor of Scarborough in Yorkshire the place of my nativity'. The money was to be invested and the interest divided between the paupers a few days before Christmas day each year. Two other non-relatives received bequests. John Salmon was given five pounds, and Peter Greene was to have all of John's woollen apparel that was on board his ship.

In his will, John asked that his family be given whatever consideration Sir Hugh Cholmley wished to allow for the value of the engines, boats and materials for the mole in Tangier over and above the two thousand pounds given to them for buying the equipment[6].

Just a few months later, Hugh Cholmley wrote to Lady Lawson. Despite his affection for John he said, he would be forced to take legal action if the money he was owed for their joint endeavour in Tangier were not paid by the executors. He enclosed a set of detailed accounts. There is no reference of a court case taking place and, when Cholmley met with Pepys the following January to settle some accounts over Tangier, the two men became great friends. No mention of John was made then or at any of their subsequent meetings. It is telling that John Lawson's name is conspicuous by its absence from Cholmley's memoir of Tangier and the building of the mole[7].

John's executor and cousin, the grocer John Lawson of Lyme Street and his son Samuel, quite evidently did not fulfil their duties. For nearly forty years after the vice-admiral's death, his widow, daughters and sons-in-law would be embroiled in legal disputes to retrieve profits and prizes due to John from his time in Tangier and patrolling the Mediterranean coast of Algiers, Tunis and Tripoli.

Cousin John appears to have borne the brunt of the complaints. The long and complicated proceedings included the presentation of detailed accounts by cousin John to support his defence, which list numerous payments for a wide range of personal and work-related expenses from surgeon and apothecary bills, grave preparation, guns and fixtures and fittings for the home and ships – five shillings to the glass man for a cabinet, for instance. Then there were the supplies for Tangier and the loan of the cousin's house and his goods to Lady Isabelle and her daughters during the great contagion – the plague – of 1665, then again the following year for the great conflagration, as the fire of London was known[8].

John the grocer and his wife Martha had moved to Wanstead in Essex by 1667, where Isabelle was living. Within six years, the Lawson family and John and Samuel were in court arguing over who was responsible for what payments and whether money was still owed to the vice-admiral's Tangier venture. Isabelle Lawson made a claim for two thousand pounds against cousin John, the exact amount that had been granted to the vice-admiral for building the mole. The court papers included depositions from Richard Norton, Isabella's father-in-law, about the dowry arrangements between her and his son and how much of it had been paid. The legal proceedings saw a number of court appearances by Isabelle, her daughters and their husbands and the attorneys representing them and John and Samuel Lawson until 1693, well after most of the parties directly involved were dead[9].

In 1674, Isabelle Lawson obtained a judgement against cousin John Lawson for non-payment of the debt of two thousand pounds, plus costs awarded by the chancery court. He was arrested and sent to the Fleet debtors' prison. After he petitioned the court, she subsequently permitted him to have his freedom in order that he could follow his trade and make money to pay the debt, so saving on the charges and fees of prison.

On 26 June 1693, Isabelle Lawson sold the remaining debt to Francis and Daniel Dashwood, local gentlemen who acted as attorneys for her in some matters. Today Francis Dashwood would have been excluded from doing so as he also undertook legal work for and on behalf of Samuel Lawson in relation to his will. The sale contract is one of the few documents on which Isabelle's signature appears and she sealed it with the imprint of a wax seal in the shape of a deer[10].

The following March, cousin John's son Samuel wrote his will before setting off on a voyage to East India in a ship called the *African of London*, captained by Edward Cooke. Samuel made no mention of his relatives on the vice-admiral's side of the family, but left everything he had to some friends in Wapping and Jamaica and to his cousin, yet another John, of Bocking in Essex, the son of William Lawson. Some time later, Samuel died in the East Indies and his will was proved back in England in 1693 once his relatives received the news.

Cousin John Lawson's fortunes recovered sufficiently for him to have enough assets to make it worth his while drawing up a will shortly before he died in London in 1682. Some of this money may have come from his returning to the grocery trade, but he and his wife Martha had also started selling and leasing out property in Wanstead before he went to jail. Martha remained in Wanstead until her death a few years later, but neither of them mentioned the other Lawsons in their wills. This was in marked contrast to the comments made by contemporaries over the number who had served under the vice-admiral in the navy, or worked with him, which reveal connections by blood that transcended geography and social position. Now, for this branch of the family at least, it was as if John, Isabelle and their daughters no longer existed[11].

By 1668, John and Isabelle's daughter Isabella was a widow with a two-year old son, named after his grandfather Richard Norton. Isabella spent several years in legal disputes with her husband's father. Suits and counter-suits continued between Richard Norton, his executors and Isabella's children and even grandchildren into the 1730s, proving Samuel Pepys to be correct in his assessment of the man's character and discontent over monetary arrangements.

Isabella was not a widow for long. She married Sir Thomas Chicheley and had another five children. Outliving her second husband, she died in 1706 and asked to be buried with him in the parish of St Giles in the Fields. Isabella had remained close to her sisters, leaving Anna a mourning ring, set with a diamond over a lock of her hair, a ring to Anna's daughter and a gold watch and ten pounds to Elizabeth's daughter.

Anna Lawson also married twice. Her wedding to Walter Attwood took place in London in 1677. They had a daughter, Mary, before Walter died in 1690. By the time Anna married for the second time two years later to Sir Thomas St George, she had moved to Wanstead where her mother was living. Anna and Thomas settled in the nearby parish of Woodford, and in 1695 she sold her share of the Scarborough properties. Anna remained in Woodford until her death in 1720 and was buried with her husband. She also left a will, naming her Norton and Chicheley nephews and asking them to take particular care of her granddaughter.

Elizabeth Lawson married Francis Kinaston and their daughter Anne was born in London in 1677. After Elizabeth's death in 1696,

Anne inherited the house in Alresford and a house and land in Sandgate in Scarborough that had been John's. Anne Kinaston made the Alresford house her home until her death in 1721, leasing out the farm and quay. In an intriguing glimpse of how superstitions and puritanical fervour still had a strong hold, Anne's tenant John Winch was involved in an assault connected to witch hunting in Alresford in August 1701. He was fined by the local courts for his part in riotously assembling, assaulting and throwing a man into the sea under the pretext that he was a wizard. One of the other participants was his brother, who was also prosecuted in another case on the same date for ducking a woman in the River Colne, where she died[12].

Holding a witch under water was the most commonly known method for identifying one. The Catch-22 of course, was that if they floated they were guilty, and if they sank they were innocent. Historically, such accusations tended to take hold where there was strong economic, religious and social disharmony, and may represent a wider malaise in the community. The persecution and executions across Europe of hundreds of thousands of people believed to be witches – mainly women – had reached its peak in the 1630s, but executions continued until the early 1700s, and the belief in witchcraft still held strong well into the eighteen hundreds, especially in rural areas.

In 1698, John Lawson's granddaughter Anne Kinaston sold her share of the lands and the house in Scarborough that he once lived in, thus severing the family's final, direct link to Yorkshire. He was one of the greatest people to have come out of Scarborough, yet barely a trace of him remains in the town he served and loved so well[13].

In 2005, 340 years after it sank, the wreckage of John Lawson's ship the *London* was rediscovered during work in advance of the

London Gateway Port development. The wreck was deemed to be of such archaeological importance that it was designated under the Protection of Wrecks Act, with all artefacts belonging to the crown. Some of the shipping channels into the mouth of the Thames were altered in order to protect the remains. Ten years later, one of the ship's wooden gun carriages was deemed to be seriously at risk after being exposed to the air. This led the Historic England organisation to employ a team of divers to raise it from the sea bed. The carriage had remained in almost pristine condition, having been buried in silt since the ship sank. At the time of writing excavation work continues.

The shadow of the many battles John Lawson had during his time at sea has reached the present day. In 2015, in a case of modern piracy, one of the professional divers who had worked on the wreck was jailed for two years for selling three unique bronze cannon branded with the crest of the city of Amsterdam. He had taken them from the ship's wreckage, as well as artefacts from other shipwrecks, to sell to an American buyer for £50,000[14].

John Lawson had lived through fifty of the most turbulent years in English history. It was an era in which the world was truly turned upside down. John witnessed religious wars, the transformation of England into a republic then back again and the early stages of England's metamorphosis into a global economic power. Yet he did not just watch from the sidelines: he was at the heart of local, national and international events that shaped the country's future.

John Lawson, a man who started life as a merchant collier hauling coals from Newcastle, worked his way up through the navy as tarpaulin captain; a radical republican and army volunteer: pragmatic and devout, a political agitator and stubborn ideologue and a plain, down-to-earth but tough and at times belligerent Yorkshireman. He was known for his devotion to the republican cause, but still became a loyal servant to the king and was a loving husband and father to the end. He was all these and more.

John Lawson was an ordinary man, who led an extraordinary life.

# NOTES

Abbreviations

| | |
|---|---|
| BHO | British History Online |
| BL | British Library |
| Bodl. | Bodleian Library, Oxford |
| BTs | Bishops' Transcripts |
| ClarCSP | Clarendon Calendar of State Papers |
| CSPD | Calendar of State Papers Domestic |
| CSPV | Calendar of State Papers Relating to English Affairs in Venice |
| ER Archives | East Riding Archives |
| ERO | Essex Record Office |
| HoCJ | House of Commons Journal |
| HoLJ | House of Lords Journal |
| LMA | London Metropolitan Archives |
| MI | Monumental Inscriptions |
| MLB | Marriage Licence Bond |
| NYRO | North Yorkshire Record Office |
| ODBN | Oxford Dictionary of National Biography |

| PCC | Prerogative Court of Canterbury |
| PCY | Prerogative Court of York |
| PRs | Parish Registers |
| SoG | Society of Genealogists |
| SP | State Papers |
| TNA | The National Archives |
| TRS | Transcript |

## Prologue

1. Lawson, John, *A Narrative of the Proceedings of the Fleet...* (22 Dec 1659); Lawson, John, *Two Letters from Vice-Admiral John Lawson and the Commanders of the Fleet to the Lord Mayor, Aldermen and Common-Councilmen of the City of London* (13 & 21 Dec. 1659).

2. Firth, C. R., Ed., *The Memoirs of Edmund Ludlow, lieutenant-general of the horse in the army of the Commonwealth of England 1625-1672*, Vol. II (Clarendon Press, 1894), p.176.

3. Warwick, Sir Philip, *Memoirs of the Reign of King Charles the First* (Edinburgh: 1702, Reprint 1813), p.476.

4. Clarendon State Papers, Vol. IV, 1657-1660 (Clarendon Press, 1932); Binns, Jack. *Sir John Lawson*, in *Oxford Dictionary of National Biography* (Oxford: 2000); Penn, Granville, *Memorials of the professional life and times of Sir William Penn from 1644 to 1670* (London: J. Duncan, 1833), Vol. 2, p.185.

5. Hinderwell, Thomas, *The History and Antiquities of Scarborough* (London: Bye, 1798 and 3rd edn., 1832).

6. Hunt, Tristram, *The English Civil War: At First Hand* (Weidenfeld and Nicolson, 2002), p.xii.

7. Manley, Professor Gordon, *Central England temperatures: monthly means 1659-1973*; Historical Weather Reports; Hunt, p.xii.

8. Lawson, *A Narrative*, 1659; *Two Letters*, 1659.

9. Lawson, John, *A declaration of Vice-Admiral John Lawson...*, *in order to the removal of the interruption that is now put upon the Parliaments the 13th of October last* (London: 13 Dec. 1659).

10. Lawson, *Letter*, 21 Dec. 1659.

11. Lawson, *A declaration*, 1659; *ODNB*; *Burke's Peerage* (107th Edition, 2003).

12. Ibid; Letters from John Lawson (various); *CSPD* 1649-1660.

13. *The Monthly Intelligencer*, Dec. 1659 - Jan. 1660.

14. Transcripts to London Freemen Records, (SoG); Webb, Cliff, London Apprenticeship Abstracts, 1442-1850 (at Findmpast).

15. *The Monthly Intelligencer*.

16. Latham, Robert and Matthews, William, Eds., *The Diary of Samuel Pepys, Vol. 1, 1660* (Bell & Hyman, 1970), p.1.

## Chapter One

1. Ludlow, Vol. I, p.viii.

2. Ibid, Vol. 1, p.176; Penn, p.185.

3. Ludlow, Vol. 2, p.427.

4. Ibid, I, p.176.

5. *Pepys*, Vol. 1, p.4.

6. Ibid, Vols. 1-6.

7. Will Vice-Admiral Sir John Lawson, PCC 1665, TNA PROB/11/317.

8. *Paver's Marriage Licences* (Yorkshire: Archaeological Society Record Series, XL, 1909).

9. Baker, Joseph Brogden, *The History of Scarborough from the earliest date* (London: Longmans, Green & Co., 1882), p.440; Binns, Jack, *Sir John Lawson: Scarborough's Admiral of the*

Red, in *Northern History*, No. 32, (1996), pp.92-93; *ClarCSP*, Vols., 3-5; Hinderwell, 1798, pp.100-107; Lawson, John, Letter to Sir Henry Vane, 12 Feb 1652/53, in TNA, SP 18/47, fo.113; *ODNB*; Penn, p.185;

10. Ashcroft, M. Y., Ed., *Scarborough Records 1600-1640: A Calendar* (North Yorkshire County Record Office Publications No. 47, 1991); Binns, Ibid, pp.92-93; Hinderwell, pp.100-107; Scarborough Churchwardens' Papers, 1607-98, ER Archives, PE 165/241; Scarborough Society of Shipowners, Masters and Mariners, NYRO, DC/SCB.

11. *Scarborough Records, 1600-1640*, p.330.

12. Scarborough PR and BT, NYRO; *Transcript to Scarborough BTs 1602-1683* (Yorkshire Archaeological Society).

13. *Scarborough Records 1600-1640*.

14. Binns, Ibid, pp.92-93; Hinderwell, p.107; Lewis, Samuel, *Topographical Dictionary of Yorkshire*, 1835.

15. *Pepys*, Vols. 1-12; Tomalin, Claire, *Samuel Pepys: The Unequalled Self* (Penguin, 2002).

16. Binns, Ibid; Scarborough Churchwardens' Papers, p.6; TNA Currency Converter; *Scarborough Records*, 1600-1640; Scarborough Society of Shipowners, 1636.

17. Binns, Ibid; Scarborough Shipowners, 1639; Scarborough PRs, BTs and TRS; Will Samuel Lawson, Merchant in the good Ship or Vessel called the African of London, PCC 1693, TNA: PROB11/414/307.

18. *Scarborough Records, 1600-1640*, pp.358-359.

19. London Apprenticeship and Freemen Records; Will John Lawson 1665; Will John Lawson, Citizen and Grocer of London PCDC 1683, LMA: MS 9052/24, no. 46; Will Samuel Lawson 1693 et al.

20. Tinniswood, Adrian, *The Rainborowes: Pirates, Puritans and a Family's Quest for the Promised Land* (London: Vintage, 2014).

21. *Pepys*, Vol. 6, p.52; Rugge, Thomas, Mercurius *Politicus redivivus, or a collection of occurrences*, 1659-1672, Vols.1-2, BL Add MS 10117, Vol. 1, fo.134.

22. CSPD 1656-7, p.228.

23. Boyd's Marriage Indexes, 1538-1840; Binns, Ibid, pp.92-93; CSPD 1653-4, p.581; Letter, Lawson to Vane, 12 Feb 1652/53; Papers of Edward Montagu, 1st Earl of Sandwich. Bodl. MS Carte 73, fo.567; Lythe and Whitby, Yorkshire PRs; *ODNB*; *Paver's*; Scarborough PRs, BTs and TRS; *Scarborough Records 1600-1640*;

24. Binns, Ibid, pp.100-12; Hinderwell, pp.100-107.

25. Binns, pers. comm; Hinderwell, p.100; Indenture from Madam Kinaston, 1698, in Sperling Family of Dynes Hall Deeds. ERO: D/DGd E38; Letters to Captain Baynes, 1641-66: BL. Add MS 21417-23; Will Sir John Lawson 1665.

26. Hinderwell, pp.100-107; Lewis, 1835.

27. Ibid; Rushton, John, *Scarborough Coal Trade*, Scarborough Maritime Heritage Centre website; Units of Weight; Ashcroft, M. Y., *Scarborough Records 1641-1660*, (NYRO No. 49, 1991), pp.33-34.

28. Tate, W. E., *The Parish Chest* (Cambridge: Phillimore, 3rd edn., 1983); Tinniswood, Adrian, *Pirates of Barbary* (London: Vintage, 2011); Wood, Phil, *Britons Could Be Slaves*, in *Ancestors*, No. 80 (March 2009).

29. *CSPD 1642-1660*; Davies, J. D., *Gentlemen and Tarpaulins: The Officers and Men of the Restoration Navy* (Oxford, Clarendon Press, 1991), pp.71-72.

30. *CSPD 1655-56*, p.160.

31. Lawson, *A declaration*, 13 Dec 1659; *ODNB*.

32. Binns, Jack, *Yorkshire in the Civil Wars: Origins, Impact and Outcome* (Yorkshire: Blackthorn Press, 2004), pp.2, 10; Capp, Bernard, *Cromwell's Navy: The Fleet and the English Revolution 1648-60* (Oxford: 1989). pp. 1-11; *CSPD 1635*, p.275; Tinniswood, pp. 21-34; *Scarborough Records 1600-1640*, pp.267-268; TNA Currency Converter.

33. *Scarborough Records 1600-1640*, p.250.

34. Tinniswood, pp.14-17.

35. Lawson to Vane, 1652/53.

36. Ibid.

37. Binns, *Lawson: Scarborough's Admiral*, pp.98-99; *Yorkshire*, pp.114-119; *CSPD 1642-1646*; Hinderwell, 1798, pp.97-99; Lawson to Vane, 12 Feb 1652/53; Informations: John Harrison the elder, Nicholas Ducke, John Barry et al., July 1650, in *Scarborough Records 1641-1660*, pp.167-168; Travis-Cook, John, *Vice-Admiral Sir John Lawson: A Reminiscence of the Civil War* (London: W. Andrews & Co., 1896), pp.3-6.

38. Binns, *Scarborough's Admiral*, pp.94-95; *CSPD 1643*, pp.554-562; TNA Currency Converter; Travis-Cook, p.4.

39. Lawson to Vane, 12 Feb 1652/53.

40. Ibid.

41. Lawson, in Travis-Cook, p.16.

42. Ibid.

43. *Scarborough Records 1641-1660 A Calendar* (NYRO No. 49, 1991), pp.17-18.

44. Binns, Jack, Ed. *Memoirs and Memorials of Sir Hugh Cholmley of Whitby 1600-1657* (Yorkshire Archaeological Society, Boydell Press, 2000), p.144; Binns, *Scarborough's*

*Admiral*, pp.93-99; Binns, *Yorkshire*, pp.97-119; Cholmley. Hugh, *The Memoirs of Sir Hugh Cholmley* (Cholmley, 1787, reproduction 1870), p.25; *CSPD* 1645, pp.629-638; Goodall, J. A. A., *Scarborough Castle* (English Heritage, 2000), pp.29-31; Hinderwell, pp. 97-99; Informations, Ibid; Lawson to Vane, 12 Feb 1652/53; Leask, Paul, *Valour is the Safest Helm: The Life of Sir Hugh Cholmley and Scarborough During the English Civil War* (Yorkshire: Jacobus Publications, 1995); Page, W., Ed., *The Borough of Scarborough*, in *A History of North York Riding* (London: St. Catherine's Press, 1923), pp.538-560.

45. *CSPD* 1642-1644; Lawson to Vane, 12 Feb 1652/53; Correspondence, Montagu, Bodl. MSS Carte 73, fo.567; Will Sir John Lawson 1665.

46. Lawson to Vane, 12 Feb 1652/53.

47. Binns, *Scarborough's Admiral*, p.98; Goodall, Ibid; Hinderwell, Ibid; Informations, Ibid; Lawson to Vane, 12 Feb 1652/53; Page, pp.538-560; Travis-Cook, pp.3-4.

48. Binns, *Memoirs of Cholmley*; Cholmley, *Memoirs*; Hopper, Andrew, *Turncoats and Renegadoes: Changing Sides during the English Civil Wars* (OUP, 2012), pp.6, 46-47, 143-144, 145-149, 168.

49. Lawson to Vane, 12 Feb 1652/53.

50. Binns, *Memoirs of Cholmley*; Cholmley, *Memoirs*, pp.42, 49-52; Fraser, Antonia, *The Weaker Vessel: Woman's Lot in Seventeenth-Century England* (London: Phoenix, 2002), p.198.

51. Cholmley, *Memoirs*, p.42.

52. Binns, *Yorkshire*; Cholmley, *Memoirs*; Ibid; Fraser, pp.197-198; Hinderwell, pp.97-98.

53. Binns, *Yorkshire*, pp.114-119; Fraser, pp.197-198; Leicester University Conference, *Care, Mortality and Welfare During the Civil War*, 7-8 Aug 2015.

54. Binns, *Scarborough's Admiral*, p.94; CSPD 1645, pp.629-638.

55. Binns, Ibid, p.98-100; *Scarborough Records 1641-1660*, pp.29-30.

56. Lawson to Vane, 12 Feb 1652/53.

57. Hopper, Andrew, Ed., *The Papers of the Hothams, Governors of Hull During the Civil War* (Cambridge: CUP for the Royal Historical Society, 2011); Hopper, Andrew, *Treachery and Conspiracy in Nottinghamshire during the English Civil War*, in East Midlands History and Heritage, 1 (June 2015), pp.21-23; Hopper, *Turncoats*, pp.112-113, 131, 171; Stirling, A. M. W., *The Hothams: The Story of the Hothams and Their Family Papers 1066-1771*, Vol.1 (Herbert Jenkins, 1918), pp.28-38.

58. Binns, *Scarborough's Admiral*, pp.94-95; Lawson to Vane, 12 Feb 1652/53; Hopper, *Papers of Hothams*, pp.26-27, 156. Hopper, *Treachery and Conspiracy*, pp.21-23; Hopper, *Turncoats*, pp.96-97, 112-113, 131, 172; Travis-Cook, pp.3-4.

59. Binns, *Memoirs of Cholmley*, pp.25-26.

60. Binns, *Scarborough's Admiral*, p.98; CSPD 1644, pp.220-223; Rushworth, John, *Historical Collections: Parliamentary and civil occurrences, 1645*, in *Historical Collections of Private Passages of State*, Vol. 6, 1645-47 (London: 1722); pp.141-228; Travis-Cooke, p.6.

61. Baker, pp.79-82; Binns, *Memoirs of Cholmley*, pp.155-157; Binns, *Yorkshire*, p.116-119; Cholmley, *Memoirs*; Goodall, pp.29-31; CSPD 1644, pp.331, 447, 452; Lewis, 1835; Page, pp.538-560; Rushworth, pp.141-228.

62. Binns, *Memoirs of Cholmley*, p.158.

63. Baker, pp.80-82; Binns, *Yorkshire*, pp.116-119; Goodall, pp.29-31; Cholmley, *Memoirs*; Lawson to Vane, 12 Feb. 1652/53; Page, pp.538-560.

64. Binns, Ibid, pp.96-98; Hinderwell, p.100; *Scarborough Records 1641-1660*, p.46; Travis-Cook, pp.9-10.

65. Hinderwell, p.72; *Scarborough Records 1641-1660*, p.64.

66. Ibid.

67. *HoLJ*, 1646, Vol.8, in British History Online (BHO), pp.298-300; *HoCJ*, 1646, Vol. 4, in BHO, pp.527-531: SP, 6 May 1646, Parliamentary Archives, HL/PO/10/205.

68. Hunt, Tristram, *The English Civil War: At First Hand* (London: Weidenfeld and Nicolson, 2002), p.140.

69. Hunt, p.140.

70. Whitaker, Mark and Saunders, Frances Stonor, *When Christmas was illegal*, in *New Statesman*, 129, 4518, (2000), p.72.

71. Binns. *Sir John Lawson*, pp.95-100; *CSPD* 1646; *Scarborough Records, 1641-1660*.

72. *CSPD* 1656-7, pp.335, 351, 500-521; Letters, W. Wright [Rumbold] to John Martyn [Hyde], 2 Jan.1660; W. Wright to the King, 6 Jan. 1660, in *ClarCSP* Vol. 3, pp.638-642; *Publick Intelligencer*, 1656-1660; *Mercurius Politicus*, 1653, Issue 50; *The Monthly Intelligencer*, Dec. 1659 to Jan. 1660.

73. Hinderwell, pp.100-107; Ludlow. Vol. 1, pp.6-7; Lawson, *A declaration*, 1659; *A Narrative*, 1659; *Two Letters*, 13 & 21 Dec. 1659; Lawson to Vane, 12 Feb. 1652/53; *ODNB*.

74. Hopper, Andrew, *The language of treachery in newsbooks and polemic.* (Oxford: University Press Scholarship Online, 2014), p.7; Mortimer, Sarah, *What was at stake in the Putney Debates*, in *History Today* (Jan. 2015), 65, 1; Raymond, Joad, *Pamphlets*

*and Pamphleteering in Early Modern Britain* (Cambridge: CUP, 2006), pp.226-228.

75. *CSPD* 1642-1650; Hinderwell; Lawson to Vane, 12 Feb 1652/53; Baynes, 1641-66, BL, Add MSS 21417-23; *ODNB*; Hinderwell, pp.100-101; Penn, pp.184-186.

76. Mortimer; Raymond, *The Literature of Controversy* (www.academia.edu 2007), pp.197-198; Raymond, *Pamphlets*, pp.226-306.

77. Lawson, *A declaration*, 1659; *ODNB*; Burke's Peerage.

78. Mortimer; Ibid; Peacey, Jason, *The hunting of the Leveller: the sophistication of parliamentarian propaganda, 1647-53*, in *Historical Research*, (Feb. 2005), No. 78, p.199; Raymond, *Controversy*; Smith, Nigel, *Non-conformist voices and books*, Barnard, John and McKenzie, D. F., Eds., *A History of British Publishing* (London: Routledge, 2nd edn., 2002), pp.410-415.

79. Smith, pp.410-415.

80. Binns, *Scarborough's Admiral*, p.98; Hopper, *Turncoats*, p.220; Informations, Ibid.

81. Binns, *Yorkshire*, pp.135-136; *HoLJ*, 1646, Vol.8; BHO, pp.298-300; Lawson to Vane, 12 Feb 1652/53.

82. Baynes, BL Add MSS 21417, fos.13-15, 37-38.

83. Ibid, fo.14.

84. Ibid; *HoLJ*, 1646, Vol.8; BHO, pp.298-300.

## Chapter Two

1. Binns, *Scarborough's Admiral*, pp.101-102; Binns, *Yorkshire*, pp.114-119; *CSPD* 1648-50; Hinderwell (1798), pp.97-99; *HoLJ*, Vol. 10, BHO, pp.639-641; Lawson, letter to Vane, 12 Feb 1652/53, SP 18/47, fo.113; *Scarborough Records: A Calendar 1641-1660*, pp.119-126.

2. Lawson, *A declaration*, 1659; *Narrative*, 1659; *Two letters*, 1659; Letter to Vane, 12 Feb 1652/53.

3. Warwick, Sir Philip, *Memoirs of the Reign of King Charles the First* (Edinburgh: 1702, reprint 1813), p.275.

4. Ibid, pp.275-277.

5. Scurr, Ruth, *John Aubrey: My Own Life* (London: Vintage, 2015), p.78.

6. *The Monthly Intelligencer*, Dec 1659-Jan. 1660; *Publick Intelligencer*, 26 Dec 1659-2 Jan 1660.

7. Binns, *Yorkshire*, p.166; *Scarborough Records*, 1641-1661, p.vi.

8. Binns, *Scarborough's Admiral*, pp.101-103; *CSPD* 1648-1650; *HoCJ*, Vol. 6, 1650, BHO, pp.473-474; *HoLJ*, Vol. 10, 1648, BHO, pp.639-641; Papers of Captain Baynes, BL Add MSS 21417-21418; *Scarborough Records*, 1641-1660, p.152;Travis-Cooke, p.7.

9. *Scarborough Records*, 1641-1660, pp.vii, 149-158, 174.

10. Ibid, pp.vii, 149, 174.

11. Ibid, p.157.

12. Ibid, pp.157-158, 174-175.

13. Ibid, pp.vii, 157-158.

14. Baker, *Scarborough*, pp.109-114; Rowntree, Arthur, Ed., *The History of Scarborough* (London & Toronto: J.M. Dent & Sons Ltd., 1931), p.237; *Scarborough Records*, 1648-1650.

15. *Scarborough Records*, 1641-1660, p.135.

16. Baynes, BL Add MSS 21417-21418; Binns, *Scarborough's Admiral*, pp.102-103; *CSPD* 1648-1650; *HoLJ*, Vol. 10, BHO, pp.639-641; *Scarborough Records*, 1641-1660, pp.138-139; Travis-Cooke, p.7.

17. Ibid; *Scarborough Records*, 1641-1660, pp.145-147.

18. *CSPD* 1648-1653; Travis-Cooke, p.7; Papers relating to naval affairs, Petitions, 1648, 1649, 1652, BL Add MS 22546, fo.76; Baynes, Ibid; Baynes, Add MS 21427, fos.37-28, 70.

19. Baynes, Add MSS 21417-21423.

20. Baynes, 21418, fos.10, 207.

21. Ibid, fo.207

22. Peace, *The hunting of the Leveller*.

23. Ibid.

24. Ibid; Hopper, *The language of treachery*, p.7.

25. Ibid; Mortimer, pp.226-229; Raymond, *Pamphlets*; Raymond, *Literature*; Robertson, Geoffrey, *Geoffrey Robertson presents The Levellers: The Putney Debates* (Verso, 2007), pp.vii-xv.

26. Lawson, *A declaration*; *Narrative*; *Two letters*; 1659; *Monthly Intelligencer*, Dec. 1659-Jan. 1660; *Publick Intelligencer*, 26 Dec. 1659-2 Jan. 1660.

27. Baynes, Ibid.

28. Hopper, Andrew, *Social mobility during the English Revolution: the case of Adam Eyre, Social History*, Vol. 38, No. 1 (2013), p.39.

29. Ibid.

30. Baynes, Add MSS 21418, fos.193, 218, 248.

31. Ibid, fos.248, 260, 285, 287-88, 291, 296, 326, 336.

32. Baynes, Add MSS 21427, f.70.

33. Baynes, Add MS 21418, fo.336.

34. *HoCJ*, 1650, Vol. 6, pp.375, 473-474; Lawson to Vane, 12 Feb 1652/53.

35. *Scarborough Records 1641-1660*, p.268.

36. Hill, Christopher, *The Century of Revolution* (London: Routledge, 2nd edn., 1980), p.131.

37. Capp, *Cromwell's Navy,* pp.1-10, 42-53, 71, 78-83, 113-134; Hill, *Century*, p.131.

38. Davies, *Gentlemen and Tarpaulins*, pp.5, 17, 27-28, 119.

39. Adamson, J. H. and Folland. H. F., *Sir Harry Vane: His Life and Times* (Bodley Head, 1973); Capp, pp.42-48, 55

40. Capp, pp.60-65, 70-72; *CSPD* 1650, pp.263-314, 410-450; 1651-2, pp.578-621; *JoHC*, 1650, Vol. 6, BHO pp.375, 473-474; Vol. 7, 1651, BHO pp.31-33. Lawson to Vane, 12 Feb 1652/53.

41. Binns, *Lawson: Scarborough's Admiral*, p.103; Capp, pp.58-68; *CSPD* 1651-2, pp.578-621; 1652-3, pp.538-557; *Deeds, Town House, Wanstead Essex, 1663-1710*. ERO: D/DGn 182-222; *HoCJ*, Vol. 6, in BHO pp.375, 473-474; Vol. 7, BHO pp.31-33, 68-71, 154; Lawson, John, *Copy journal covering service aboard HMS Fairfax and HMS George during the First Dutch War, 1652-53*, BL RP 1071/2, original at Lilly Library, Bloomington, Indiana, USA, June-July 1653; *ODBN.*; Penn, pp.184-190; Tuffs, Jack Elsden, *The History of Wanstead*, Vol. 3, 1649-1727 (Author: 1942-? [pre-1977]); Wilford, J., *The History of England during the Reigns of the Royal House of Stuart*, Vol. 2 (London: 1732-1735), p.410

42. Lawson to Vane, 12 Feb 1652/53.

43. Ibid.

44. *CSPD* 1652, p.618.

45. Lawson to Vane, 12 Feb 1652/53.

46. Ibid.

47. Capp, pp.71-77

48. Lawson, *A declaration*, 1659.

49. Capp, Ibid.

50. Papers naval, BL Add MS 22546, fo.76.
51. *CSPD* 1653, pp.538-557; Lawson, *journal*, 1652-53; Letter from John Lawson, 9 May 1652, in SP 18/48/102.
52. Lawson, *journal*, 14 Feb 1652/53.
53. Ibid, 18 Feb 1652/53.
54. *CSPD* 1653, pp.538-557; Lawson, *journal*, 19 Feb 1652/53.
55. Ibid; Davies, pp.10-14; Travis-Cook, pp.7-9.
56. Lawson, *journal*, Ibid.
57. Ibid.
58. *CSPD* 1653, pp.538-557; *A Collection of the State Papers of John Thurloe*, Vol. v, in BHO, p.260; Lawson, *journal*, 1652-53; Travis-Cook, p.9.
59. Capp, p.81; Lawson, *journal*, 15 March 1652/53.
60. Lawson, John, Letter to Luke Robinson, Esq., 18 March 1652/53, in Hinderwell, pp.106-107.
61. Ibid.
62. *CSPD* 1653-54, pp.77, 220, 280; Lawson, *journal*, 1653.
63. *CSPD* Ibid; Lawson, *journal*, April-June 1653; *Scarborough Records*, 1641-1660.
64. Baker, *Scarborough*, pp.87-88; Binns, *Yorkshire*, ch.11; *Scarborough Records*, 1641-1660.
65. Scurr, pp.90-93,
66. Cromwell, Oliver, *A Declaration of Oliver Cromwell, captain general of all the forces of this Common-wealth, Whereas the Parlament being dissolved...* (London: William Dugard, April the last 1653); Wilford, p.412.
67. Ibid.
68. Ibid.
69. Ibid.
70. Warwick, p.406.

71. *Mercurius Politicus*, 21-28 April 1653, No.150.

72. Anon, *Another declaration...* (London: 1653); Cromwell, *Whereas, the Parlament beeing dissolved.*

73. Ludlow, Vol. I, p.365.

74. Warwick, p.407.

75. S. S., *The Parliament Routed* (London: G. Horton, June 1653).

76. Ibid.

77. Ibid.

78. Purnell, Robert, *Englands remonstrance...* (London: 14 Nov. 1653).

79. *A Christmas Song When the Rump was first Dissolved*, in Macky, Charles, *The Cavalier Songs and Ballads of England*, 1642-1684.

80. Ibid.

81. *Mercurius Politicus*, 21-28 April 1653, No.150.

82. Lawson, *Narrative*, 1659: *Two Letters*, 1659.

83. Capp, pp.122-123; *CSPD* 1653, pp.249-302; Lawson, *journal*, 25 April 1653.

84. Lawson, *journal*, 2 June 1653.

85. Ibid.

86. Capp, pp.81-82.

87. Ludlow, Vol. I, pp.361-362.

88. Ibid.

89. *CSPD* 1653, pp.538-557; Lawson, *journal*, June 1653; Ludlow, Vol. I, pp.361-363.

90. Travis-Cook, pp.10-11.

91. *CSPD* Ibid; Lawson, *journal*, Ibid; Ludlow, pp.361-364; *Thurloe*, Vol. v. BHO, p.297; Travis-Cook, Ibids.

92. *CSPD* 1653-4, p.77; *Guibon Goddard's Journal*, August 1653, in Diary of Thomas Burton, Esq, Vol. 1, 1653-1657, ed. John Towill Rutt (London: 1828), pp.iv.x; *HoCJ* 1653, BHO,

pp.296-297;*Thurlow*, August 1653, Vol. 5, BHO, pp.435-445; *Wilford*, p.416.

93. Ibid.

94. Sperling Deeds; Will Sir John Lawson, 1665.

## Chapter Three

1. *CSPD* 1656-7, p.243.

2. Ibid.

3. *CSPD* 1642-60; Lawson to Vane, 12 Feb 1652/53; *ODNB*; Penn, *Memorials*, Vol. 2, p.185.

4. Capp, pp.125-126; *CSPD* 1653; Ludlow, Vol. 1, pp.361-362.

5. *CSPD* 1652-3, pp.249-302, 557-576; 1653-4, pp.108-109; Lawson, *journal*, 1652-3.

6. *CSPD* 1653-4, Ibid.

7. Lawson, *journal*, 25 Aug 1653.

8. *CSPD* 1652-3, Ibid; 1653-4, Ibid, 280-578; *Thurloe*, Vol. xviii, BHO, pp.591-605.

9. Anon, *Another declaration... of the just grounds and reasons of the dissolving the Parliament by the Lord Generall...* (London: T. Brewer, 3 May 1653); Anon, *The Army No Usurpers...* (London: Giles Calvert, 20 May 1653); Cromwell, Oliver, *A declaration of Oliver Cromwell...* (London: William Du-Gard, April the last 1653); *Mercurius Politicus*, 21-28 April 1653, Issue 150; Hill, *The Century of Revolution*, pp.163-164; Purnell, Robert, *Englands remonstrance...* (London: E. Alsop, 14 Nov 1653); S. S., *The Parliament routed* (London: 1653).

10. Aspinwall, William, *A brief description of the fifth monarchy...* (London: 1653); Coward, p.240; Green, Ian and Peters, Kate, *Religious publishing in England 1640-1695*, in Barnard and McKenzie, Eds., *The Cambridge History of the*

*Book in Britain Vol. IV. 1557-1695* (Cambridge: CUP, 2002), pp.70-74; Hunt, p.211; Raymond, *Controversy*; Raymond, *Pamphlets*, pp.234-238.

11. *The Weekly Intelligencer of the Commonwealth*, No.126, June-July 1653.

12. Little, Patrick, *Oliver Cromwell and the Regicides*, in *Cromwelliana* (Cromwell Association, 2011), pp.10-19.

13. Ludlow, Vol. I, p.7

14. Warwick, pp.405-406.

15. Evans, Arise, *The bloudy vision of John Farly...* (London: 1653); Green and Peters, pp.70-73; Kaye, William, *Gods presence with the present government... answering the Fifth Monarchists, and anarchists arguments...* (London: T. Mabb for Richard Moon... 1655).

16. Little, Ibid, p11.

17. Anon, *A true narrative of... dissolution of the late Parliament...* (London: 12 Dec 1653).

18. Adamson and Folland, p.321; Ludlow, Vol. 1, p.368.

19. Anon, *By the council. Whereas the late Parliament dissolving themselves...* (Dublin: 16 Dec 1653 & 30 Jan 1653/54); Little, Ibid, pp.11-12.

20. Ludlow, Vol. 1, pp.365-68, 372-379.

21. Fraser, pp.309-320.

22. Lawson to Bourne, 25 Feb 1653/54, in SP 18/79/335.

23. Capp, p.128; *CSPD* 1654, p.581; Lawson to Bourne; Tinniswood, *The Rainborowes*, p.320.

24. Capp, p.85; *CSPD* 1654, pp.175-76, 578.

25. *CSPD* 1654, pp.175-176.

26. Ibid, pp.147, 175-6; Ludlow, Vol. I, p.378.

27. Autograph Letter from John Lawson to Cromwell, 15 June 1654: Text courtesy of Jarndyce Antiquarian Booksellers, London; *CSPD* 1654, pp.459-584; Ludlow Ibid.

28. Baker, *Scarborough*, pp.228, 245-246; Capp, p.135; *Scarborough Corporation Records*, 1601-1660; *Thurloe*, Vol. xxiv, BHO, p.71.

29. Little, Patrick, *Oliver Cromwell and the Good Old Cause*, in *Cromwelliana* (2011), p.4.

30. Capp, pp.135-136; *Thurloe*, Vol. xviii, BHO, pp.591-605; Vol. xxiv, p.71.

31. Capp, p.136; *CSPD* 1654, p.371.

32. Ibid, pp.86-92.

33. Capp, pp.136-137; 160-161; Davies, *Gentlemen and Tarpaulins*, pp.5, 9-27, 34-66, 124 *Thurloe*, Vol. xviii, BHO, p.136.

34. Capp, Ibid; Examination and Information of Samuel Dyer, Feb 1657/58, in *Thurloe*, Vol. lvii, BHO, pp.403, 409; *Thurloe*, Ibid.

35. Capp, p.137; *Thurloe*, Vol. x, BHO, p.30; Vol. xviii, BHO, pp.591-605; Vol. xxiv, BHO, p.71; Vol. xxvi, BHO, p.17.

36. Capp, pp.136-137; Dyer 1658, in *Thurloe*, Vol. lvii, BHO, p.403; *Thurloe*, 1655, Vol. xxxvii, BHO, p.43;

37. Ludlow, Vol. I, p.380.

38. *CSPD* July 1656-7, pp.194-198; Hunt, pp.238-239; Ludlow, Vol. I, p.6.

39. Capp, p.141; Dyer, in *Thurloe*. Ibid; Little, *Oliver Cromwell and the Good Old Cause*, pp.1-4.

40. Capp, pp.139-141.

41. Ibid; *CSPD* 1655-6, pp.61-111.

42. *CSPD* Ibid.

43. Capp, p.137; *CSPD* 1655-6, preface, pp.18, 192; *Thurloe*, Vol. xviii, BHO, pp.591-605; Vol. xxiv, BHO, p.71; Warwick, p.415.

44. *CSPD* 1656-7, pp.194-198; Ludlow, I, p.6; *Thurloe*, Vol. xxiv, BHO, p.71; Vol. xxiii, BHO, pp.81, 89; Vol. xxxiii, BHO, p.632.

45. *ClarCSP* 1656-7, p.420; *Thurloe*, vol. xxxvi, BHO, p.17.

46. Capp, pp.142-144; *CSPD* 1655-6, pp.138, 141; 1656-7, p.17; Ludlow, Vol. II, ch.4.

47. *CSPD* 1653-4, pp.220, 280; 1655-6, pp.xvi, 135, 141, 196-197, 209, 476, 492; 1656-7, pp.228, 581; *Publick Intelligencer*, No.79, 13-20 April 1657.

48. *CSPD* 1655-6, p.472.

49. Ibid, p.476.

50. *Thurloe*, Vol. xxxvii, BHO, pp.43-45.

51. *CSPD* 1655-6, p.196.

52. Ibid, p.209.

53. *Thurloe*, Ibid, p.43.

54. Capp, pp.143-145.

55. *Thurloe*, Vol. xviii, BHO, p.136.

56. Adamson and Folland, pp.319-325. Little, *Oliver Cromwell and the Regicides*, pp.18-19; Peacey, Jason, *Cromwellian England: A Propaganda State?* in, *History* (The Historical Association and Blackwell Publishing, April 2006), Vol. 91, Issue 302, p.177.

57. Capp, pp.87-92; 136-145; *CSPD* 1656-7, pp.194-198; Penn, pp.184-190; *Thurloe*, Vol. xviii, BHO, p.136; Tuffs, *The History of Wanstead*.

58. Adamson and Folland, ibid; Capp, p.145; *CSPD* 1656-7, pp.98, 194; Little, *Oliver Cromwell and the Regicides*, pp.18-19; Little, *Oliver Cromwell and the Good Old Cause*, pp.1-4;

Peacey, *A Propaganda State?*, p.177; *Thurloe*, Vol. xli, BHO, p.528; Vol. lxiv, BHO p.141.

59. *Thurloe*, Vol. xl, BHO, p.159.

60. Capp, p.145; *CSPD* 1656-7, p.56; 1657-8, p.244; *Thurloe*, Vol. xli, BHO, p.528.

61. Butler, Samuel, *As Close as a Goose*, 1657, in *Cavalier Songs*.

62. *Saxby to Father Talbot*, 26 April 1657, in *ClarCSP*, Vol. 3; *Ludlow*, Vol. 1, pp.38-39; *Publick Intelligencer*, No.79, 13-20 April 1657; *Thurloe*, Vol. lxiv, BHO, p.141.

63. Anon, *The Downfall of the Fifth Monarchy*... (London: John Andrews, at the White Lion in the Old Baily, 1657), p.3; *Thurloe*, Ibid.

64. *CSPD* 1656-7, p.351; *Publick Intelligencer*, No.78, 6-13 April 1657.

65. *CSPD* 1656-7, pp.324-362; *Publick Intelligencer*, Ibid; *Thurloe*, Vol. lxiv, BHO, p.141.

66. Thurloe, Ibid.

67. *Publick Intelligencer*, Ibid.

68. *CSPD* 1656-7, p.344; Ludlow, Vol. I, p.39; *Thurloe*, Vol. lviii, BHO, p.200.

69. Ibid, preface, p.243; Historic Royal Palaces.

70. Anon, *The Downfall of the Fifth Monarchy*.

71. *CSPD* 1656-57, p.250.

72. Ibid, preface.

73. Ibid, p.6; *Publick Intelligencer*, No.79, 12-20 April 1657; No.80, 4-11 May 1657.

74. Ludlow, Vol. I, p. 39.

75. *CSPD*, 1655-6; Lovelace, Richard, *To Althea from Prison*, 1642.

76. Lovelace.

77. *Publick Intelligencer*, No.80, 27 April-4 May 1657.

78. Ibid, No.83, 18-25 May 1657; No.84, 25 May-1 June 1657.

79. Ibid, No.81, 4-11 May 1657.

80. Raymond, Joad, *An Eye-Witness to King Cromwell*, in *History Today* (July 1997), Vol. 47, Issue 7, pp.37-38.

81. *Publick Intelligencer*, No.88, 22-29 June 1657.

82. Raymond, *An Eye-Witness*, p.38.

83. Ibid.

84. *CSPD* 1657, pp.19-20; *Publick Intelligencer*, No.88, 22-29 June 1657; No.91, 13-20 July 1657; No.92, 20-27 July 1657. Raymond, *An Eye-Witness*, p.38; Warwick, pp.420-1.

## Chapter Four

1. *CSPD* 1656-7, pp.228, 320-337, 344, 351, 420, 581; 1657-8, pp.346: *Publick Intelligencer*, 1657, Nos.79-88; *Thurloe*, 1656, Vol. 5, BHO, pp.316-332.

2. Binns, *Scarborough's Admiral*, p.104; Hinderwell, pp.100-107, 230; Penn to Sandwich, 8 Aug 1661, in Correspondence, Montagu, Bodl., MS Carte 73, fol.567; London St Dunstan in the East PRs; *ODNB. Pepys*, Vol. 2, pp.131-132; *Scarborough Records*, 1641-1660; Will, John Lawson, 1665; Sperling Deeds.

3. *Scarborough Records*, 1641-1660, pp.242, 244-245.

4. Ludlow, Vol. 2, pp.44-45.

5. Ibid, pp.45-48.

6. *CSPD* 1659; *CSPV, 1659*; Rugge, Vol. 1, fo.26.

7. *Scarborough Records*, 1641-1660, p.251.

8. Ibid; *CSPD* 1659; *CSPV 1659;* Rugge, Ibid.

9. Capp, pp.331-336; *ClarSP*, Vol. 3, pp.469-471, 499-511; *CSPD* 1659-60, pp.449-565; *CSPV* 1659, pp,vii-lvi; Davies,

pp.119-121; *HoCJ* 1659, Vol. 7, BHO, pp.665-667; Ludlow, pp.91-92; *Pepys*, Vol. I, pp.xxiv-xxvi; Rugge, Vol. 1, fo.28; Thurloe, Vol. 7, BHO, pp.666-678;

10. Bray, William, Ed., *The Diary of John Evelyn*, (London and New York: Walter Dunne, 1901), Vol, 1, p.328-329; Capp, pp.335-342; *CSPD*; *CSPV*, Ibid; Davies, ch.10; *HoCJ*; Ludlow; *Pepys*; Thurloe, Ibid.

11. Rugge, Vol. I, fos.31-32.

12. *The Monthly Intelligencer*, Dec 1659-Jan 1660.

13. Letter, Samborne to Hyde. 14 Oct 1659, in *ClarCSP*, Vol. 3, p.581.

14. Capp, pp.342-347; *CSPD* 1659-60; *CSPV*, 1659-61, pp.vii-lvi; Hasilrigg, Arthur, *The advance of Sir Arthur Hasilrigg...* (London: George Horton, 1659); Lawson, *A Narrative*, 22 Dec 1659; Vice-Admiral Sir John Lawson: Letters from him and the Officers of the Fleet to the Lord Mayor: 1659..., in BL Sloane MS 970, fos.10, 14; Penn, Vol.2, pp.184-185; Rugge, Vol. 1, fos.35-38; Wilford, *History*, p.436.

15. Capp; *CSPD*; *CSPV*; Ibid; *ClarSP*, Vol. 3, pp.629-630; Hasilrigg, p.4; Lawson, *Letter*, 13 Dec 1659; Lawson, *A declaration*, 1659; Thurloe, Vol. xli, BHO, p.528; Letter Charles Fleetwood to Vice-Admiral Lawson, 21 Dec 1659, BL Add MS 15857, f.236; Penn, Vol.2, pp.184-186; Rugge, Vol. 1, fos.40-45.

16. Lawson, *Letter*, 13 Dec 1659.

17. Lawson, *A declaration*, 1659.

18. Capp, p.348; Lawson, *A declaration*, 1659; Lawson, A letter from the Vice-Admiral to Lord Fleetwood, 1659, Greenwich Archives 355.49"1642/1659"; Penn, Vol.2, p.185.

19. Lawson, *A declaration*.

20. Ibid.

21. *ClarCSP*, p.488; Lawson, *Narrative*, 22 Dec 1659; Broderick to Hyde, 16 Dec 1659, in *ClarCSP*, Vol. 3, pp.629-630; Penn, Vol.2, pp.184-186; Rugge, Vol. 1, fo.41.

22. Adamson, and Folland, *Sir Harry Vane*, introduction; Penn, Vol.2, pp.184-185.

23. Ibid, pp.387-388.

24. Anonymous. *Sir Harry Vane's last sigh for Committee of Safety...* (London: 17 Dec 1659).

25. Penn, Vol.2, pp.185-188.

26. Lawson, *A Narrative 1659; Two Letters*, 1659, Penn, Vol. 2, pp.188-194; *Vane's last sigh*.

27. Penn, pp. Vol.2, 189-190.

28. Capp, pp.148-149; Rugge, Vol. 1, fo.41.

29. Capp, Ibid; Hasilrigg; Lawson, *A declaration, Narrative*; Rugge, Vol. 1, fos.41-44.

30. Hasilrigg, pp.3-5.

31. Lawson, *A declaration*; Penn, Vol.2, pp.188-194.

32. Capp, pp.148-149; Hasilrigg, pp.7-8; Letters, BL Sloane MS 970, fos.10, 14; Penn, Ibid.

33. *ClarSP*, Vol. 3, pp.653-666; Wilford, *History*, Vol. 6, p.159; Ludlow, Vol. 2, p.180; Penn, Vol.2, pp.194-195.

34. *Pepys*, p.1.

35. *Vane's last sigh*; Green and Peters, pp.68.69; Peacey, Jason, *Editing and Editorial Interventions in English Journalism from the Civil Wars to the Restoration,* in *Media History*, Vol. 18, (August 2012), Issue 3/4, pp.259-273; *Pepys*, Vol. 1, pp.62, 253; Rugge, Vol. 1, fos.33-36; Scurr, pp.111, 119-120.

36. Albemarle, George Monck, Duke of, *A Letter of advice to his excellencie the Lord General* Monck (London: 1660); Anon,

*Letters to the council of state, from the commissioners of the militia... and a letter from the Lord Montague...* (London: 1660).

37. *HoCJ* 1660, Vol.7, BHO, pp.793-802; Penn, Vol. 2, pp.194-195; Rugge, Vol. 1, fos.47-52.

38. *HoCJ*, Ibid, pp.801-802.

39. *ClarCSP*, Vol. 3, pp.638-642; *CSPD* 1660, pp.500-521; *HoCJ*, Ibid, pp.817-818; Penn, Ibid; Rugge, Ibid.

40. Capp, pp.351-352; *CSPD* 1660, pp.500-521; *ClarCSP*, Vol. 3, pp.637-642; *Pepys*, Vol. 1, p.13.

41. Rugge, Vol. 1, fo.48.

42. *CSPD* 1660, pp.488-521, 550; *ClarCSP*, Ibid; Penn, Vol.2, p.197-201; Rugge, Vol. 1, fos.52-54.

43. Albemarle, *A Letter of advice*; Anon, *Letters to the council of state, from the commissioners of the militia... and a letter from the Lord Montague...* (London: Abel Roper and Thomas Collins, 1660); Anon, *The Glory of the west...* (London: Charles Gustavus 1660); J. W., *Englands heroick champion. Or the ever renowned General George Monck... to a pleasant new northern tune* (London: John Andrews at the white Lion near Pye-corner, 1660); *ClarSP*, Vol. 3, pp.653-666; Raymond, *Pamphlets*, p.251; Rugge, Vol. 1, fos.52-60.

44. *ClarSP*, Vol. 3, p.677; *Publick Intelligencer*, 1659-60. Raymond, *Pamphlets*, p.218; *Weekly Intelligencer*, 1659-60.

45. *Pepys*, Vol. 1, p.45.

46. *CSPV* 1659-61, pp.vii-lvi; *ClarSP*, Vol. 3, p.681; Lister, T. H., Ed., *Life and Administration of Edward First Earl of Clarendon with Original Correspondence*, Vol. 3 (London: Longman, Orme, Brown, Green and Longman, 1837), pp.83-84; Rugge, Vol. 1, fos.52-53; Scurr, pp.123-124.

47. *Life of Clarendon*, pp.83-84.

48. Wilford, p.456; Ludlow, Vol. 2, pp.215-216; *Pepys*, pp.22-25; Rugge, Vol. 1, fos.53-54.

49. Ludlow, Vol. 2, p.216.

50. Ibid, pp.215-216; *Pepys*, Vol. 1, p.45.

51. *CSPD* 1660, p.550; Davies, pp.120-121; Rugge, Vol. 1, fo.67.

52. Ibid; Collins to Hyde, in *ClarCSP*, Vol. 3, p.681; *Evelyn*, pp.330-331; *Monthly Intelligencer*; Ibid; *Pepys*, Vol. 1, pp.79, 99-100; Scurr, p.124.

53. Capp, pp.353-354; *CSPD* 1660, p.xiii; Ludlow, p.243; Major Wood to -, 21 Feb 1660, in *ClarCSP*, Vol. 3, p.688; Samborne to Hyde, 24 Feb 1660, in *Life of Clarendon*, p.85; Ludlow, Vol. 2, pp.242-244; Penn, Vol.2, p.203; *Pepys*, Vol. 1, p.79.

54. *CSPD* 1660, p.xiii; Ludlow, p.243; Penn, Vol.2, p.203; Scurr, p.123.

55. Capp, pp.354-356; Correspondence, Montagu, 1st Earl of Sandwich, Oxford, Bodleian Library, MS Carte 71, fol.185; MS 72, fos.229, 347; *CSPD* 1660, pp.564-565; Davies, pp.121-125; SP 29/9, fol.15-16.

56. Ludlow, p.243.

57. Capp, Ibid; Correspondence, Montague, Bodl., MS Carte 73, fol.355; *ODNB*; *Life of Clarendon*, pp.89-90.

58. Slingsby to Hyde, 16 March 1660, Samborne to Hyde, in *Life of Clarendon*, Vol. 3, pp.91-93; *Pepys*, Vol. 1, pp.99-100; Rugge, Vol. 1, fo.73.

59. Capp, pp. 354-356; Davies, pp.121-128; *ODNB*; Lawson, *Declaration*, 1659; Lawson, *Letters*, 1659; Will John Lawson, 1665; London Apprenticeship and Freemen Records; *Scarborough Records*, 1601-1660.

60. Capp, Ibid; Correspondence, Montague, Bodl., MS Carte 71, fol.185; MS Carte 72, fos.229, 347; *CSPD* 1660, pp.564-565; Davies, pp.121-125; SP 29/9, fol.15-16.

61. *Pepys*, Vol. 4, pp.372-377.

62. *Life of Clarendon*, Vol. 3, p.93; Lawson, John, Aboard the James at Gravesend, John Lawson to the Mayor, Aldermen and Common Council of Rye, 19 March 1659/660, East Sussex RO, RYE/47/161/1; *Pepys*, Vol. 1, pp.95, 98.

63. *Pepys*, Vol. 1, pp.99-109.

64. *Pepys*, Vol. 1, pp.99-110.

65. *CSPD* 1660, p.19; *Pepys*, Vol. 1, p.122; Rugge, Vol. 1, fo.103.

66. *Pepys*, Vol. 1, pp.130-131.

67. Rugge, Vol. 1, fo.86.

68. Ibid, fo.95.

69. *Pepys*, Vol. 1, p.153; Rugge, Vol. 1, fo.96.

70. *Pepys*, Vol. 1, pp.154-155.

71. Ibid, Vol. p.159.

72. Ibid.

73. Anon, *Englands Gratulations on the landing of Charles the Second...* (London: printed for Charles Prince, 1660); *Evelyn*, pp.332-333; Rugge, Vol. 1, fos.88-100.

74. *Evelyn*, p.332.

## Chapter Five

1. *Pepys*, Vol. 1, pp.130-131.

2. Burke's Peerage; Penn, pp.249-50; *Pepys*, Vol. 1, pp.253-54.

3. Ludlow, p.278; Penn, pp.250-51.

4. *CSPD* 1661-2, pp.16-54; 1663-4, pp.81-96; Davies, *Gentlemen and Tarpaulins*, p.126; *HoCJ* 1660, Vol. 8, BHO pp.213-215; Penn, pp.247-254; *Pepys*, Ibid; Travis-Cook, p.36.

5. Capp, *Cromwell's Navy*, pp.359-360, 371-375; *Pepys*, Vol. 4, pp.xxx-xxxi, 372-377.

6. Capp, Ibid; *Pepys*, Ibid.

7. *CSPD* 1665, pp.401-17; Scarborough PRs and TRS; Will of Jane Lawson of Scarborough, Borthwick, YPC 1694.

8. Capp, pp.376-77; *CSPD* 1660 Charles II, pp.1-24.

9. *CSPV* 1659-61, pp.vii-lvi; *Pepys*, Vol. 1, pp.1, 122, 265; Rugge, Vol. 1, fos.103, 125, 177.

10. *CSPV* Ibid; Little, *Oliver Cromwell and the Regicides*, p.9; *Pepys*, Vol. 1, p.265; Rugge, Ibid.

11. *CSPV* Ibid; Rugge, Vol. 1, fo.149; Vol. 2, fos.9-10.

12. Anon, *Hells master-piece discovered... the damnable plot...* (London: Francis Grove, [1660?]; *CSPV* Ibid; *Pepys*, Vol. 2, p.1.

13. Capp, pp.374-75; *CSPD* 1660-1 Charles II, pp.1-30, 107-150; *Pepys*, Vol. 2, pp.45, 50.

14. Capp, p.256; Davies, pp.90-92.

15. Anon, *The holy sisters conspiracy...* (London: T. M., 1661); *CSPV* 1659-61, Ibid; *Pepys*, Vol. 2, pp.1, 10-11, 18; Rugge, Vol. 1, fos.149-150.

16. *Pepys*, Vol. 2, pp.26-27, 31; Rugge, Vol. 1, fos.152-154.

17. Traditional late 17 century rhyme edited by Benjamin Britten, 1938.

18. Jordan, Don and Walsh, Michael, *The King's Revenge: Charles II and the Greatest Manhunt in British History* (Abacus, 2012); Little, *Oliver Cromwell and the* Regicides, p.9; Ludlow.

19. *Pepys*, Vol. 2, p.65; Rugge, Vol. I, fo.200; *Mercurius Politicus*.

20. Butler, Lawrence, *Whitby in North Africa*, in *Yorkshire Archaeological Journal* (Yorkshire: 2004), Vol. 76, pp.171-175; Tinniswood, *Pirates*, p.204.

21. Tinniswood, pp.4-13; Wood, *Britons Could Be Slaves*.

22 Butler, Ibid; Capp, p.375; Davies, p.177; Davies, J. D., *Montagu, first earl of Sandwich*, in *ODNB* (Oxford: UP,

online edn., Jan 2008); Tinniswood, pp.204-205; Tomalin, p.144; Travis-Cook, p.36.

23. *Pepys*, Vol. 2, pp.131-138, 155; Penn to Sandwich, in Correspondence, Montagu, Bodl. MS. Carte 73, fol(s). 567; St Dunstan in the East PRs; Will John Lawson, 1665.

24. Penn to Sandwich, Ibid.

25. A plan or bird's-eye view of Algiers, 1661... presented by Sir John Lawson, BL King George III's Topographical Collection, K.Top.117.73.b; *Pepys*, Vol. 2, p.184; Rugge, Vol. I, fos.453-459.

26. *CSPV* 1661-4, pp.42-62; Rugge, Ibid.

27. Correspondence, Montagu, Bodl. MS Carte 73/565; Plan of Algiers, 1661; *Pepys*, Vol. 2, pp.184, 189; Rugge, Vol.1, 453-459; Vol. 2, fos.2, 4, 10-14.

28. Rugge, Vol. 2, fos.2-3.

29. Cholmley, Hugh, *An Account of Tangier. By Sir Hugh Cholmley, Bart...* (Gale ECCO Edition), p.16; Rugge, Vol. 2, March 1661/62, fos. 3-8, 14.

30. Cholmley, *Tangier*, pp.39-40; Rugge, Vol. 2, fos.10, 29; Tinniswood, *Pirates*, pp.206-208.

31. Cholmley, Ibid; Montagu, in *ODNB*; *Pepys*, Vol.2, P.189; Rugge, Vol. 2, fos.4, 29; Tinniswood, Ibid.

32. Butler, Ibid; Cholmley, *Tangier*, pp.4, 9, 16; Rugge, Vol. 2, fos.3-8, 13-15.

33. Cholmley, *Tangier*, pp.8-9; Colonel Henry Norwood, Esquire of the Body to Charles II., Treasurer to the Colony of Virginia, Lieutenant-Governor of Tangier, and Commander in Chief of the English Forces in Africa: Correspondence and papers... Sloane MS 3509: 1660-1680, BL, f.15.

34. Rugge, Vol. 2, fo.29.

35. Butler, Ibid; Cholmley, *Tangier*, p.48; Letter Book of Sir Hugh Cholmley, 1664-66. NYRO Cholmley MSS ZCG/V1/1/1, pp.96-100, 110-118, 190-197, 286.

36. Contract for building a mole at Tangier, 1662, in: Norwood, Ibid, f.18.

37. Butler; Cholmley, Ibid Correspondence, Montagu, Bodl. MS Carte 75, fo.110; Letter Book, Cholmley, Ibid.

38. Cholmley, *Tangier*, p.41.

39. Butler; Contract for mole; Cholmley, *Tangier*; Letter Book, Cholmley. Ibid.

40. Lawson to Vane, Feb 1652/53.

41. Letter Book, Cholmley, ibid, pp.193, 197.

42. *Pepys*, Vol. 3, pp.121-22, 79, 89 Vol. I, fos.453-459; Travis-Cook, p.36.

43. *CSPD* 1662, pp.396-426; *CSPV* 1662, pp.137-168; Rugge, Vol. 2, fo.33.

44. *Pepys*, Ibid.

45. Correspondence, Montagu, Bodl. Carte MS 75, fos.38, 52, 56; *CSPV* 1662, pp.146-158, 182-204.

46. Little, *Oliver Cromwell and the* Reigcides, p.9; Rugge, Vol. II, fo.29-33.

47. Lawson to Vane, 1652/53; Little, Ibid; *Pepys*, Vol. 3, pp.258, 260, 264; Rugge. Vol. II, June 1662, fo.30; Tomalin, p.144.

48. Articles of Peace between Charles II... and the Kingdom of Tunis, 5 Oct 1662, BL B.J.6(6); Correspondence, Montuagu, Bod;. MS Carte 75, fo.86; *CSPV* 1662, pp.146-168; *Pepys*, Vol. 3, p.263; Rugge, Vol. 2, fos.56-61.

49. *CSPD* 1662, pp.592-609; *Pepys*, Vol. 4, pp.3-4, 12, 73; Travis-Cook, p.36; Correspondence, Montagu, Bodl. MS Carte 75, fo.86.

50. Deeds, Alresford alias Easthall Manor Court Records. ERO: D/DJo MJ; Sperling Deeds; Tuffs, *History of Wanstead*, p.49; Lawson Probate Records (various); Alresford, Bocking and Wanstead PRs; Will John Lawson, 1665.

51. Hopper, Andrew, *The Farnley Wood Plot and the Memory of the Civil Wars in Yorkshire*, in *The Historical Journal*, (Cambridge: UP, June 2002), Vol. 45, No. 2, pp.281-303.

52. Hopper, Ibid.

53. Letter Book, Cholmley. Ibid; from Admiral Sir John Lawson, 1663-1664, National Maritime Museum, The Caird Library, Greenwich, A/GC/L/1/18; *Pepys*, Vol. 4, pp.13, 26-27, 31, 35-36, 88; Will John Lawson, 1665.

54. *CSPD* 1669, pp.350-391; Davies, *Gentlemen and Tarpaulins*, pp.63-64; *Pepys*, Vol. 4, pp.369-70; SP 82/11/172.

55. Letters from Admiral Sir John Lawson, Greenwich AGC/L/1/1-7.

56. Ibid.

57. Cholmley, *Tangier*; Letter Book, Cholmley, pp.286-7; *Pepys*, Vol.4, pp. 104, 325 Vol. 5, pp.303, 343; Vol. 6. p.71, 101; Tinniswood, *Pirates*, pp.229-32.

58. Cholmley, *Tangier*, pp.66-67.

59. Letters Admiral Sir John Lawson, Caird A/GC/L/1/11.

## Chapter Six

1. Chancery Records, Lawson v. Lawson, TNA: C/7/576/88, C5/514/49, C5/616/95, C10/198/34; Papers in suit in Chancery decree 1668, Hampshire Archives and Local Studies, SM50/388-390; *Pepys*, Vol. 4, p.23; Vol. 5, p.7; Vol. 6, pp.60, 150-151; Vol. 7, p.264.

2. Chancery Records, Ibid; Papers in suit, Ibid; *ODNB*; *Pepys*, Vol. 6, pp.60, 150-151, Vol. 7, p.264.

3. *Pepys*, Vol. 6, Ibid.

4. Anon, *The holy sisters conspiracy*, 1661, Ibid; Chancery Records, Ibid; Clarendon, Bodl., MS Carte 75, fol.273; *Pepys*, Vol. 5, pp.295&n, 299.

5. *Pepys*, Ibid.

6. Rugge, Vol. 2, fos.134-5.

7. *CSPV* 1664-6, pp.v-lv; Davies, *Gentlemen and Tarpaulins*, pp. 133-158.

8. *CSPV* Ibid; Davies, pp. 133-136; Penn, Vol. 2, pp.311-4; *Pepys*, Vol. 7, p.195; Vol. 8, p.125.

9. Assignment of Judgement and Power of Attorney, Isabelle Lawson 1693, ERO: D/DGn 22; Chancery Records, Ibid; Sperling Deeds; Alresford alias Easthall Manor Court Records; London Apprenticeship and Freemen Records; Papers in suit, Ibid; *ODNB*; *Pepys*, Vol. 6, pp.39, 61, 100-1, 119, 185; Will Sir John Lawson, 1665; Will John Lawson, 1683, LMA MS 9052/24, No.46 ; Will Samuel Lawson, 1693, TNA: PCC PROB 11/414.

10. Davies, *Gentlemen and Tarpaulins*, p.15; Pepys, Vol. 6, p.52; Pepys, Vol. 1, pp.114-5.

11. *Pepys*, Vol. 6, p.52.

12. Ibid, &n, 55; Rugge, Vol.2, fos.134-36; The London Ship Trust.

13. De Beer, Ed, *The Diary of John Evelyn* (Oxford: Everyman's Library, 2006 edn.) pp.424, 428; *Pepys*, Vol. 6, pp.52-3; Rugge, Vol. 2, fos.134-136.

14. Penn, Vol. 2, p.315; *Pepys*, Ibid; Rugge, Vol.2. fo.134.

15. *CSPD* 1667, pp.542-561; *Pepys*, Vol. 6, pp.52-3; Rugge, Vol. 2, fos.135-6.

16. Rugge, Vol. 2, fo.135; *The City and the Navy: An Opportunity for History to Repeat Itself*, in Pall Mall Gazette (23 Jan 1896).

17. Chancery Records, Lawson v Lawson, TNA: C5/616/95.

18. *The City and the Navy*, Ibid.

19. Chancery Records, Ibid, Rugge, Ibid.

20. Rugge, Vol. 2, fo.139.

21. Will John Lawson, 1665.

22. Lawson Wills (various).

23. Penn, Vol. 2, p.336.

24. Grant of Annuity, 1665, Lincolnshire Archives, 1-Dixon/1/E/93; Penn, Vol. pp.336-7; Sperling Deeds, Ibid; Calendar of Treasury Books, Vol. 1, 1660-1667, BHO, 1664, p.27; 1665, pp.258, 292.

25. *CSPV* 1664-6, pp.v-lv; Davies, pp. 133-158; Pepys, Vol. 6. pp.116-7, 122-3, Rugge, Vol. 2, fo.140.

26. Clarendon, Edward, *The life of Edward Earl of Clarendon, Lord High Chancellor of England and Chancellor of the University of Oxford in which is included his history of the grand rebellion written by himself*, Vol. 2, (Oxford: Clarendon Press, 1827) p.391; Conference: Care and Mortality; *CSPV* 1664-6, pp.v-lv; Penn, Vol. 2, pp.337-8; *Pepys*, Vol. 6, pp.121-123, 129, 138

27. Chancery Records, TNA: C5/616/95; *Pepys*, Vol. 5, p.332&n; TNA Currency Converter.

28. Rugge, Vol. 2, fo.141.

29. *Pepys*, Vol. 6, pp.131-2.

30. *Pepys*, Vol. 6, p.138.

31. *Pepys*, Vol. 3, pp.121-2&n; Vol. 6, pp.145, 276&n.

32. Chancery Records, Ibid; *Pepys*, Vol. 6, p.145.

33. Will of John Lawson 1665.

34. Papers in suit, Ibid; *Pepys*, Vol. 6, p.145; Rugge, Vol. 2, fo.142; St Dunstan in the East London PRs; Will John Lawson, 1665.

35. Clarendon, *History*, p.391.

## Epilogue

1. Calendar of Treasury Books, 1660-1700 at BHO; Grant of Annuity, 1665, Lincolnshire Archives 1-Dixon/1/E/93; *Pepys*, Vol. 6, pp.150-1&n; Vol. 7, p.264; Sperling Deeds; Will John Lawson, 1665.

2. Calendar, Ibid; Grant, Ibid; Chancery Records, Lawson v Lawson; Letter Book, Cholmley, pp.286-7; *Pepys*, Vol. 6, pp.150-1&n; Vol. 7. p.264; Sperling Deeds; Will John Lawson, 1665.

3. Assignment of Judgement and Power of Attorney, 26 June 1693, ERO: D/DGn 222; Chancery Records; Wanstead PRs; Wanstead PRs; Will, John Lawson, 1665.

4. Will, Ibid.

5. Ibid.

6. Ibid.

7. Cholmley, *Tangier*; Letter Book, Cholmley Ibid; *Pepys*, Vol, 7, pp.18-19, 98-99, 323.

8. Assignment of Judgement, Ibid; Conveyances, John and Martha Lawson, 1674, ERO: D/DG/182-229; Chancery Records, Ibid.

9. Wanstead Essex PRs; Will Dame Anna St George of Woodford, Essex, 1720, TNA: PROB 11/579; Will John Lawson, 1683, LMA: MS 9052/24, No.46; Will Martha Lawson, of Wanstead, widow 1687, ERO: D/AEW 27/252.

10. Assignment of Judgement; Chancery Record, Lawson v Lawson, 1674, C/7/57/6/88.

11. Will Martha Lawson; Will John Lawson, 1683; Will Samuel Lawson, 1693, Ibid.

12. Calendars of Essex Quarter Sessions and Assize Records at Essex Record Office; Sperling Deeds.

13. Calendars of Treasury Books; LMA PR Indexes & PRs at Ancestry; Papers in suit in Chancery; *Pepys*, Vol. 6, Ibid; Sperling Deeds; Will Anne Kinaston of Alresford, Spinster 1721, LMA: D/ABW 84/1/107; Will Dame Isabella Chicheley, 1706, TNA: PROB 11/516; Will Dame Anna St George; Wanstead and Woodford St Mary the Virgin Essex PRs

14. *Diver jailed for fraud over £50,000 sale of cannon*, 5 Sept 2015, in *The Guardian*, p.18; The London Shipwreck Trust.

# APPENDICES

*Letter from John Lawson to Sir Henry Vane*
12 February 1652/53
TNA: SP 18 47 f113

Right Honrble
It pleased the Lord in the beginning of these times to Convince
mee of the Justice of the p[ar]l[i]am[e]nts proceedings soe that
in the year 1642 I voluntarily Ingaiged in the service and Ever
since the Lord has kept my heart upright to the Honest Interest
of the Nation, Although, I have been nessesitated twice to
Escape for my freedom, and danger of my liefe, att the trecheres
of Sr Hugh Cholmly and Colonell Boynton, at Scarbrough in the
First and second war: my wife and Children being Banished two
years to Hull, where it pleased god to make mee an Instrument
in discovering and (in some measure) preventing the Intended
treacherie of Sr Jo: Hotham, having mett with other tossings and
removals to my outward loss, suffering many times by the enemy

at sea, my livelihood being by trade that way: during part of the first war I served at sea in a small ship of my own and partners, in which time receiving my freight well I had subsistence; since that I commanded a foot company at land near five years, and about three years last past was called to this employment in the State ships, at which time my foot company was disposed. In the aforesaid service at land and this last at sea, by reason of the treacheries and revolutions ashore and smallness of salary at sea, I assure your honour myself and family has not had maintenance from the public, nor I have not used those ways of plundering that others have. At my return from the Straits the last summer I resolved to have left the sea employment and to have endeavoured some other way to provide for my family; but this difference breaking out betwixt the Dutch and us, I could not satisfy my conscience to leave at this time being very well satisfied that this service is in order to the design of God in the exaltation of Jesus Christ, and therefore with much cheerfulness shall spend myself in this cause where the glory of God and the good of his people is so much concerned. May it please your honour, I have one suit I shall humble beg for favour in, which is, that if the Lord shall have appointed my course to be finished and shall take me to Himself while I am in this employment (which at the appointed time I trust through His rich mercy & free grace in Jesus Christ He will do) that your honour will become instrumental that my wife and children may be considered in more than an ordinary manner, for they have suffered outwardly by my embracing this sea service last: my wife is dear to me, and I have good ground to believe she is dear to God ^and therefore I assure myself your honour will be more willing in such a case to take the trouble upon you. I beg pardon for this presumption, beseeching the Lord to preserve your honour and all faithful ones at land, and that His presence may be with, and providence over us at sea. My most humble and bounden service presented, I crave leave to subscribe myself, Right Honourable,

Your Honour's and the Interest of God's people's faithfull Servant whilst I am

Jo. Lawson

Aboard the States Frigot the *Fairfax* in Dover Road, this 12th of the 12th mon: 1652.

## Extracts from the journal of John Lawson

Lawson, Sir John, Copy journal covering service aboard HMS *Fairfax* and HMS *George* during the First Dutch War

16 November 1652 to 20 September 1653

Copy at British Library (ref. RP 1071/2)

Original held at and courtesy of Lilly Library, Bloomington, Indiana, USA

1652

Decemb: 1

The first in ye morning... Anchored in Margett Rode it being thicke weather and the winde Southerly, at 12 oclocke it cleared the wind came to the N.W. soe weighed arrived in the Downes where the Genll. of fleete was, but they had ingaiged ye Dutch fleete the day before, the Garland and Capt. Hoxon being taken.

[Dec.] 3

The 3d: had a Councell of war on board the Genll. in ye morning where it was judged fitt sometime longer in the Downes but about noone there was one of yᵉ Dutch men of war stood in w[thin]

in the South and head, having English Colors, & viewed the fleete, & it blowing fresh went away soe ye Genll. Called another Councell of war, in ye afternoone, and there it was put to the Question, whether it was judged fitt for the fleete to ride there will or noe, & resolved in the negative, the 2nd question was putt, whether wee should goe out and fight y^e Hollandrs. they being plying up betwixt the Heads (the condicon of the fleete being considered) Resolved in the negative. The 3rd question was put – whether the fleete should move for most safety, & most expeditious reinforcem[en]t. Resolved for Lee Road and that in ye morning to sett sail.

Feby: [1652/53] 14

The wind came Westerly, fair weather stood to & againe was thwart of Beachy, the same day resolve aboard the Genll. at a Councell of the Flagg officers, that is winde & weather served, wee should indeavo^r. to gett thwart of the start and there to ply in expectacon of ye Dutch fleet, and that the Rendeavous, in case of parting company, w[i]th the winde westerly should be S^t. Hollings Road, if to ye westw[ar]d of it, & if to the Eastw^d. of ye Isle of Wight, the Downes and for an Easterly winde, to keepe the sea, & if parte the next fair weather, five leagues of the start.

[Feb 1652/53] 18

The 18th Instant the morning Discovered the Dutch fleet off St. Albans …. About Nine of the clock wee Ingaiged them, and continued till sunset, the Tryumph & some others were forelorne that day wee had many men slaine & wounded, there was about 7 or 8 of there men of war taken Suncke & burned, one of them taken was an East India Shipp, of 1200 tuns wee had one Flemish ship of 28 guns sunck, her name the Sampson, she was taken last year. A Convoy, wee had some of o[r] ships near taken but regained Capt. Ball. Capt. Mildmay w[th] some of the Comand[rs] and many officers slaine.

Feby: 19

*Margin note*: There was about 20 men off Warr in all taken and suncke and 50 mrcht ships.

The 19[th] about noone wee began againe, w[hi]ch was as soone as wee could get up w[th]. them, continued fighting till night... ... ... about halfe an houre before sunset, I steared aboard one of 38 guns, and came of w[i]th her, my selfe & Company that had escaped being much spent, I had slaine both days 27 men & wounded 56, some of w[hi]ch are dismembered and will hardly escape besides my selfe & many others rec~ed blowes & bruses w[i]th Splenters, among those slaine my Boatsw[ai]n... but I desire of the Lord that I may whilest I live in this tabernackle of Flesh, acknowledge his great power Providence & goodness in my profervacon [sic], & those others w[i]th me that were proscribed the Instrum[en]ts of Death flying very thick about us, on every side, yet had no Comission to touch us, and the Lord kept upp o[r]. Spirrits and struck terror to the harts of o[u]r enemyes for they Runn. The 19th at night, I put my Lieut. and 30 men into the Prize, being willing to save her she being a ship of 500 Tunns, there was two men of war more taken then I see, that night I steared after o[r]. Fleete w[i]th w[ha]t sails wee could, but in the morning they were in pursuite of the Enemy, as farr as wee could see them, soe I steared towards the English shoare I know not w[ha]t execution was done ye 20th day when they left y[e] Enemy.

Feby: 26

The 26<sup>th</sup> Reced ordr. From Comr. Bourne at Deale to repaire with the Fairfax for Chattham.

Feby: 28

The 28th. Weighed gott into the Gore that night.


March

The first day weighed to goe over the flatte the winde Southerley, but the Rylott weighed to soone by two houres, for that wee came aground in ye narrow and lay wringing till the Pitch of high water, yet then it pleased the Lord send us of w[hi]ch was a great mercy and that night wee arrived safely at Quinbrough where I mett ordrs. For my stay there, and to goe on board the George w[i]th w[ha]t seamen were here in this Frigt. Soe Anchored and Mored.


*George* March 1652/53

March 12

The 12th Instant by ordr. of ye Honorble. Comrs. for the affairs of the Admlty. I tooke possession of ye George at Quinbrough, w[hi]ch day the Fairfax sailed towards Chattam, & arrived at Gillingham.

15 The 15<sup>th</sup> Instant I rece~ed a Comission from ye Rt. Honrbl the Genll. of the Fleete to be Rear Admll. of the Fleete, a very high favor. & great trust, w[hi]ch I beseech the Lord inable mee to discharge to his glory & the Comfort of my soule, I rec~ed from ye Honrbll. Commrs. of ye Admlty. Notice, that upon debate w[i] th the Genrlls. at Portsmouth, they had presented to mee to the Rt. Honrble. Councell of State ye 8th, w[hi]ch was approved by theire Honors. for ye Comand.

19

This 19th sett saile for Lee Road [arrived there crossed out] the 20th in the morning arrived there, this day the Beare and Violett, sailed towards Newcastle to Convoy the Collyers.

21

This 21st came upp about 35 saile of Vessells from Hull out of w[hi]ch I gott 40 men.

26

The 26th the Greyhound arrived here from Chattam as alsoe ye unhappy newes of ye Fairfax being burned.

27

The 27ᵗʰ Little Betty arrived here in Lee Road.

The 28 I was ready to saile.

Aprill 1653

The 6ᵗʰ of Aprill I rec[eive]d ordrs. From ye Rt Honrble. Councell of State to sett saile to ye Swine, date ye 5th in ordr. to a Conjunction w[i]th the Vice Admrll. Who was to come from the Downes.

7

The 7th w[he]n the Rylott came sett saile ye Greyhound in Company as alsoe the Wildman & Hunter the Fireships and ye Hope.

8

The 8th weighed & standing downe the Swine, w[i]thin ye Spitts, wee see A Ship side, soe sent ye Greyhound to see w[ha]t shee was, it proved A Fireship called the Golden Faulcon whereof Capt. Litle is Comr. Who was then on shoar arrived thwart of Hrwidge ansured advice of some shipps of Flambrough has supposed those…

April 25

The 25th weighed went into the Downes anchored at the Southern most part of the same yt [that] rec~d a letter from the Gen[ll]. directed to ye Commadrs. & writt one jointly in answer declares o[u]r resolutcon to continue faithfull in the discharge of o[u]r trust at sea against the people of the United Provences and all other Enemys to the Como~n wealth notw[i]thstanding the Desolution of the Parliamt.

Maye 1

The first, wee all anchored of Dungeonness.

Maye 2

The 2d weighed & going about ye southsand head see 10 or 12 saile of ships stood w[i]th them they proved Lubockes and Hamburgers who told us that Trump lay off the Taxell soe resolved by a Councell of war to sale towards him.

June 1

The first weighed the winde. N. W. stood to ye Longsand head anchored there, in ordr. to a Conjuncon, w[i]th the ships then comeing out of the River, about an houre before wee then anchored, there was two Galliote hoyes, w[i]th Dutch Clowes stood towards o[u]r Fleete, and was very near soe they discovered us, and o[u]r Frigts. upon that chased the Dutch Fleete soe stood back againe (all but the Nonsuch Pearle & Martin Gally). and fired guns making signs, soe wee all weighed stood towards them, but night came on, soe anchored againe But that afternoone the George struck upon the Galloper sand, 4. or 5. times & weny over w[i]thout harme, praised be the Lord, w[hi]ch was a great mercy confirming the sea was troublesome.

June 2

The 2d Instant in ye morning discovered Van Trums [sic] fleet to the Leeward of us the winde at N. N. W soe we weighed stood towards them they plyed up towards us Small winds soe about nine of the Clocke he came w[ith]in shott, and presently after wee were ingaiged, but it fell almoste Calme, my selfe and o[u]r squadron, was on the left wing, & nearest, about noone it was very little winde, and came about to the N. E. soe Ruter & his Squadron w[hi]ch was on their left wing taked upon us and wethered my Squadron, most of w[hi]ch tacked, and soe all the Dutch fleet tacked, and soe bore up a little towards o[u]r owne fleete w[hi]ch was Leewards my vice Admll. and Rear Admll. came to mee, wee three fought alongst all the Dutch Fleete being hotly ingaiged, yet it pleased the Lord miraculously to preserve us, soe that I had but one man slaine, & one Dangerously wounded that day, soe the Dutch Fleete bearing up after us, put themselves to the Leeward, and o[u]r Genll, and Fleet Tacking, weatherd the Dutch Fleete againe, in w[hi]ch God appeared mercifully towards us, that night, Genll. Dean was slaine, then, the Enemy lost, some 3 ships suncke & one blowne up as some observed soe night parted us.

[July] 19

... had a Councell of Warr, where it was debated whether we should ply of the Texell or Fly, having intelligence that parte of the Dutch fleet was at ye Texell still & ready, and Turing alsoe ready, it was resolved to ply of the Texel and w[i]th fair weather, or the winde of the shore, to anchor at a fair berth off, and keepe some to Ride close into the shore, to see none of the Enemy sailes upon the night.

July 31

The 31ht in the morning the wide came to ? S.W. soe wee tackt &
steered clear through Trumps Fleete w[i]th o[u] whole Fleete
ingaiged Hotly at w[hi]ch time many of those ships was disabled in
there Masts, some shott by the Board to the Deck, wee had four of
o[u]rs had their Mainmasts shott by the Board, they endeavoured
to have fired severall of or. great ships, but the Lord prevented
them, onely the Oake was burned by a fire ship soe we were clear
through them, they tacked upon us and wee Upon them, and soe we
continued tacking Upon them & they Upon us, till we had passed
one the other three times besides the first Encounter by w[hi]ch
time many of there ships was suncke & disabled to the numb~. was
supposed by moste, or about twenty amongst w[hi]ch the Garland
was one, w[hi]ch had her great Masts both shott by the board near
the Decke. And Trumpes Mainttopmast & Flagg was shott by the
Board soe then they began to Run, w[hi]ch was about 3 'clock we
pursued them close to their owne shore, till ten o'clock at night in
the Pursuitte one vice Admll was sunke, nighte came ...

August 25

... Capt. Saunders in the Ruby told us he had spoken one that
came from the Soun. with a fleet of Dutch Merchant ships who
said they we near about where wee plyed, after 12 A Clocke see
some sailes, soe we sett our maintop sale and after our foreto saile,
stood after them that afternoon, severall fleetes were taken, which
came from Lisbona St Oves [sic] laden with salt and one or two
were suncke, that night tacked to the Westward late W. S. W. Vice
Admiral Goodson came aboard, halfe an houres before sunset, told
mee that one of our ships to leeward had handed all her sails but
Mirzon and fired guns upon which three of our ships bore too her,

A *816. m. 1.*
98.

# DECLARATION

OF

*H. 116.*

## Vice-Admiral John Lavvſon;

### Commander in Chief of the Fleet in the narrow Seas, by Authority

OF

# PARLIAMENT:

### With the Commanders of the ſeveral ſhips now with him in the *Downes,* in order to the Removal of the Interruption that is put upon the *Parliament*, the 13th. of *October* laſt.

VVHereas on the ninth inſtant there was a Letter, from the Lord *Fleetwood*, came on board the Ship *James*, directed to the Vice-Admirall, in which he deſired, that he, and thoſe concerned, might give the Freedome of their thoughts touching a Government for the Common-Wealth : In Anſwer to the which was Retorned by the Vice-Admiral, and all the Commanders preſent, That being burthened in Spirit, at the ſence of the unhappy breaches and diſtractions amongſt the good people in the Nation ; it was their humble apprehenſion, that the hopefulleſt wayes and means to make up the breaches and diviſions, was a happy compoſure betwixt the Parliament and Army, and that the Parliament might return to their Truſts, which when the Lord pleaſe to Grant, they could heartily joyn with any in Petitioning, that all words ſpoken, or things done by any perſon whatſoever, concerned in the difference betwixt the Parliament and Army, ſince the 13th of *October* 1659, might be for ever obliterated.

Now foraſmuch as the ſame burthen lyes upon our Spirits ſtill, in the Apprehenſion of the ſad Conſequences that are like to. enſue ; for that We do not hear of any Compoſure, but that the Breach growes wider, thereby eminently threatning the loſſe and utter Ruine of the Cauſe and Intereſt of Chriſt and His People, which for ſo many years hath been ſo conteſted for, and coſt much Blood and Treaſure, both by Sea and Land. We apprehending ſtill that there's no other Viſible means under Heaven to heal the Breaches, and ſecure the Nation from the Common Enemy ; Do Declare, That through the Lords Aſſiſtance, We ſhall in all Chriſtian wayes and means, Endeavour the begetting aright Underſtanding betwixt the *Parliament* and Army, and a happy Compoſure (if it may be) without Blood-ſhed : But if there be yt an Endeavour by Force to hinder the *Parliament* ; That was Interrupted the 13th of *October* (1659;) from returning to the Exerciſe an d Diſcharge of their Truſt ; Who have ſo often been Declared the Supream Authority of theſe Nations, That then We ſhall to the utmoſt of our Power, with our Lives, and all that is Dear to Us, uſe our whole Intereſt for the Removing of that Force, and reſtore Them to their Freedom and Priviledges.

And we do further Declare, (as in the preſence of the Lord) that we have no Aym nor Ends to Advance particular Intereſts, but the Intereſt of Chriſt , and the Good and Weal of all the People of God ; in their Rights, Civil, and Religious ; and of our poor ſuffering Nations in General. And do utterly diſclaim the Intereſt of *Charls Stuart*, and all His Adherents, or the Intereſt of any Single Perſon whatſoever, or Houſe of Lords ; Therefore We doubt not but to find the Concurrence and Aſſiſtance of all the and Upright-harted in the Land. For whoſe ſakes, next to the Cauſe of Chriſt, (God being our Witneſs) We have Engaged.

And We therefore Invite all our Brethren of the Churches, Army, Navy, and Militia of the City of *London* and *Country*, and all that profeſſe Love to God, and His People, to joyn with Us, and give Us their Chriſtian Ayd and Aſſiſtance in the performance of the Premiſes, whereunto We are perſwaded the Lord hath Called Us; leaſt when too late, They and Us have Cauſe to lament the non-Improvement of the Opportunity that God hath put into our Hands, once more to Aſſert the Priviledges of Parliamen, and Liberty of the good People of this Nation.

And that it may appear to all People, That We have no Rancor or Malice againſt the Perſons of any, or thirſt after Blood : We do Reſolve, when the Lord ſhall pleaſe to Reſtore the Parliament to the Exerciſe of their Truſt ; Humbly to Petition Them, according to the Heads following, *Viz.*

1. That Indempnity and Oblivion may be Granted to every Perſon and Perſons, that have acted in the late unhappy differences, betwixt the Parliament and Army, ſince the 13th of *October*, 1659. that ſhall not further perſiſt in Obſtructing their retorn to their Truſt.

2. That the Intereſt of Chriſt may be advanced in Juſtice and Uprighneſſe ; that the Government of the Nations may be ſetled upon theſe Foundations, and that all Laws not agreeable to the Word of God, may be repealed, and all Laws that ſhall be enacted, may be Conſonant to the Word of God.

3. That all people of God, may be preſerved in their Liberty to Worſhip God, as the Lord Jeſus ſhall lead them out, ſo that they make not uſe of this to the prejudice of others. And that Superſtition, and Idolatry, and profaneneſſe, be not Countenanced.

4. That care be taken for the maintenance and Incouragement of pious and learned Godly Miniſters within the Nation, otherwiſe then by the way of Tythes.

5. That all poſſible encouragement may be given to Navigations, and the much decayed Trade of the Nation ; and to that end, as ſoon as poſſible, thoſe great Impoſitions (as Exciſe, and other new Impoſts,) may be taken off, and ſome other way found for defraying the Charge of the Nation.

6. That no man be impreſſed, or forced, to ſerve in any Military Employment either by Land or Sea, otherwiſe than in the defence of his Country; and that the Sea-men might be paid every 10 or 12 Months, at the fartheſt, to Them or their certain Attorney.

7. That a comfortable Proviſion may be made for any man that ſerves at Sea, that ſhall be maimed or diſmembred, and to the Widdow and Orphans of ſuch as ſhall be ſlain, which may be out of the Cheſt, and Prize-mony, which is the price of their Blood.

8. That ſome way and means may be found out for the Employment of the poor of the Nation, that are able ; and ſuch as are impotent and lame may have a Maintenance for their Subſiſtance,

*Signed on board the James in the Downes, the 13th of December, 1659.*

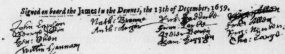

soe wee hoped they would furnish her with what she wanted & stand by her we made saile.

September 16

We see Vice Admll & triumph, to the seaboard of us Hull downe, but were plying towards the shore.

The 17th in the morning I rec~ed a lett[r]. from ye Genll. implying his being without, and plying upp and that when wee see him, wee should weigh & goe to him the same day, see him, soe weighted, gott into Alborough Bay, all of us anchored.

The 19th weighed plyed towards the Swine, the winde Southerly.

The 20th Arrived at the Bouy of the Ouse Edge.

## Letters regarding John Lawson in *The Life of Edward Earl of Clarendon*

*The life of Edward Earl of Clarendon, Lord High Chancellor of England and Chancellor of the University of Oxford in which is included his history of the grand rebellion written by himself,* Vol. 3, (Oxford: Clarendon Press, 1827), pp.89-95.

XLVI

MR SAMBORNE TO THE LORD CHANCELLOR HYDE.

[From the Bodleian Library. *Orig.*]

9 March.

MONTAGUE is to go to sea with 23 shipps, which bee ready about 10 dayes hence. Lawson endevours to make a mutiny among the seamen, but there is noe great danger of any thing hee can doe. By the next I will send you a list of the shipps and their commanders, which will bee all moderate men, but there will be noe gaining any of them without Montague, who I believe will be honest.

The Parliaments having in a manner declared for the King by ordering the printing of the Covenant, and setting it upp in all churches and in the houses, has much startled the armyes, as well as Gl. Monks as the other. Overton, in Hull has declared against the present power; soe has some about Chester and North Wales. And yesterday Gl. Monk's officers brought to him a remonstrance against a single person. They were high on both sides, but the Genlls. Stout and discreete behaviour has quelled them for the present; yet tis feared wee shall have some combustions, w[hi]ch makes well for the King; for some of the chief Presbyterians exprest great bitternesse against the Kings party, especially against his councell, and would insist upon rigid conditions with the King; but now their feare of the army makes them more mild. Let not the King lose any time in his preparations, at all events. It is all over the towne here that the King is gone into France, which I cannot believe. I heare also the Irish have sent to the King. If they bee reasonable, the Kind would doe well to agree with them a part from these, and so devide them as much as he can. Lockhart has received 4 thousand pounds, & is to have 6 more, and then to returne to Dunkirke. His instructions I know not.

Endorsed by L[or]d Chr Hyde – '"Mr Samborne, March 9th 1660"'.

XLVII.

TO THE LORD CHANCELLOR HYDE

[From the Bodleian Library. *Orig.*] The name of the writer of this letter is not known.

London, March 16. 1660.

This afternoon the Parliament dissolved; the act for the militia in all countys being first printed 7 published. Monke, being put upon by some humoursome men, writt a letter to the house a little before they rose, to stopp the publishing of the sayd act: but the letter was layd aside, and nothing done upon it. In a few dayes we shall see how the game will foe. If the discontented part of the officers can compass their ends, we shall yet be in blood for a time, though it is hardly possible they doe any thing to that purpose, unlesse it be to give the King an opportunity of com~ing in freely without any conditions, while they are struggling. However, they have a declaration ready, if they can get Monck to sett his hand to it, against the King and that line, or a House of Lords.

Montague goes to the sea the beginning of the next weeke. Lawson is in the Downes, & carrys faire to him till he have an opportunity to shew his teeth. Montague has quite left Thurloe, St John, & all that cabal, & cleaves to his father in law, Crew, Pierpoint, and the rest, for the King upon conditions. He told me yesterday an intimate friend of his & mine, yt [that] he was now for the settlement of the King, though he knew he must be the sufferer by it. Thurloe is simper idem: but I hope his hornes will never grow so long as formerly to push the Kings friends. St John is a great pike that's loath to be beaten into the next. He & Thurlow have been labouring of late to blow up the sectarys and discontented officers, but I hope it will come to nothing. Noe letters from Ireland these last two posts: Jones, Coote, and Broughill, are the chief actors there. Soe farr as we understand they are all there disposed for the King.
Endorsed by L[or]d Chr Hyde – '"1660, March 16"'.

XLVIII.
Mr. Samborne to the Lord Chancellor Hyde.
[From the Bodleian Library. *Orig.*]
I have yours of the 19th, and know you to be soe full of businesse, that I expect noe more then to know myne are received, unlesse you

have something to command mee. Since my last Lawson has made his submission, where upon hee and all his captaines, save one, are continued in employment. Montague is gone downe to the fleete to give orders, but returnes again, for most of the shipps will not yet be ready these 8 or ten dayes. I send you a list of the shipps and their commanders; those marked with crosses are Annabaptists; few of them were formerly better than gunners and ship carpenters; men that have noe sence of honour or conscience, that will change with the winde, and keepe to of the strongest side as the most profitable.

You at that distance may well thinke our proceedings heere to be riddles, since wee upon the place doe the like. I shall tell you my sence of them. Those contradictions are bones cast among them by a discontented party in the house, as that concerning Hampton Court, w[hi]ch if granted would cause jelosy, if denyed would disobleege Monke. I now begin to have a better opinion of Monke, for he is noe foole, and he must now doe the King's business, or he had undone his owne. The ill temper of his army may well excuse his walking hitherto in the darke.

Mr Hollis is lately come to towne and sitts in the house. The Rump has the greatest part of both armys on their side, and bragg that they will doe greate matters Suddenly. The Genll. in the mean time labours to prevent the disorders threatned by his own army. This day tis expected the house shall dissolve. I wish the King could land in any part of with 3 or 4 thousand men' the reputation of it would suddenly doe his business without a blow. Coll Tuke I heare is maliciously diligent here to prejudice L[or]d Ormond, your Lo[rdshi]p, and L[or]d Bristoll, in the opinions of every body. I beseech you cause my patent to be past before the King goes thence.

Endorsed by L[or]d Chr. Hyde – '"Mr Samborne, March 16th 1660."

XLIX.

TO THE LORD CHANCELOR HYDE (the name of the writer of this letter is unknown).]

[From the Bodleian Library. *Orig.*[

MONTAGUE is this morning gone for the Downes. Lawson is at Gravesend expecting orders, and carryes faire, but in truth hopes the Sectarys may get up againe, & then he is sure to be one, if he can but make a party. There is in the army, here and in the countreys, a very discontented party, who will probably resist in blood, before the King can come in; and though this Councell of State have prohibited their meetings, ye they find wayes of a correspondence. Whaly is a great stickler against the King, and Goff another; but the su~me of all of this is, if the Kings friends be the strongest party in the next Parliament, he surely wins the day, and the opposers will be too weak. God Almighty grant that we may see that day. Thurloe and St Johns begin to be very sick of this already, and there has been caballing of late to sett up Monke or Richard.

Letters from Ireland speake but darkely. Their Convention still sits: they lately sent to expresses to signify their adhering to the late declaration of the officers there: they likewise sent a list of officers for Ireland' but its thought the Councell of State will alter it, and desire their Convention to dissolve. Coote, Jones, Broughill and Clotworthy are the main men and their designe is to bring Ireland into the same posture as before 49. Yesterday the writs were proclaimed for a Parliament, upon w[hi]ch all depends. This Councell of State has noe other designe then to secure all things till the next Parliament, and to help us back the Parlmt. with the Presbiterians, who will I feare lay very hard upon the King, as to conditions, being a cinical generation. Old Noll's Wife sends often for Thurloe. She would faine see Dick up agaiine.

I forgot to tell you in my last, that Thurloe told Gibs lately, that if the King married Manchini, it would be the best news he ever heard in his life; for 9said he) that would be the only meanes to unite all partys against the King. Thurlow was first Sr Gamalaell Capell's butlers man, then Sr Wm Massams clearke, then St John's man; and when St Johns had beaten something into him with trenchers, w[hi]ch he often threw at his head, he then gott him first Clearke, and then Secretary to the old Councell of State, where Noll met with him, and gave him the key of his jugglers box. I can assure you that in all the series of old Noll's projects, when ever there was the least difficulty and danger, St Johns was his constant Achitophell, and either was visited by, or visited Thurloe or him every night; sometimes till past midnight: and yet he pretends the contrary, and would be accounted innocent; but he is the most deadly enemy the King has in England. What Monk is, God knows. He comes once a day into the Councell of State. Time will discover whether he be a wise man or a foole. He lately wish'd his right hand might rott off if he were reconcilable to the King. Endorsed by L[or]d Chr. Hyde – '"1660 March 23d"'.


L

MAJOR WOOD TO THE LORD CHANCELLOR HYDE.
[From the Bodleian Library. *Orig.*
London, March 30
Sr
Two dayes since I writt you by Massy's servant, and this is to the same purpose. Upon the 27th pr[e]sent, I was tould from a sure

hand, that this day fortnight, L[or]d Mordant sent Mr Rumball to the King to do his best to destroy you. He is to engage you with keeping intelligence with Thurloe, and, to make it good, hath carried two men along with him, to justify their seeing of several of your letters to him; allso that you have for many yeares receive a pention of 4000 pounds per year. Mr Corrant and Mr Scot, I heare, are upon the same imployment. Pray God pr[e]serve you from this horrid conspiracy. I must desire you to conceale from whom you rec[eive]d this accompt, least I loose my intelligence hereafter, & thereby made less able to serve you. I much want a good addresses. L[or]d Mordant helpes me not as formerly. Pray let me have y[ou]r directions how in the above sayd affaire I may best serve you, whoe am desirous of noething more then in manyfesting myselfe to be.

Sr. y[ou]r most faythfull & humble servant. 940.925.

## Extract from An Account of Tangier

From Cholmley, Hugh, *An Account of Tangier. By Sir Hugh Cholmley, Bart. With some account of himself and his journey through France and Spain to that place, Where he was engaged in building the mole in the time of King Charles the Second; and a Journal of the Work carrying on. And Also Some of his Speeches in Parliament. Taken from Manuscripts now in the Possession of Nathaniel Cholmley of Whitby and Howsham, in the County of York, Esquire, 1787.* Gale ECCO Edition.

Pages 39-40

The Continuation of the Story of Tangier, under the Command of the Earl of Peterburg, [sic] until the Arrival of the Earl of Tiviot.

So many brave men, unused to an idle war, could not keep themselves within the walls of Tangier; but, passing about the fields in lesser parties, had several encounters with the Moor, parting still with little loss and equal revenge: the Governor sometimes marched with greater numbers farther into the country, but always made a false retreat, where he himself was to head the party. Gayland at this time seemed so well inclined to peace, that he advised our countrymen might not pass so freely into his territories. However, was continued the foresaid skirmishing war, without any more considerable loss at any one time than what befell one Baker, who was cut off with about five or six others, that ventured with him to a little hill, which was then too far from relief though within the present lines, and now commonly called Baker's Folly. But, upon the third of May following, happened a great disaster; for the Moors appearing not far from the walls of the place, several of the garrison to the number of about five hundred men, led by one Lieut. Col. Fines, ran in a confused manner to the attack, thinking to fall in upon the enemy with the but-end of the musket, but they were themselves destroyed by much greater numbers, placed on purpose in ambush under the shelter of some vallies, that lie commodious for that surprising kind of war. This misfortune added a new grief to the sufferings of the place, and brought so much fear upon the garrison, as to keep the gates almost continually shut, emboldening the Moors by their nearer appearing, even unto the carrying cattle from under the very walls and guns of the town. The Earl of Peterburg found his presence in England was of absolute necessity, to inform his Majesty rightly of all that passed, and to supply such defects as were not foreseen at first, or could not then be remedied. Leaving the command to Col. Fitzgerald, Lieutenant-governor, he appeared at Court about the middle of summer, where he made a very short stay; and though he could not in that time have those supplies he desired, yet was he not from this, and the sense of the former inconveniencies, kept from a second journey, which he undertook in October following: in which his resolution was the more commendable, as his quality and his fortune were removed from the confinement and the sufferings at that time indispensable with the government of that place; but it being known, that his Excellency, contented with the honour of conducting first his Majesty's troops into Africa, was willing enough to leave the command to another; and by the surrender of Dunkirk the Lord Rutterford wanting at the same time employment, his Majesty was pleased to honour him both with the government of Tangier and the Earldom of Tiviot, so that his Excellency repaired to his charge in May, one thousand six hundred sixty-three; and my Lord Peterburg left the place the beginning of June that followed.

Pages 63-69

The Death of the Earl of Tiviot, and coming of the Lord Ballafys to Tangier.

The Earl of Tiviot found the common soldiers in Tangier much dejected, from the common cause of bad accidents that had happened in the loss of their countrymen: and such was the fear they harboured of the Moor, as to keep the gates almost continually shut, and few there were greatly willing to hazard themselves out of the city walls; but his Excellency presently set them open, and began to build a small and near redoubt, more especially to embolden the men, which he effected in a few days, notwithstanding the opposition of the enemy that appeared continually in lesser parties; and, besides this, cast up several lines and ditches, which he afterwards maintained, and laid the foundation of a considerable redoubt, called Fort Catherine, situate upon an eminence not above three hundred yards from Catherine Port, the gate that passes into the country; and this he kept against all the power of Gayland's army, that came to attack it about the ninth of June, in the year one thousand six hundred sixty-three, although there was nothing of this fort finished, farther than the out-walls, carried up for about ten feet in height; but in this attack Gayland lost so considerable a number of men, and had the horse of his army so much galled by those triangular pointed irons, called Crow's feet, with which my Lord had every where strewed the fields, that Gayland became so well inclined to peace, as presently to conclude a truce for six months, which gave his Excellency so much leisure as to pass into England, September following, where he obtained such necessary supplies, and regular settlement of affairs, as were before wanting; Col. Fitzgerald, in my Lord's absence, discharging the trust that was reposed in him as Lieutenant-governor of the place. About the end of August this year, were laid the first foundations of the Mole; the stones being brought in some sailing-boats that were about ten tons in burden, though framed in England, had been above three months setting together on the place, because of its being destitute of all kind of conveniencies necessary for an expeditious preparation; and this made it requisite to build places for all sorts of stores, warehouses, and work-shops, as well as quarters for the men and horses; but from hence followed so necessary a delay, that the larger engines of cranes in boats were many months in putting together and framing. However the principal officers of the garrison, they were all destroyed by Gayland's army, which accidentally (as conjectured) happened to lodge themselves in that place, but a few hours before their coming; and this is believed, because most certainly in the night my Lord caused several spies to pass up and down those woods; who returned with this assurance, "That they neither heard noise, nor made any other discovery that might denote an enemy's being there." Besides the foresaid party, which was all foot, the General had ordered about one hundred horse, as a guard unto the rear; but these, upon the appearance of far greater numbers, which they could not resist, retreated safe within the lines, by the conduct of Sir Tobias Bridges, excepting about six of them that pricked their horses with more heat towards the point of land, where was places the rear of my Lord Tiviot's party; and these few horse were so happy in their assistance, as from the little check they put upon the enemy, to make more easy the escape of near a hundred of our countrymen; and from hence some conclude, had the whole body of horse followed to the same point of land, many more of the English had saved themselves; but as this is said to have been against the instructions of the General, so it is certain, they could have contributed nothing to the security of his own person, or those that were with him, because they were engaged far in the wood, and in passages that are not accessible by horses. Some say the occasion of this unhappy march into the Moor's country was from a defect of lime and other materials, which put a stop to the fortifications; and that the General, wanting employment; pitched upon this, as one that hated to have the soldier idle; others think it was intended to supply the want of fuel, by cutting down those woods, as also to disappoint the enemy at the same time, by thus clearing the places of their usual ambush: some say my Lord designed this expedition to take away the superstitious fear which our men had conceived, because of the anniversary day that had been formerly fatal, by the destruction of considerable numbers of our men. It is unhappy that we have nothing of better reason left to justify so unsuccessful a proceeding; the causes given not being of weight to excuse the seeming precipitation of the action, which was unfortunate to the glory of so great a man, that freed Tangier from being a perfect prison, and to whom she owes at this day all the refreshment of the adjoining fields; that restored the courage of the soldier, that was become drooping enough; and in a few months made them as great a dread unto the Moor as not long before these had been a terror to themselves. But the place had, in the General's death, a loss almost ireparable; considering he was a man of indefatigable industry and labour, and had by his successful proceedings got a mighty esteem and reputation in the country; and that in great truth he was a great Captain, even among the greatest of the age in which he lived; it may well be presumed, had his life been spared a few years longer, Tangier would not at this day have wanted a circumference of land perfectly secured, and in sufficiency at least to the being of the place, and would have been besides in great measure free from the strokes and wounds which called afterwards in question, the very keeping of the place, from arguments and reasons that were only heated because of its misfortunes. Sir Tobias Bridges was chosen, after my Lord's loss, to the chief command, and kept the possession of all the outworks, which the Moors (notwithstanding their success) had not so much as courage to attempt; but presently after the news of what had happened reached England, Col. Fitzgerald, being then there, was dispatched to his charge with money and recruits necessary; who employed his time in perfecting the works that were not finished, and in making others that were designed; in repairing the fountains and quarters, and doing other works that were for the public good of the place; his power continuing but a few months, because of my Lord Bellafys's arrival the following April, one thousand six hundred sixty-five, who commanded all under the same character that had been given to the preceding Governor of that place.

## Will of Vice-Admiral Sir John Lawson
PCC 1665, TNA: PROB 11/317.

In the Name of God Amen The desires and will of Sr John Lawson this Nyneteenth of Aprill One Thousand Six Hundred Sixty Five When the Almighty shall call for my immortall Soule out of this Earthly Tabernacle ys trust through the Lords free grace and mercy in Jesus Christ hee will receive my soule unto the eternall armes of his love to live with him and Jesus Christ for evermore unto whom I bequeath it Amen, (If it fall soe out that with conveniency it may be done) I desire my body may be laid by my Children in the great Isle of Dunstans Church in the East without any great noyse But if God in his Providence soe order it That there be not convenency for it his will be done., My will is as to my outward estate That my Deare wife Isabell Lawson enjoy my house in Alresford in Essex called the warren house And the out houses with All the Farme and land of myne thereunto belonging As alsoe all my proffitts of the Ballast Key with all the Advantages I have dureing her naturall life And that after her decease the aforesaid house and Land to be equally devided to my Two daughters Elizabeth Lawson and Anna Lawson and their heires for ever My Will is That my wife Isabella Lawson enjoy dureing her naturall life my house att Scarbrough in Yorkshire and Three closes that belongs to mee in that parish And after her decease To be equally devided to my Two Daughters Elizabeth and Anna and their heires for ever: Whereas the Kings Majesty hath beene pleased Gratously to settle upon mee a Pention of Five hundredth pounds per Annum during my naturall life. And was Gratiously pleased to declare to the Earle of Southampton Lord High Treasuror of England aboute a moneth agoe That if God take mee away in his Majesties Service That the aforesaid Pention of Five hundredth Pounds per Annum should be setled upon One of my Daughters During her naturall life my humble desire is That the said Sum of Five hundredth pounds may be equally devided And the one moiety might be setled upon my daughter Elizabeth Lawson And the Other moiety might be setled upon my daughter Anna Lawson During their naturall lives But if the Kings Majesty shall settle the whole upon one of them I desire it may be upon my daughter Anna And that then shee give unto her Sister Elizabeth Satisfaction for the vallue of the moiety But I hope it will not be denyed to be setled upon them both equally I intreate Sr Phillip Warwicks care and kindnesse in this business I give out of my personall Estate one hundredth pounds to the poore of Scarbrough in Yorkshire the place of my Nativity To be paid unto Bayliffs and Co~mon Counsells hands for the tyme being To be by them put out att Interest and never to be Lessened nor diverted otherwayes And that the Interest money be given to the poore of the towne every yeare some few dayes before the Feast of the Nativity of our blessed Saviour Jesus Christ And that Security be taken of the Bayliffs and Co~mon Councell for that end according to Law by the Overseers of this my will. I give to the Two William Lawsons now on board the Royall Oake Five pounds a peece And to John Salmon Five pounds I give to my

Daughter Isabella Norton for her First Sonne Or for want of Sonne to her First Daughter a Gold Chayne That was Given mee in the Dutch Warre in the yeare One Thousand Six Hundred and Fifty Three if God give her noe Child to dispose as shee please I give unto my daughter Isabella Norton Two of my best silver dishes And Six Silver Plates. I give to my Sonne Daniell Norton All my Gunns Pystolls Scimiters and Swords on board not otherwise disposed by name in this my will afterward I give unto my Cosen John Lawson Grocer of London a blacke new velvet Coate And my Flea bitten Gelding att home I give unto my Cosen Samuell Lawson Merchant a Long Gunn Mr Henry Crane gave me and my best silver hilted Rapier I give unto my daughter Elizabeth Lawson A Gold chayne that was given mee in Portugal in the yeare One Thousand Six Hundred and Sixty Three for her eldest sonne or eldest daughter if noe sonne If God give her noe Child to dispose as shee please I give unto my Two daughters Elizabeth and Anna All the rest of my Gold or Silver Plate and all my moneys (debts and Legacies being First paid All my Shipping And all my personall Estate to be equally divided betwixt them And what consideracon Sr Hugh Cholmeley shall allow for the valleu of the Engines Boates and all materialls for the Mole of Tanger that is in being above and beyond Two Thousand pounds which was the Sum~e allowed us to buy Engines withal. I give unto Peter Greene All my weareing woollen Apparell on Board. I desire my wife may have the Tuition of my Two Daughters Elizabeth and Anna while Shee lives a Widdow But if she marry againe Then I desire and my Will is That my Personall Estate and Pention or Pentions be improved for the good of my Two Daughters Elizabeth and Anna there being paid to my wife dureing her life Annually out of the Pention or Pensions one hundred pounds over and above the Revenue of the houses and the Land ^If the Kings Majestie be gratiously pleased to give my Wife and Children any thing If the Overseers of this my will to see his Majesties Pleasure fulfilled I make and constitute my wife Sole Executor of this my Will I make and constitute my Cosen John Lawson Cittizen and Grocer of London liveing in Lyme Streete and Samuel Lawson his Sonne Merchant Overseers of this my Will.

Jo: Lawson.

Witnessed by Jerom Collins. Pet: Greene.

Probate:... London vicesimo quinto Septembris 1665

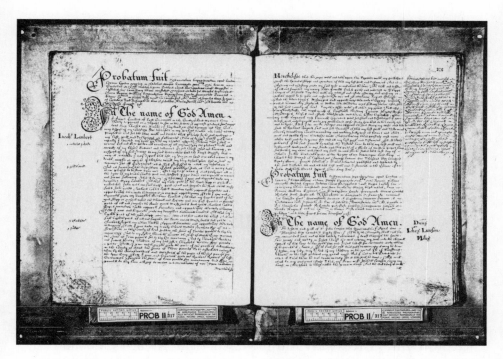

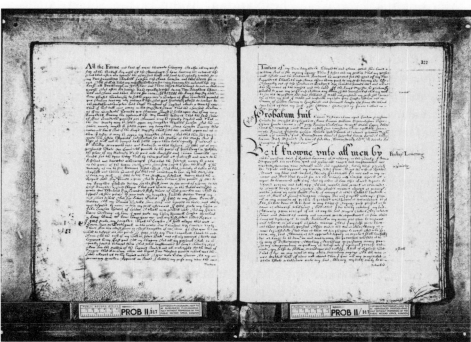

# SOURCES AND BIBLIOGRAPHY

The majority of sources used are held at the Bodleian Library in Oxford, the Borthwick Institute in York, British Library, Essex Record Office, Greenwich Naval Museum and Archives, London Metropolitan Archives, The National Archives, the Society of Genealogists and Yorkshire Archives. Copies of broadsheets and newspapers were accessed via Gale Gengage Learning and are held at the British Library unless otherwise specified.

Some material was accessed online via the genealogical websites Ancestry, British History Online, FamilySearch Findmypast and The Genealogist, as well as via Academia, the British Library, Gale, Gengage Learning, googlebooks, Internet Archives, Project Gutenberg and the Society of Genealogists.

## Abbreviations

| | |
|---|---|
| BHO | British History Online |
| BL | British Library |
| Bodl. | Bodleian Library, Oxford |
| BTs | Bishops' Transcripts |
| ClarCSP | Clarendon Calendar of State Papers |
| CSPD | Calendar of State Papers Domestic |
| CSPV | Calendar of State Papers Relating to English Affairs in Venice |

| ER Archives | East Riding Archives |
|---|---|
| ERO | Essex Record Office |
| LMA | London Metropolitan Archives |
| NYRO | North Yorkshire Record Office |
| ODBN | Oxford Dictionary of National Biography |
| PCC | Prerogative Court of Canterbury |
| PCY | Prerogative Court of York |
| PRs | Parish Registers |
| SoG | Society of Genealogists |
| SP | State Papers |
| TNA | The National Archives |

## MANUSCRIPT SOURCES, INDEXES AND TRANSCRIPTS

*Bodleian Library, Oxford*

Montagu, Edward, *Correspondence, Papers of Edward Montagu, 1st Earl of Sandwich*. Bodleian Library MSS Carte 31, fols. 552, 557; Carte 47, fols. 416; Carte 71; Carte 72; Carte 73, fols. 347, 349, 353, 355, 491, 565, 567, 569, 572, 604; Carte 75, fols. 38, 40, 42, 48-50, 52, 54-56, 71-72, 86, 110, 145-146, 273; Carte 222, fols. 8-9, 68-69.

*British Library*

A plan or bird's-eye view of Algiers; drawn on parchment about 1661... presented to His R.H (the Duke of York, afterwards James II.), by Sir John Lawson, BL King George III's Topographical Collection, K.Top.117.73.b

Articles of Peace between ... Charles II ... King of Great Britain ... and the most excellent Signors, Mahomet Bashaw, the Duan ... of Tunis, Hagge Mustapha Dei, Morat Bei, and the rest of the souldiers in the Kingdom of Tunis, concluded by Sir John Lawson ... Fifth of October 1662. B.J.6.(6).

Colonel Henry Norwood, Esquire of the Body to Charles II., Treasurer to the Colony of Virginia, Lieutenant-Governor of Tangier, and Commander in Chief of the English Forces in Africa: Correspondence and papers... Sloane MS 3509: 1660-1680, BL, f.15.

*Contract for building a mole at Tangier:* 1662, in Colonel Henry Norwood, Esquire of the Body to Charles II., Treasurer to the Colony of Virginia, Lieutenant-Governor of Tangier, and Commander in Chief of the English Forces in Africa: Correspondence and papers... BL Sloane MS 3509: 1660-1680, f.18.

*Dispatch of Capt. William Fenner to the Lord High Admiral...* Add MS 37425, f.56.

Haselrigg, Sir Arthur, *The advance of Sir Arthur Hasilrigg, from the garrison of Portsmouth, toward the city of London: and his letter to the Lord Mayor, aldermen, and Commoun Council. Also, the number both of horse and foot; the names of the regiments revolted from the Army; together with the Isle of Wight and most of the castles thereabouts. Likewise, the answer agreed upon by the Lord Mayor, aldermen, and Common Council at Guild-Hall yesterday, and the names of the commissioners, sent to Sir Arthur Hasilrigg, and Vice-Admiral Lawson, to communicate the sense of the city* (London: George Horton, 1659).

Lawson, John, *A declaration of Vice-Admiral John Lawson, commander in chief of the fleet in the narrow seas by authority of parliament, with the commanders of the several ships now with him in the Downes, in order to the removal of the interruption that is now put upon the Parliaments the 13th of October last* (London: 13 Dec. 1659).

Lawson, John, *A Narrative of the Proceedings of the Fleet, giving an Account of what hath passed since their arrival at Gravesend; between divers hon. Members of parliament and vice admiral Lawson etc. 22 Dec. 1659.* (London: 22 Dec. 1659).

Lawson, John, *Copy journal covering service aboard HMS Fairfax and HMS George during the First Dutch War,* 1652-53, BL RP 1071/2, original at Lilly Library, Bloomington, Indiana, USA.

Lawson, John, Letters, Lord Fleetwood to Vice-Admiral Lawson: 1659, in Add MS 15857, f.236.

Lawson, John, *Two letters from Vice-Admiral John Lawson and the commanders of the fleet to the Lord Mayor, Aldermen and Common-councilmen of the city of London, dated the 13th of*

*December, 1659 from the Downes: the other the 21 instant from Gravesend* (London, 13 and 21 December 1659).

Lawson, Sir, John, Agustus van Holsteyn: Journal of voyage to Tripoli: 1675-1676, includes Treaty concluded by, between England and Tripoli: 1662, Sloane MS 2755, f.44b.

Letters to Captain Baynes, 1648-55, British Library Manuscript Collection, Add MSS 21417-23.

*Miscellaneous* orders, accounts, petitions, and correspondence of Captain Adam Baynes... 1645-1689. John Lawson, Captain in the Army, and afterwards Vice-Admiral: Petitions: 1648, 1649, 1652. Add MS 21427. f.70.

*Original* papers relative to the navy office; 1644-1699; consisting of orders of the navy commissioners, letters of naval officers, reports, petitions, etc. ; and containing autographs of the following persons; viz .,... Admiral John Lawson; 9 Oct. 1659, Add MS 18986, f.317

Papers relating to naval affairs; 1643-1677: John Lawson, Captain in the Army, and afterwards Vice-Admiral. Add MS 22546, f. 76.

*Petitions* addressed to Charles II., chiefly after the Restoration, with orders thereon and reports of referees; 1649-1675... John Lawson, Captain in the Army, and afterwards Vice-Admiral: Petitions: 1648, 1649, 1652. Egerton MS 2549 f.76.

Richard Skeffington 4th Bart., of Fisherwick to his cousin Sir E. Dering; Coventry, Vol. II, 1640-1664, Stowe MS 744, f.88.

Rugge, Thomas, *Mercurius Politicus redivivus: 1659-1672. Charles II of England: Mercurius politicus redivivus, or a collection of occurrences, by T. Rugge.* Vols.1-2. Add MS 10116-10117.

Vice-Admiral Sir John Lawson: Autograph signature: circ. 1654. Sloane MS 645, f. 46.

*East Sussex Record Office*

Lawson, John, Letter 19 March 1659-60, *Aboard the James at Gravesend.* John Lawson to the Mayor, Aldermen and Common Council of Rye. RYE/47/161/8.

*Essex Record Office*

1861 hand-coloured copy of 1810 copy of survey of the parish and manor of Alresford by William Braiser, 1730, ERO: C306 Box 1.

A Particular of Alresford Lodge, circa 1710, in Sperling Family of Dynes Hall Deeds, 1698-1715, ERO: D/DGd E38.

Abstract of title of lands called Little Pannels alias Pinnels, copyhold of Manor of Alresford, 1748-1777, ERO: D/DEI T2/3.

Alresford alias Easthall Manorial Court Rolls, 1624-1741, ERO: D/DEt MM4 & D/DJo MJ; M10.

Alresford, Essex Parish Registers.

Calendars of Essex Quarter Sessions and Assize Records. ERO.

Copies of documents in support of title to the Manor Alresford and Fishery, 1085-1877, ERO: T/P 46/1.

Deeds relating to Town House and Lands in Wanstead, Essex inc. Conveyances, Mortgages, Final Concords and Assignment of Judgement and Power of Attorney, 1663-1711, in: Miscellaneous Records; Records of William Bullock of Shelley, Clerk of the Peace, ERO: D/DGn 182-222.

Essex Wills Beneficiaries Index 1505-1916. Essex Family History Society.

Johannes Blaeu's Map of Essex, 1645. Reproduction by Essex Record Office.

Sperling Family of Dynes Hall Deeds of messuage called Gylotts, 1634-1716, ERO: D/DGd T47.

Sperling Family of Dynes Hall Deeds, 1698-1715, ERO: D/DGd E38.

Will (1698 copy) of John Lawson, 1665, in Sperling Family of Dynes Hall Deeds, 1698-1715. D/DGd E38.

Woodford, Essex Parish Registers.

*Hampshire Archives*
Papers in suit in Chancery: Richard Norton of Southwick v Isabella Norton (nee Lawson) widow of Daniel, son and heir of Richard Norton, concerning agreement as to management of estates to descent to Richard Norton (grandson) upon death of Richard Norton and jointure of £800 of Isabella Norton, 1668, Hampshire Archives and Local Studies, SM50/388-390.

The Visitation of Hampshire 1686 (Harleian Society, 1991).

*Lincolnshire Archives*
Grant of Annuity of £250p.a., Charles 2 to Elizabeth, dau. of late Sir John Lawson, kt, 28 August 1665. Lincolnshire Archives 1-Dixon/1/E/93

*London Metropolitan Archives and Guildhall Library (and online via Ancestry and Findmypast)*
Indexes and Transcripts to LMA London Parish Registers at Ancestry.

London Livery Company Apprenticeship Indexes, 1442-1850. Transcript by Cliff Webb of records at Guildhall Library via Findmypast.

St Dunstan in the East, London Parish Registers.

St Helens, Bishopgate, London Parish Registers.

*National Maritime Museum: The Caird Library Manuscripts Section Greenwich*
Lawson, Sir John (d 1665) Knight Admiral, Letters, 1663-1664, AGC/L/1-18.

Copy of letter from James, Duke of York arranging for stores to be issued to the fleet under the Earl of Sandwich and Sir John Lawson. Also, fragments of receipts of the Ordnance Store keepers, 1661, AGC/7/1.

Gilbert, Thomas. Purser's bond for £500, signed John Lawson, Geo Penn, 11 Feb 1657, ADL/Q/31.

Lawson, John, *A declaration of Vice Admiral John Lawson, commander in chief of the fleet in the narrow seas ... to which is added a letter from the Vice-Admiral to the Lord Fleetwood* (London: 1659), 355.49"1642/1659"(42):0941 12630-1001 Rare Book

*Oxford University, Worcester College Archives*
Vane, Sir Henry, miscellaneous correspondence, 1649-59. HMC[51] Leybourne-Popham MSS.

*Society of Genealogists, London*
Boyd's Marriage Indexes, 1538-1840.
Pedigree collection.
Burke's Peerage.

*The National Archives*
Chancery Court Records. Lawson v Lawson, 1673-1710: TNA
C6/445/65; C5/514/49; C5/616/95; C7/576/88; C10/198/34;
C22/670/52; 671/35.
State Papers Domestic (various)

*Yorkshire Archives at North Allerton and Beverley*
Ashcroft, M. Y., Ed., *Scarborough Records 1600-1640
A Calendar*, North Yorkshire County Record Office Publications
No. 47, 1991.
   Ashcroft, M. Y., Ed., *Scarborough Records 1641-1660
A Calendar*, North Yorkshire County Record Office Publications
No. 49, 1991.
   Letter Book of Sir Hugh Cholmley, 1664-66. NYRO: Cholmley
MSS ZCG/V1/1/1, pp.96-100, 110-118, 190-197, 286.
   Lythe Yorkshire Parish Registers and Bishops' Transcripts,
NYRO and online via Ancestry, FamilySearch and Findmypast.
   Scarborough Churchwardens' Papers, 1607-98, ER Archives, PE
165/241.
   Scarborough Society of Shipowners, Masters and Mariners,
NYRO, DC/SCB.
   Scarborough, Yorkshire Bishops' Transcripts and Parish
Registers. NYRO and online via Ancestry, FamilySearch and
Findmypast.
   Whitby, Yorkshire Parish Registers. YRO.

# PROBATE RECORDS
Indexes to Prerogative Court of Canterbury, Prerogative Court of
York and Local Church Courts in Essex, London and Yorkshire:
Lawson 1580-1800.
   Indexes to Prerogative Court of Canterbury, Prerogative Court
of York and Local Church Courts in Yorkshire: All Jefferson in
Lythe Scarborough and Whitby 1610-1750.

*Selective Wills and Administrations*
Will (1698 copy) of PCC Will of John Lawson of Alresford, Essex,
1665, in ERO: Sperling Family of Dynes Hall Deeds, 1698-1715,
ERO: D/DGd E38.

Will of Anne Kinaston of Alresford, Spinster, 1721, Commissary of Bishop of London, ERO: D/ABW 84/1/107.

Will of Dame Anna St. George of Woodford, Essex, PCC 1720. TNA PROB/11/579.

Will of Dame Isabella Chicheley, Widow of Saint Giles in the Fields, Middlesex, PCC 1710. TNA: PROB 11/516/296.

Will of Elizabeth Kinaston, Widow of Oatley, Shropshire, PCC 1704. TNA: PROB 11/474/194.

Will of Elizabeth Lawson of Bocking, widow. Archbishop of Canterbury: Peculiar of Deanery of Bocking, 1700. ERO: D/APbW 2/22.

Will of Jane Lawson of Scarborough, YPC 1694. Borthwick.

Will of John Lawson of Braintree, Sherman, Commissary of Bishop of London, 1603. ERO: D/ABW/24/52.

Will of John Lawson, Citizen and Grocer of London Peculiar Court of the Dean and Chapter of St. Paul 1683. LMA: MS 9052/24, number 46.

Will of Joseph Lawson of Bocking, carpenter. Archbishop of Canterbury: Peculiar of Deanery of Bocking, 1686. ERO: D/APbW 1/235.

Will of Martha Lawson of Wanstead, widow, Archdeaconry of Essex, 1687. ERO: D/AEW 27/252.

Will of Nicholas Lawson of Raistrop, PCC 1657, TNA: PROB 11/272.

Will of Nicholas Lawson, citizen and grocer of London, PCC 1656. TNA: PROB 11/256/277.

Will of Samuel Lawson, Merchant in the good Ship or Vessel called the African of London, PCC 1693. TNA: PROB 11/414/307.

Will of Sir John Chicheley of Saint Giles in the Fields, Middlesex, PCC 1708. TNA: PROB 11/501/376.

Will of Sir Thomas St. George, Knight of the Garter Principal King of Arms, 1703. TNA PROB 11/469/168.

Will of Vice-Admiral Sir John Lawson, PCC 1665, TNA: PROB 11/317.

Will of William Lawson of Braintree, freeman of the Company of Skinners of London, Commissary of Bishop of London, 1672, ERO: D/ABW 66/350.

Will Sage Lawson, Scarborough, PCY 20 Jun 1666, fol.543, Dickering. Borthwick.

Will William Jefferson, Lythe, Yorkshire, PCY 1642-3, page 97. Borthwick.

Will: 1698 copy of PCC Will of John Lawson of Alresford, Essex, 1665.

## OTHER

LAWSON, Sir John. CROMWELL, Oliver. Autograph letter signed from Vice-Admiral Sir John Lawson, on board his ship 'Fairfax', to Cromwell, reporting on the disposition of Parliament's ships and in particular the dispatch of the 'Bristol' to Jersey and the 'Maidstone' to Guernsey, 15 June 1654. Text courtesy of Jarndyce Antiquarian Booksellers, London Albemarle, George Monck, Duke of, *A Letter of advice to his excellencie the Lord General Monck* (1660).

## PRINTED PRIMARY SOURCES, INCLUDING BROADSHEETS AND NEWSHEETS

*A Collection of the State Papers of John Thurloe.* (London: Fletcher Gyles, 1742). British History Online.

Anon, *A true narrative of the cause and manner of the dissolution of the late Parliament, upon the 12. of Decemb. 1653. By a member of the House, then present at that transaction* (London: 1653). William Andrews Clark Memorial Library, University of California, Los Angeles, California.

Anon, *Another declaration wherein is rendred a further account of the just grouunds [sic] and reasons of the dissolving the Parliament by the Lord Generall and his Council of Officers* (London: Printed for T. Brewer, 1653). British Library.

Anon, *Awake O England, or, The peoples invitation to King Charles being a recital of the ruines over-running the people and their trades, with an opportune advice to return to obedience of their kings, under whom they ever flourished* London: Printed for Charles Prince, and are to be sold at the East end of St. Pauls, 1660). Beinecke Rare Book and Manuscript Library.

Anon, *By the council. Whereas the late Parliament dissolving themselves, and resigning their powers and authorities, The government of the Common-wealth of England, Scotland, and Ireland, by a Lord Protector* (Dublin: Printed by William Blade, 1653). Library Company of Philadelphia.

Anon, *Englands gratulation on the landing of Charles the Second, by the grace of God King of England, Scotland, France, and Ireland, at Dover and his advance from thence to the city of London, May the 29, being his birth day, attended with all the ancient nobility and gentry of this nation and a great part of the army commanded by His Excellence the Lord Generall Monk, his magnificent entertainment in the city of London by the Right Honourable the lord mayor and his brethren, and the great preparation for his coronation which wil be more ful of state and tryumph then ever King of England had before* (Printed for Charles Prince., 1660). Harvard University via Early English Books.

Anon, *Hells master-piece discovered: or Joy and sorrow mixt together. Being a breife [sic] and true relation of the damnable plot, of the invetrate [sic] enemies of God, and the King; who intended to a mixt our joy for the nativitie of Christ, with the blood of the King, and his faithfull subjects. Being a fit carrall for Royallist to sing, that alwaies fear God, and honour the King. To the tune of, Summer time* (London: Francis Grove, [1660?]. University of Glasgow Library.

Anon, *Letters to the council of state, from the commissioners of the militia of several counties, &c. informing them of the several marches of Colonel Lamberts forces, and shewing their readiness to suppress them and a letter from the Lord Montague, expressing the fleets obedience to the council and Parliament, also a letter from Col. Ingoldsby, who with his own hands took Col. Lambert prisoner. With some further information given by the messenger that came first with the news and was in person at the randezvous on Edge-hill, when Col. Okey and Major Creed appeared there* (London: Printed by Abel Roper and Thomas Collins, London, 1660). Henry E. Huntingdon Library and Art Gallery.

Anon, *London and England triumphant: At the proclaiming of King Charls [sic] the Second, by both the Houses of Parliament, the Judges of the Land: with the Lord Mayor, the Court of Aldermen, and Council of the City, as it was performed with great*

*solemnity, and loud acclamations of joy by the people in general..*
*To the tune of, I am a jovial batchelor* (London: Printed for F.
Grove, 8 May 1660).University of Glasgow Library.

Anon, *The Army no usurpers, or, The late Parliament not*
*almighty and everlasting shewing that the present army in their*
*former opposing and late dissolving of the Parliament have done*
*nothing contrary to law, but according to equity, and that late*
*Parliaments claim of power to do what they please, until they*
*should be dissolved by their own consent, is long since made void*
*by their own act* (London: Printed for Giles Calvert, 1653). British
Library.

Anon, *The Downfall of the Fifth Monarchy. Or, The personal*
*reign of Christ on earth, confuted. Discovering the desperate and*
*dangerous principles and designes of these frenzy-conceited men*
*of the Fifth Monarchy; who pretending to do the work of their*
*generations, seek to involve these nations again in bloud and*
*misery, had not the Lord prevented them in their designe; with a*
*brief manifestation of the true generation work which every good*
*Christian ought to do.* (London: Printed for John Andrews, at the
White Lion in the Old Baily, 1657). British Library.

Anon, *The Glory of the west, or, The Tenth renowned, worthy*
*and most heroick champion of this Brittish island being an*
*unparallel'd commemoration of General Monck's coming towards*
*the city of London.* (London: Printed for Charles Gustavus,
[1660]). Harvard University Library.

Anon, *The holy sisters conspiracy against their husbands, and*
*the city of London, designed at their last farewell of their meeting-*
*houses in Coleman-street; together with their Psalm of mercy*
(London: Printed by T. M., 1661).

Anon, *The loyal subjects exultation, for the coronation of King*
*Charls the Second. To the tune of, When the king comes home in*
*peace again.* (London: Printed for F. Grove, 1660). University of
Glasgow Library.

Anonymous Satire, *Sir Harry Vane's last sigh for Committee of*
*Safety, etc. with the Right Honourable Vice-Admiral John Lawson,*
*17 Dec 1659* (London: 17 Dec. 1659).

Aspinwall, William, *A brief description of the fifth monarchy*
*or kingdome that shortly is to come into the world the monarch,*

*subjects, officers and lawes thereof, and the surpassing glory, amplitude, unity and peace of that kingdome: when the kingdome and dominion, and the greatnesse of the kingdome under the whole heaven shall be given to the people, the saints of the most high, whose kingdome is an everlasting kingdome, and all soveraignes shall serve and obey him : and in the conclusion there is added a prognostick of the time when the fifth kingdome shall begin, by William Aspinwall* ... (London: Printed by M. Simmons and are to be sold by Loverwell Chapman, 1653). New York Library.

Bray, William, Ed., *The Diary of John Evelyn, Vols. 1-2* (London and New York: Walter Dunne, 1901).

*Calendars of State Papers Colonial: America and West Indies, 1656- 1700* (London: HMSO: 1893-1910). British History Online.

*Calendars of State Papers Relating to English Affairs in the Archives of Venice, 1659-1669* (London: HMSO, 1931-1933). British History Online.

*Calendars of State Papers, Domestic. 1640-1679* (London: HMSO, 1887-1915). Printed copies and BHO.

Cholmley, Hugh, *An Account of Tangier. By Sir Hugh Cholmley, Bart. With some account of himself and his journey through France and Spain to that place, Where he was engaged in building the mole in the time of King Charles the Second; and a Journal of the Work carrying on. And Also Some of his Speeches in Parliament. Taken from Manuscripts now in the Possession of Nathaniel Cholmley of Whitby and Howsham, in the County of York, Esquire,* 1787. Gale ECCO Edition.

Clarendon, Edward, *The life of Edward Earl of Clarendon, Lord High Chancellor of England and Chancellor of the University of Oxford in which is included his history of the grand rebellion written by himself,* Vol. 3, (Oxford: Clarendon Press, 1827).

Cromwell, Oliver, *A declaration of Oliver Cromwell, captain general of all the forces of this Common-Wealth. Whereas, the Parlament beeing dissolved...* (London: William Du-Gard, 1653).

Evans, Arise, *The bloudy vision of John Farly, interpreted by Arise Evans. With another vision signifying peace and happiness. Both which shew remarkable alterations speedily, to come to pass here in England, also a refutation of a pamphlet, lately published* by one Aspinwall: called a *Brief discription of the fifth Monarchy. Shewing that the late Parliament was that beast mentioned, Rev. 13. that this representative is the image thereof, and that the fifth Monarchy will shortly be established in the person of Charles Stewart* (London: 1653).

Firth, C. R. Ed., *The Memoirs of Edmund Ludlow, lieutenant-general of the horse in the army of the commonwealth of England 1625-1672*. Vols. 1-2. (Oxford: Clarendon Press, 1894).

Firth, Sir Charles and Routledge, F. J. Eds. *Calendars of the Clarendon State Papers Preserved in the Bodleian Library,* Vols. 3-5, 1642-1726 (Oxford: Clarendon Press).

Foster, Joseph, Ed., *Alumni Oxonienses, 1500-1714* (Oxford University Press, 1891).

*Guibon Goddard's Journal, August 1653*, in Diary of Thomas Burton, Esq, Vol. 1, 1653-1657, ed. John Towill Rutt (London: 1828). British History Online.

Hopper, Andrew, Ed., *The Papers of the Hothams, Governors of Hull During the Civil War* (Cambridge: CUP for the Royal Historical Society, 2011).

J. W., *Englands heroick champion. Or the ever renowned General George Monck through whose valor and prudence Englands antient liberties are restored, and a full and free Parliament now to be called, to the great joy of the nation. Let the trump of fame sound forth the name of honorable actions to free this land from factions. Then except of what is meant and pray for a free Parliament. To a pleasant new northern tune* (London: Printed for John Andrews at the white Lion near Pye-corner, [1660]). British Library.

*Journals of the House of Commons, 1642-1666* (London: HM Stationery Office, 1767-1830). British History Online.

*Journals of the House of Lords, 1642-1666* (London: HM Stationery Office, 1767-1830). British History Online.

Kaye, William, *Gods presence with the present government plainly, remonstrated to the light that is in all men, whereby a word in season is hinted, especially to those that were in open hostility, shewing just grounds for their subjection, as they will apparently avoid fighting against God, through their resisting his chosen instruments, ordained for the suppressing of poperie, or antichrist, and for the preservation of all saints in their profession of reformation, the way to peace, and blessednesse / written by William Kaye, minister of the gospel at Stokesley in Yorkshire...; unto which is added, A further discovery in answering the Fifth Monarchists, and anarchists arguments, wherein the dominion of saints is truly stated, for their satisfaction* (London: T. Mabb for Richard Moon, and are to be sold at his shop in Pauls Church-yard, at the Seven Stars, 1655). Beinecke Rare Book and Manuscript Library.

Laughton, J. K. July 7 1883, *A Letter from Sir John Lawson to Sir Henry Vane, 1652[/53]* in, *Notes And Queries*, Volume S6-VIII, Issue 184, at Internet Archive.

Lister, T. H., Ed., *Life and Administration of Edward, First Earl of Clarendon. With Original Correspondence and Authentic papers.* Vol. III (London: 1837)

*Mercurius Politicus*, 21-28 April 1653, Issue number 150.

Morrice, Reverend Thomas, Ed.. *A Collection of the State Letters of the Right Honourable Roger Boyle, The first Earl of Orrery, Lord President of Munster in Ireland. Containing A Series of Correspondence between the duke of Ormonde and his Lordship, from the Restoration to 1668* (London: James Bettenham, MDCCXLII)

*Paver's Marriage Licences* (Yorkshire: Archaeological Society Record Series, XL, 1909).

Penn, Granville, *Memorials of the professional life and times of Sir William Penn: from 1644 to 1670*, Vol. 2 (London: J. Duncan, 1833).

*Publick Intelligencer* (various).

Purnell, Robert, *Englands remonstrance. Or, a word in the ear to the scattered, discontented members of the late Parliament. Shewing, that self-seekers are self-losers; and that no member ought to feather his own nest, but freely permit every bird to enjoy his own feathers, and every honest man to sit under his own vine, and enjoy the fruits thereof. Likewise, a word to the present assembly at Westminster, and the councel of state at White Hall, in order to their present power, rule, government; and the peoples rights, liberties, and priviledges. By Robert Purnel* (London: Printed by E. Alsop, [1653]). British Library.

Rushworth, John, *Historical Collections of Private Passages of State.* Vol. 6, 1645-47 (London: 1722).

S. S., *The Parliament routed: or, Heres a house to be let. I hope that England after many jars, shall be at peace and give no way to wars O Lord protect the General, that he may be the agent of our unity. To the tune of, Lucina, or, Merrily and cherrily* (London: Printed for G. Horton, June 1653). Harvard University Library.

Shaw, William Ed., *Calendar of Treasury Books, Volume 1, 1660-1667* (London: 1904), pp. 520-527. British History Online.

*The Monthly Intelligencer.* Dec. 1659 to Jan. 1660. London.

*The Monthly Intelligencer.* Dec. 1659 to Jan. 1660. London. British Library.

*The Weekly Intelligencer of the Common-wealth.* 28 June-5 July 1653: Issue number: 126. British Library.

Venn, J. A., Ed., *Alumni Cantabrigienses 1261-1900* (Cambridge University Press, 1922-1954).

Warwick, Sir Philip, *Memoirs of the Reign of King Charles the First* (Edinburgh: 1702, Reprint 1813).

## GENERAL BIBLIOGRAPHY

Adamson, J. H. & Folland, H. F., *Sir Harry Vane: His Life and Times* (Bodley Head, 1973).

Ashley, Maurice, *General Monck* (Jonathan Cape, 1977).

Baker, Joseph Brogden, *The History of Scarborough from the earliest date* (London: Longmans, Green & Co., 1882, CD reproduction Colin Hinson)

Barber, Sarah, *Charles I: Regicide and republicanism*, in *History Today*, (January 1996), Vol. 46 Issue 1.

Barnard, John and McKenzie, D. F., *The Cambridge History of the Book in Britain. Vol. IV. 1557-1695* (Cambridge: University Press, 2002).

Binns, Jack, Ed., *Memoirs and Memorials of Sir Hugh Cholmley of Whitby 1600-1657* (Yorkshire Archaeological Society, Boydell Press, 2000).

Binns, Jack, *Sir John Lawson*, in *Oxford Dictionary of National Biography* (Oxford: 2000), Vol. 32.

Binns, Jack, *Sir John Lawson: Scarborough's Admiral of the Red* (*Northern History* (1996), Volume, 32, XXXII.

Binns, Jack, *Yorkshire in the Civil Wars Origins, Impact and Outcome* (Yorkshire: Blackthorn Press, 2004).

*Burke's Peerage*, 107th Edition (2003).

Butler, Lawrence, *Whitby in North Africa*, in *Yorkshire Archaeological Journal* (Yorkshire: 2004), Vol. 76.

Capp, Bernard, *Cromwell's Navy: The Feet and the English Revolution 1648-60.* (Oxford, 1989).

Coward, Barry, *The Stuart Age* (Longman, 2nd edn., 2004).

Davies, Godfrey, *The Restoration of Charles II* (Oxford: OUP, 1995).

Davies, J. D., *Gentlemen and Tarpaulins: The Officers and Men of the Restoration Navy* (Oxford: Clarendon Press, 1991).

Beer, Ed, *The Diary of John Evelyn* (Oxford: Everyman's Library, 2006 edn.).

*Diver jailed for fraud over £50,000 sale of cannon.* 5 Sept 2015, in *The Guardian*, p.18.

Feather, John, *A History of British Publishing* (London: Routledge, 2nd edn., 2006).

Foxley, Rachel, *The Levellers: Radical Thought in English Revolution* (Manchester University Press, 2013).

Fraser, Antonia, *The Weaker Vessel: Woman's Lot in Seventeenth-Century England* (London: Phoenix, 2002)

Gaunt, Professor Peter, Ed. *Cromwelliana Journal* (Cromwell Association)

Goodall, J. A. A., *Scarborough Castle* (English Heritage, 2000).

Granger, J., *A Biographical History of England* (Project Gutenberg https://archive.org/details/biographicalhist177903gran, 1779)

Harding. Edward, *Naval Biography; Or, The History and Lives of Distinguished Characters in the British Navy*, Vol. 1 (London: 1805).

Hill, Christopher, *The Century of Revolution* (London and New York: Routledge, 2nd edn. 1980),

Hill, Christopher, *The World Turned Upside Down: Radical Ideas During The English Revolution* (Penguin, 1972, reprint 1991).

Hinderwell, Thomas, *The History and Antiquities of Scarborough* (York and London: 1788 &1833).

Hopper, Andrew, *Social mobility during the English Revolution: the case of Adam Eyre*, in *Social History* (2013), Vol. 38, No. 1, pp.26–45, http://dx.doi.org/10.1080/03071022.2013.755329.

Hopper, Andrew, *The Farnley Wood Plot and the Memory of the Civil Wars in Yorkshire*, in *The Historical Journal*, (Cambridge: UP, June 2002), Vol. 45, No. 2, pp.281-303.

Hopper, Andrew, *The language of treachery in newsbooks and polemic*. (Oxford: University Press Scholarship Online www. oxfordscholarship.com, 2014).

Hopper, Andrew, *Treachery and conspiracy in Nottinghamshire during the English Civil War* in, *East Midlands History and Heritage* (June 2015), Issue 1, pp.21-23.

Hopper, Andrew, *Turncoats and Renegadoes: Changing Sides during the English Civil Wars* (Oxford: University Press, 2012).

Hunt, Tristram, *The English Civil War: At First Hand* (London: Weidenfeld and Nicolson, 2002).

Jordan, Don and Walsh, Michael, *The King's Revenge: Charles II and the Greatest Manhunt in British History* (London: Abacus, 2012).

Latham, Robert and Matthews, William, Eds., *The Diary of Samuel Pepys*, Volumes I-XI (London: Bell & Hyman, 1970-1983).

Leask, Paul, *Valour is the Safest Helm: The Life of Sir Hugh Cholmley and Scarborough during the English Civil War* (Yorkshire: Jacobus Publications, 1995).

Lewis, Samuel, *Topographical Dictionary of Yorkshire*, 1835.

Miller, John, *The English Civil Wars Roundheads, Cavaliers and the Execution of the King* (Constable and Robinson, 2009).

Mortimer, Sarah, *What was at stake in the Putney Debates* (In: *History Today*, January 2015), Vol. 65 Issue 1.

Page, W., Ed., *The Borough of Scarborough*, in *A History of North York Riding* (London: St. Catherine's Press, 1923).

Peacey, Jason, *Cromwellian England: A Propaganda State?* in *History* (April 2006), Vol. 19, Issue 302.

Peacey, Jason, *Editing and Editorial Interventions in English Journalism from the Civil Wars to the Restoration*, in *Media History*, Vol. 18, (August 2012), Issue 3/4.

Peacey, Jason, *The hunting of the Leveller: the sophistication of parliamentarian propaganda, 1647-53*, in *Historical Research* (Feb. 2005), Vol. 78, Issue 199.

Purkiss, Diane, *The English Civil War: A People's History* (Harper Press, 2006).

Ravelhofer, Barbara, *Censorship and Poetry at the Court of Charles I: The Case of Georg Rodolf Weckherlin*: Essay, in *English Literary Renaissance*. (May 2013), Vol. 43 Issue 2.

Raymond, Joad, *An Eye-Witness to King Cromwell* in *History Today* (7 January 1997), Issue 7.

Raymond, Joad, Ed., *News, Newspapers and Society in Early Modern Britain* (London: Frank Cass, 1998)

Raymond, Joad, *Pamphlets and Pamphleteering in Early Modern Britain* (Cambridge: CUP, 2006).

Raymond, Joad, *The Literature of Controversy* (www.academia.edu, 2007).

Robertson, Geoffrey, *Geoffrey Robertson presents The Levellers: The Putney Debates* (Verso, 2007).

Rowntree, Arthur, Ed., *The History of Scarborough* (London & Toronto: J. M. Dent & Sons Ltd., 1931).

Rushton, John. *Scarborough Coal Trade*. Scarborough Maritime Heritage Centre website:http://www.scarboroughsmaritimeheritage.org.uk/acoal.php.

Scurr, Ruth, *John Aubrey My Own Life* (London: Vintage, 2015)

Sharpe, Kevin, *Ideas and Politics in Early Stuart England*, in, *History Today* (January 1988), Vol. 38, Issue 1.

Smith, Nigel, *Non-conformist voices and books*, in Barnard, John and McKenzie, D.F. Eds., *A History of British Publishing* (Routledge, 2nd edn., 2002)

Tate, W. E., *The Parish Chest* (Cambridge: Phillimore, 3rd edn., 1983)

*The City and the Navy: An Opportunity for History to Repeat Itself*, in Pall Mall Gazette (23 Jan 1896).

Tinniswood, Adrian, *The Rainborowes: Pirates, Puritans and a Family's Quest for the Promised Land* (London: Vintage, 2014).

Tinniswood, Adrian, *The Rainborowes: Pirates, Puritans and a Family's Quest for the Promised Land* (London: Vintage, 2014).

Tomalin, Claire, *Samuel Pepys: The Unequalled Self* (London: Penguin, 2002).

Travis-Cook, John, *Vice Admiral Sir John Lawson. A reminiscence of the Civil War* (London, W. Andrews & Co., 1896).

Tubb, Amos, *Independent Presses: The Politics of Print in England During the Late 1640s*, in *The Seventeenth Century* (Manchester University Press, Autumn 2012), Vol. 27 Issue 3, pp.287-312.

Tuffs, Jack Elsden, *The History of Wanstead. Vol. 3. 1649-1727*, (Author, 1942-? [pre-1977])

Whitaker, Mark and Saunders, Frances Stonor, 'When Christmas was illegal', in *New Statesman* (2000), Vol. 129, Issue 4518, p.72.

Wilford, J., 'The History of England During the Reigns of the Royal House of Stuart... And several Original Letters from King Charles II, King James II, Oliver Cromwell, etc... The whole Collected from the Most Authentick Memoirs', in *The London Magazine, or, Gentleman's Monthly Intelligencer*, Vol. 2 (London: 1732-35).

Womack, Pamela, *An illustrated Introduction to The Stuarts* (Stroud: Amberley Publishing, 2014).

Wood, Phil, *Britons Could Be Slaves*, in *Ancestors* Magazine (March 2009). Issue 80.

## OTHER SOURCES

Binns, Jack. *Pers. Comm.* April 2015.

Conference. 7-8 August 2015: *Care, Mortality and Welfare During the Civil War*. Leicester University at: Newark Civil War Centre.

Hopper, Andrew. *Pers Comm.* April 2015.

Pepys Club.

Smith, Dr. David L. Lecture at Cambridge Museum 02/03/2015. *Oliver Cromwell: Hero or Villain*.

The Scarborough Maritime Heritage Centre

## WEBSITES

Ancestry

British Civil Wars (BCW) Project http://bcw-project.org

Central England temperatures: monthly means 1659-1973 by Professor Gordon Manley www.rmets.org/sites/default/files/qj74manley.pdf

Currency Converter www.nationalarchives.gov.uk/currency/results.asp#mid

FamilySearch

Findmypast

Historic Royal Palaces www.hrp.org.uk

Historical Weather Events: http://booty.org.uk/booty.weather/climate/1650_1699.htm

Internet Archive

Mackay, Charles, Ed. *The Cavalier Songs and Ballads of England, 1642-1684* (Transcribed from the 1863 Griffin Bohn and Co. edition) www.gutenberg.org/files/1030/1030-0.txt

The Cromwell Association www.olivercromwell.org/cromwell_association.htm

The Genealogist

The London Gazette www.thegazette.co.uk

The London Shipwreck Trust www.thelondonshipwrecktrust.co.uk

The Project Gutenberg eBook, The Cavalier Songs and Ballads of England, 1642-1684 by Various, Edited by Charles Mackay. Transcribed from the 1863 Griffin Bohn and Co. edition. www.gutenberg.org/files/1030/1030-0.txt

The Scarborough Maritime Heritage Centre www.scarboroughsmaritimeheritage.org.uk/aadmiraljohnlawson.php

Units of Weight http://sizes.com/units/chaldron.htm

# INDEX